GOD *and* CAESAR *in* CHINA

GOD *and* CAESAR *in* CHINA

POLICY IMPLICATIONS OF CHURCH-STATE TENSIONS

Jason Kindopp
Carol Lee Hamrin
editors

BROOKINGS INSTITUTION PRESS
Washington, D.C.

ABOUT BROOKINGS

The Brookings Institution is a private nonprofit organization devoted to research, education, and publication on important issues of domestic and foreign policy. Its principal purpose is to bring knowledge to bear on current and emerging policy problems. The Institution maintains a position of neutrality on issues of public policy. Interpretations or conclusions in Brookings publications should be understood to be solely those of the authors.

Copyright © 2004
THE BROOKINGS INSTITUTION
1775 Massachusetts Avenue, N.W., Washington, D.C. 20036
www.brookings.edu

All rights reserved

Library of Congress Cataloging-in-Publication data

God and Caesar in China : policy implications of church-state tensions / Jason Kindopp, Carol Lee Hamrin, editors
    p.   cm.
  Includes bibliographical references and index.
  ISBN 0-8157-4936-8 (cloth : alk. paper)—
  ISBN 0-8157-4937-6 (pbk. : alk. paper)
    1. Church and state—China. 2. China—Religion. I. Kindopp, Jason. II. Hamrin, Carol Lee. III. Title.
  BR1285.G63 2004
  322'.1'0951—dc22   2004000193

9 8 7 6 5 4 3 2 1

The paper used in this publication meets minimum requirements of the American National Standard for Information Sciences—Permanence of Paper for Printed Library Materials: ANSI Z39.48-1992.

Typeset in Adobe Garamond

Composition by OSP, Inc.
Arlington, Virginia

Printed by R. R. Donnelley
Harrisonburg, Virginia

Contents

Acknowledgments · vii

1 Policy Dilemmas in China's Church-State Relations: An Introduction · 1
   Jason Kindopp

PART ONE
State Policy: Control of Religion

2 A Tradition of State Dominance · 25
   Daniel H. Bays

3 Control and Containment in the Reform Era · 40
   Mickey Spiegel

4 Accession to the World Trade Organization and State Adaptation · 58
   Kim-kwong Chan

PART TWO
Church-State Interaction

5 Setting Roots: The Catholic Church in China to 1949 · 77
   Jean-Paul Wiest

6   Catholic Conflict and Cooperation in the
    People's Republic of China   93
    Richard Madsen

7   "Patriotic" Protestants: The Making of an
    Official Church   107
    Yihua Xu

8   Fragmented yet Defiant: Protestant Resilience
    under Chinese Communist Party Rule   122
    Jason Kindopp

PART THREE
Religion in U.S.-China Relations

 9 Unreconciled Differences: The Staying Power of Religion   149
    Peng Liu

10 Advancing Religious Freedom in a Global China:
    Conclusions   165
    Carol Lee Hamrin

Suggested Reading   187

Contributors   191

Index   195

Acknowledgments

This book would not have been possible without the generous support of the Pew Civitas Program for Faith and Public Affairs, funded by the Pew Charitable Trusts and administered by the Center for Public Justice (CPJ). The Civitas program funded Jason Kindopp's fellowship at the Brookings Institution and also underwrote the conference from which this volume emerged. CPJ president James Skillen and Civitas program director Keith Pavlischek deserve special thanks for their vision and support in making the fellowship, the conference, and the volume a reality. Carol Hamrin's participation was made possible by support from the Maclellan Foundation, and she would like to thank Maclellan's executive director, Tom McCallie, for his unflagging personal support. We would also like to thank Cindy Lail for her very valuable help in the editing process. Authors of the chapters were enthusiastic and collegial participants at every step—from high-quality conference presentations through writing and editing.

At the Brookings Institution, E.J. Dionne i supported the project from its inception and made the initial suggestion that we compile the conference papers into an edited volume, while Robert Faherty at the Brookings Institution Press shepherded the volume's development with verve; to both of them we express our gratitude. We also thank Katherine Kimball, who edited the manuscript, Vicki Chamlee, who proofread the pages, and Sherry Smith, who compiled the index.

1

JASON KINDOPP

Policy Dilemmas in China's Church-State Relations: An Introduction

Containing religion's social and political influence has become a leading policy concern for China's leaders in recent years, and their methods of doing so have strained China's relations with the United States. The salience of religious policy within China is in part a result of unanticipated rapid growth in religious activity. When China's reform era began in 1978, religion appeared moribund. All religious venues had been closed or destroyed, and few visible signs of its survival remained. Yet by the turn of the century, China's government reported that more than 200 million religious believers worshiped in eighty-five thousand authorized venues, and estimates by outside observers are higher yet.[1]

As in previous eras, Buddhists are most numerous, with more than 100 million adherents, 320,000 nuns and monks, and sixteen thousand temples and monasteries nationwide. Tibetan Buddhism remains a vital force in Tibet and western Sichuan Province, as does Islam in the northwest region of Xinjiang, where the majority of China's 18 million Muslims and thirty-five thousand mosques are concentrated. Christianity's inclusion within China's religious revival is particularly surprising. Until recently, most outside observers viewed the Christian missionary enterprise in China as a failure, drowned in the sea of history. Yet by the end of the millennium, China's Catholic population had swelled from 3 million in 1949 to more than 12 million,[2] surpassing the number of Catholics in Ireland. China now has about five thousand officially authorized Catholic churches and meeting points and the same number of clergy, almost half of which are located in Hebei Province. Protestantism in China has grown at a faster pace during the same period, multiplying from 1 million to at least 30 million adherents—with estimated figures as high as 45 million to 60 million—serviced by twenty thousand officially authorized clergy and more than thirty-five thousand registered churches and meeting points.[3] Protestantism's growth has occurred simultaneously in diverse regions, from the southeastern coastal areas to the densely populated central provinces of Henan and Anhui to the minority regions of China's Far Southwest and Northeast. China now has the world's second-largest evangelical Christian population—behind only the United States—and if current growth rates continue, China will become a global center of evangelical Christianity in coming decades.

A host of religious and quasi-spiritual groups and sects that the government does not recognize have also sprouted up in virtually every corner of Chinese society. Dozens of colorfully named religious sects—such as Eastern Lightning, Established King, and the Heavenly Soldiers Fraternal Army—have emerged in remote corners of China's vast rural hinterland, often cohering around charismatic leaders who preach doomsday messages and claim to be the "Supreme Savior" or the "returned Jesus," attracting up to hundreds of thousands of adherents.[4] Other movements have cohered around masters of *qigong* (a quasi-mystical traditional Chinese breathing exercise) and other traditional Chinese spiritual disciplines, also attracting large followings. The banned Falungong *qigong* sect, for example, claimed tens of millions of practitioners before the government launched its nationwide campaign to exterminate the group in 1999.[5]

Church-State Tensions

Unsurprisingly, relations between China's resurgent religious groups and the officially atheistic Communist Party state have been fraught with tension. As in other communist states, China's leaders sought first to eradicate religion (during the 1950s and 1960s) and then to co-opt and control it. The policy framework established after 1978 provides limited space for religious believers to practice their faith but also calls for comprehensive control measures to prevent religion from emerging as an independent social force. At the broadest level, the government has sought to constrain religious activity by conferring recognition on only five world religions (Buddhism, Catholicism, Taoism, Islam, and Protestantism). For each, the government erected a hierarchically ordered, monolithic "patriotic" organization—patterned after other Leninist mass organizations—and gave them sole representative authority over their respective religious adherents. Political authorities appoint loyalists or even Communist Party cadres to leadership positions within the religious organizations and give them authority over all religious venues, training seminaries, and clergy appointments.

Official regulations also stipulate tight government control over every aspect of religious existence, dictating acceptable forms and contents of religious services, the publication and distribution of materials for worship and training, and interaction with foreigners. Official control extends even to the realm of beliefs. Political authorities impose boundaries for acceptable religious doctrines, denouncing beliefs that emphasize evangelism, supernaturalism, or salvational doctrines that challenge the government's religious policies or contradict its projected symbolic order, which depicts all of Chinese society as unified under Chinese Communist Party (CCP) rule. In addition to enforcing the myriad regulations governing religion—undertaken primarily by the government's Religious Affairs Bureau and the police's Ministry of Public Security—the government takes proactive measures to ensure loyalty and compliance from religious figures, organizing frequent "patriotic education" campaigns for clergy and requiring religious leaders to participate in intensive propaganda courses that cover such topics as official religious policy, CCP history, and Marxist-Leninist ideology.[6]

Within these constraints, authorities allow limited yet meaningful religious participation. Buddhist and Taoist temples, for example, teem with worshippers, and most officially authorized Catholic and Protestant churches are filled to capacity on any given Sunday, as congregants endure the constraints imposed on their parishes in exchange for the opportunity to worship in public. Churches conduct a widening range of services, catering to the spiritual needs of youth, the elderly, married couples, and other religious demographic groups and many offer an array of social and welfare services.

The government's external constraints and internal manipulations conflict with religious groups' own norms of operation, beliefs, and values, however, and underlying scenes of packed churches, temples, and mosques are profound tensions between the state's demands for control and religious identities. Political authorities structure religious organizations according to their own interests—such as reorganizing Catholic dioceses without consulting church leaders and forcing associational Protestant groups into the highly bureaucratized Three-Self Patriotic Movement

(TSPM)—and, in doing so, alienate the faithful. The party-state's practice of limiting the number of religious sites is another point of contention, as many churches are packed beyond capacity, making for an uncomfortable worship experience, or are too distant for convenient access, or both. The appointment of unpopular figures to leadership positions within the "patriotic" religious organizations and to government-mandated Democratic Management Committees within individual churches, temples, and mosques is an enduring source of friction, creating divisions within religious groups and often leading to corruption, as co-opted leaders and their political backers siphon off the revenues and resources of the organizations they were appointed to represent.

The Communist Party's explicit policy of training and installing "patriotic" religious personnel to clerical positions is an even-greater source of conflict with religious believers. The method of ordination for Catholic bishops, for example, is a long-standing litmus test for clergy legitimacy among parishioners, who reject bishops who lack Vatican approval. Although the dividing line may not be as clear for Protestant pastors or Islamic imams, congregants are keenly aware that some of their leaders' loyalties to the regime trump their commitment to serving the faithful. Tensions are exacerbated when co-opted religious figures attempt to revise religious doctrines or reinterpret sacred tenets to conform to policy imperatives. For example, political authorities have long required official Catholic clergy to endorse its policies on abortion and birth control against church tradition. Similarly, senior figures in the official Protestant church have long denounced the core Protestant doctrine of "righteousness by faith" on grounds that it creates divisions between believers and unbelievers, in opposition to the conservative theological views of the vast majority of China's Protestants.[7]

Finally, official constraints on a wide range of religious activities conflict with religious norms and values. The government's stipulations that all religious activity must occur within approved venues and be led by authorized clergy run counter to the associational traditions of many religious forms; it also suppresses their evangelical identity, which favors itinerant evangelism. Concerned with religion's mobilizational power, authorities stipulate that all activities be conducted in an "orderly" manner, implicitly prohibiting all charismatic forms of worship and other popular practices. The government's long-standing prohibition of minors' receiving religious instruction is a source of tension with all believers who seek to raise their children within their own faith traditions.

At the heart of the tensions between religion and China's political authorities lies conflicting demands for loyalty. Religious faith commands an allegiance that transcends political authority, whereas the Communist Party's enduring imperative is to eliminate social and ideological competition. Religious beliefs and doctrines equip the faithful with conceptual resources to critically assess government policies and, indeed, Communist Party rule itself. Faith also endows believers with resources for resisting state demands: the promise of salvation for the faithful, clear behavioral guidelines, and feelings of solidarity with fellow believers offer powerful motivations to remain true to one's convictions in the face of official repression. For religious believers in China, these core incentives are reinforced by shared memories that contrast sharply with the party line. All religions suffered untold abuse and calamity under China's Communist Party rule, particularly during the rule of Mao Zedong (1949–76). Moreover, official abuses occurred with the active support of the "patriotic" religious organizations that now claim sole representative authority over their respective religious populations, even though many of the organizations' current leaders were in positions of authority during the repressive Mao era.

Resistance and Repression

Irreconcilable differences between the state's demands and religion's interests have compelled large numbers of religious believers in China to reject the government's system of religious control and operate outside official boundaries. Resistance is widespread among Tibetan Buddhists who remain loyal to the Dalai Lama and among Muslims in Xinjiang who refuse to subject themselves to the government's "patriotic education" campaigns.[8] The open defiance of thousands of Falungong adherents after China's leaders promulgated a nationwide ban on the group stunned political authorities and outside observers alike.

Perhaps most surprising, however, is the systematic and widespread resistance of the majority of China's Catholics and Protestants to their representative "patriotic" religious organizations. The Vatican and independent specialists estimate that the number of Catholics worshipping in "underground" churches in China is more than double the 4 million members in the official Catholic Patriotic Association. The ratio is similar for China's Protestants: an estimated 30 million to 45 million believers worship in illicit "house churches," compared with the 15 million members of churches under TSPM control.[9] Nor are their members isolated. The

Catholic Church's integrated clerical structure endows the underground church with considerable mobilizational capabilities. Although many Protestant house churches are relatively small and autonomous, large networks have also emerged across the country, in some cases claiming millions of adherents and having operations in virtually every province.

China's authorities have responded with a mixture of accommodation and repression. In many areas, unofficial religious groups have become a relatively institutionalized—though vulnerable—part of the social fabric. In areas of the country with long-standing traditions of lax governance—such as China's Far Southwest, Northeast, and southern coastal area—local authorities grant considerable leeway to autonomous religious groups. Many local party cadres and village leaders in the minority regions of southwestern Guizhou and Yunnan Provinces, for example, are religious believers themselves, and house churches operate openly in the southern coastal city of Wenzhou and among the minority Korean populations in China's northeastern province of Heilongjiang. Local authorities often turn a blind eye to house churches within their jurisdiction, provided that they remain small and autonomous and avoid contact with foreigners. In some locales, underground Catholic priests and those in the Catholic Patriotic Association hold services in the same church.[10]

At the same time, China's rulers regularly use force against religious groups that defy its policies and threaten its monopoly over social organization. Religious repression tends to be most harsh in areas where the state lacks sophisticated control mechanisms and autonomous religious activity is growing most rapidly or is linked with separatist movements. The widespread abuses of human rights in the religious and ethnic minority regions of Tibet and Xinjiang are well documented.[11] Among the majority Han population, the poor, largely rural, central province of Henan has logged the most accounts of religious persecution, followed by neighboring Anhui and Shandong Provinces.[12] Sporadic arrests of unauthorized religious leaders are also common in large, politically sensitive cities, such as Beijing and provincial capitals, although the state's comprehensive methods of coercion in such areas usually obviate the need for extreme measures.

Regional disparities aside, nationwide trends in recent years suggest an overall rise in government repression of unauthorized religious groups.[13] The crackdowns come amid government concerns of broader social unrest. Urban unemployment now exceeds 11 percent, and more than 125 million rural workers are underemployed.[14] Official corruption is endemic, consuming a staggering 13 to 17 percent of gross domestic product.[15] The pervasive wielding of political power for private economic gain has transformed China from a highly egalitarian society into one of the world's most unequal in less than three decades.[16] These trends have eroded the regime's legitimacy and fueled social discontent, resulting in a dramatic rise in mass protest in both rural and urban areas.[17] To counter growing civil unrest, authorities launch periodic "strike hard" anticrime campaigns targeting a wide range of criminal offenses. Religious believers in unauthorized groups are often included in the dragnet along with political and labor dissidents and common criminals.

A spike in official abuse also came with the government's campaign to eradicate the Falungong. When Falungong adherents resisted, the party-state mobilized its machinery of repression, resulting in an increasingly brutal crackdown with tens of thousands of arrests, widespread psychological and physical abuse, and, according to foreign human rights reports, hundreds of deaths.[18] With the campaign against the Falungong winding down, political authorities have turned their attention to other religious groups that are capable of mobilizing large numbers of adherents, using vague definitions of "cult" to denounce them and to justify harsh repression of them. Internal documents issued by the Ministry of Public Security detail the government's designs to develop a nationwide communications system to track, infiltrate, and ultimately crush independent social and religious networks.[19] The documents offer detailed instructions to local police to compile personality profiles of leading religious figures, improve intelligence networking with other government agencies, mobilize reconnaissance teams to infiltrate religious groups, coerce the groups' own members to spy for them, and, ultimately, to arrest all members "in one blow."

A widening gulf between state demands and religious allegiance may give rise to more open conflict. In China's religious landscape, the most volatile terrain is where religious beliefs link with competing political agendas. This is most visible in the autonomous regions of Tibet and Xinjiang, where religious identities are strong and political separatist movements are active. China's leaders have long viewed Buddhist monasteries in Tibet as closely allied with proindependence activism. The same holds true for Muslim mosques in Xinjiang (particularly among the Uighur minority), which are purportedly linked with separatist movements that seek to create an independent "East Turkistan." More recently, millenarian sects espousing explicitly revolutionary agendas have arisen throughout rural China. For example, one group known as the Heavenly Soldiers Fraternal Army practiced shamanistic rituals of spirit possession and exorcism and "pledged to fight for a new, divine regime free from social classes, authorities, grades and ranks, and the like." The sect was able to recruit thousands of followers from more than one hundred villages in southwestern China before authorities took action against it.[20]

Religious Revival and Political Change: Comparative Perspectives

History suggests that China is approaching a critical juncture in church-state relations. The Cultural Revolution taught China's Communist Party that religion cannot be eradicated by force. After three decades of rapid religious growth—much of it unsanctioned by the state—China's rulers are now realizing that they are unable to control and contain religion by government dictate. Nor do current trends bode well for increased official vigilance against religion's perceived threat to the CCP's rule. Religion will continue to hold a strong appeal in a Chinese society undergoing wrenching social and economic transition, while the deepening influence of transnational forces as China integrates into the global economy will further weaken its system of comprehensive social control.

Experiences from other countries and China's own history suggest that China's rulers face two broad options: they can either accommodate burgeoning religious groups and integrate them into a broader civil society, or they can repress them and create a mobilized opposition to the established order. China's own history illustrates this choice well. Popular religious groups have been an enduring feature of China's social landscape for centuries. For the most part, one leading scholar observes, such groups met the needs of "peasants, laborers, and artisans who needed support, assurance, and a renewed sense of their own worth and continuity" in relatively peaceful coexistence with political authorities.[21] China's emperors periodically sought to eradicate autonomous religious groups, however, usually in response to the groups' growing institutionalization and influence in society. Rulers' zealotry in repressing autonomous religious groups derived from the structure of China's social and political order, which was conceived as a single, monolithic hierarchy sustained by heaven's mandate. Thus the very existence of alternative social groups offering salvation was an affront to the emperor's totalistic claims, spurring official crackdowns that, in turn, provoked popular uprisings.

These inherent tensions—which resemble church-state relations today—have endowed China with an unparalleled history of religious-based political rebellion. As C. K. Yang observes in his classic study of religion in Chinese society, "Religious rebellion crowded the records of every decade after the middle of the eighteenth century. Few political rebellions of any appreciable proportions were totally unconnected with some religious element or organization."[22] The most prominent example is the Taiping Rebellion (1850–64), which originated when Hong Xiuquan, a failed government official examinee, came upon some Christian evangelical tracts and, after a lengthy illness, convinced himself that he was the younger brother of Jesus. The sectarian religious movement that Hong founded eventually sought to topple the Qing dynasty, launching a civil war that lasted fourteen years and claimed more than 20 million lives. Although no religious group in China today is capable of catalyzing a similar catastrophe, continued government persecution may antagonize religious adherents to stage concerted protests, which, if done in tandem with other disaffected social segments, could escalate into a mass rebellion against the government.

Communist states in Eastern Europe and the Soviet Union similarly tried, and failed, to repress, control, and co-opt religion.[23] Poland's Solidarity movement, the juggernaut of social and political change in Eastern Europe, fused the material interests of labor with Polish nationalism and Catholic faith, creating an irrepressible force for political change.[24] Similarly, East Germany's "revolution of the candles" began with peaceful candle-lit demonstrations around Leipzig's Nikolai Church in September 1989 and over the following weeks grew to mass gatherings of 300,000 people. An East German sociologist studying the demonstrations has found that the core of early protesters were members of church groups who had already formed communities of trust and solidarity within an otherwise atomized society.[25] Other authoritarian states adopted less repressive policies toward their religious populations, including South Korea in the 1980s, Taiwan under Chiang Ching-kuo, and a number of authoritarian regimes in Latin America.[26] Although religion also played a catalyzing role in these countries' democratic transition, for the most part, religious leaders advocated nonviolent change, moderating more radical opposition forces.[27]

The fundamentalist attributes of many of China's resurgent religious groups today offer another point of comparison. Consistent with the emergence of religious fundamentalism in other countries, much religious revival in China today may be seen as a backlash against the secularization of society.[28] China's secularization process was even more rapid and extreme than that in most countries where fundamentalist religion has emerged. Mao-era mass political campaigns repeatedly attacked religious beliefs and practices along with other forms of traditional culture, replacing them with a quasi-religious utopian Marxist ideology and a personality cult of Chairman Mao—both of which were discredited by the Cultural Revolution's destructive culmination. As with fundamentalist religion elsewhere, China's house-church Protestants, underground Catholics, and many indigenous sects and cults—including the Falungong—claim to be the defenders of true religion (by upholding orthodoxy or orthopraxy) against the party-state's secular ideology, its restrictive policies, and the compromised "patriotic" religious organizations. Emerging in a hostile environment, many groups form separate enclaves with sharp boundaries, mobilize adherents with millenarian or messianic doctrines, and define their strategies for action against the perceived threats posed by their adversaries.

Although these attributes endow fundamentalist religious groups with considerable mobilizational capabilities, their social and political impact depends largely on the reaction of the established order to their emergence. Countries with established civic institutions have been able to absorb the energies of fundamentalist religious groups by "draining off anxiety and resentment in response to social and economic crises, and converting them into secular politics and public policy."[29] Fundamentalist religious movements in Western democratic states, India, and Latin America, for example, have largely been integrated into broader society and have even utilized the social capital they generate to promote economic development and democratic governance.[30] By contrast, interventionist states that have repressed the institutions of civil society and sought to restrict religion's expression have engendered religious radicalism and militancy. The rise of militant Islam in twentieth-century Egypt, Algeria, and Iran, for example, is intrinsically linked with the persistent efforts of their authoritarian states to repress autonomous social organization and political dissent, whereas radical Islamic movements in the more moderate states of Turkey and Indonesia have held less popular appeal.

China's leaders face similar choices today. They can either accommodate popular religious forms by adopting broader reforms that protect autonomous civic institutions, or they can attempt to repress them through coercion and brute force. China's history and experiences in other countries suggest that the latter option will only breed social unrest and rebellion. Although the CCP has stepped back from its extreme antireligion policies of the Mao era, China's leaders have not yet demonstrated the political will to embrace a more accommodative posture. Rather, they occupy a slippery middle ground in which the rhetoric of "freedom of religious belief" coexists with ongoing efforts to repress religion's most popular forms. Faced with the continued rapid growth of fundamentalist religious groups, the choice China's leaders face is an increasingly urgent one. In the absence of decisive measures to reform its policies toward religious groups and other civic institutions, however, their current middle ground may prove to be a decision against adaptation, with pernicious implications for both the state and social development.

Official Dialogue on Issues of Religious Freedom

The rise in importance of church-state relations within China remains largely unexamined either in China or in the United States. China's leaders prefer to avoid the subject entirely, enforcing a ban, until recently, on internal discussion of the subject. American concerns about violations of religious freedom, in turn, have been expressed primarily in the form of criticism over individual cases. Until the mid-1990s, religious repression was rarely mentioned in debates over China policy in Washington (with the exception of Tibet). During the 1990s, however, reports of growing persecution of Christians abroad—including in China—combined with the perceived indifference to these abuses within the U.S. foreign policy establishment gave rise to a groundswell of American popular support for legislation to advance religious freedom abroad. The resulting International Religious Freedom Act, passed in 1998, created an Office of International Religious Freedom, headed by an ambassador-at-large, within the State Department and a U.S. Commission on International Religious Freedom. The act effectively institutionalized U.S. government concern for religious freedom abroad, requiring, among other mandates, that the State Department issue an annual report on religious freedom in other countries and that the president take action against countries found to violate religious freedom.

Every annual State Department report on international religious freedom has listed China as a "country of concern." In response to the initial report in 1998, China denied requests for a dialogue from Ambassador-at-Large for International Religious Freedom Robert Seiple. By the time the George W. Bush administration came into office in 2000, religious persecution had become a leading issue in bilateral relations. Chinese officials refused to meet with officials from the International Religious Freedom

Office, however, during a U.S. embassy–sponsored trip to China in March 2001. In his first face-to-face encounter with China's president Jiang Zemin, President George Bush raised the issue of religious freedom, making clear his concern about the issue at the October 2001 Asia-Pacific Economic Cooperation summit in Shanghai. Bush also conditioned his planned trip to China in February 2002 on the Chinese government's granting him the opportunity to make a live and uncensored televised speech on religious freedom and human rights (accepting a recommendation from the Commission on International Religious Freedom).[31] China's leaders conceded—Bush's speech aired on China's CCTV on February 21, 2002—and religious freedom became one of the most prominent issues during the second trip.

The Chinese resistance to dialogue on the issue of religious freedom has recently begun to change. In July 2002, at Beijing's invitation, Ambassador-at-Large for International Religious Freedom John Hanford visited China, and exchanges on issues of international religious freedom during broader dialogues on human rights followed. But the dialogue remains sporadic and unfocused. For the most part, businesses, faith-based organizations, and other nongovernmental organizations with China portfolios have either remained on the sidelines or have harnessed discourse on religious freedom in China to domestic political agendas. As a result, the focus has been on governmental prerogatives, and policy debates have been superficial at best and manipulative at worst.

About This Book

God and Caesar in China seeks to take initial steps toward a grounded dialogue on advancing religious freedom in China. The volume grew out of a conference sponsored by the Pew Civitas Program in Faith and Public Affairs at the Brookings Institution in February 2002. The conference participants are leading specialists on church-state relations in China, yet they also hold a diverse array of perspectives, coming from Hong Kong, mainland China, and the United States, with backgrounds in academia, government, and human rights advocacy.

Rather than attempt the unwieldy task of surveying China's entire religious landscape, we decided to conduct a closer historical examination of China's Catholics and Protestants, and their interaction with the state, in greater depth. Whereas many religious forms coexist relatively harmoniously with CCP rule, Christianity's congregational form, cogent belief system, close historical links with Western churches, and the hierarchical order within the Catholic Church leading to the ultimate authority in the pope create a constant source of conflict between state demands and religious norms and values. As the representatives of the dominant religions in the United States, Catholic and Protestant churches and faith-based organizations have extensive transnational networks leading into China, and they hold the capacity to exert considerable influence.

This volume addresses three sets of related questions. The first deals with official control of religion in China. Why and how does China's government seek to regulate religion? How intrusive are the government's institutions of control? How much latitude does the government give religious groups to govern themselves and conduct religious activities? How pervasive is the Chinese government's repression of religious groups and believers who fail to comply with its policies?

Next, we examine the interaction between China's Catholics and Protestants and China's ruling Communist Party and the historical underpinnings of their relations. What were the dominant attributes of Catholic and Protestant churches that conditioned their response to China's communist revolution? To what extent have China's Catholics and Protestants adapted to, resisted, or rebelled against state demands? What are the implications of China's rapidly changing church-state relations for the nation's social and political stability? Is the church a bulwark for the existing order? A force for change? Positive or negative?

Finally, we seek to draw the implications of church-state relations in China for U.S. foreign policy and for bilateral relations more broadly. What common ground do China and the United States share in protecting religious freedoms? What place should promoting religious freedom have in U.S. foreign policymaking? What tools should be used to achieve our objectives? What role should nongovernmental actors play in improving the situation in China?

God and Caesar in China is organized around these themes. Daniel Bays begins the first section with a review of China's long history of official control of religion. Bays observes that state control and monitoring of religion is far from an invention of the Communist Party. The state's prerogative to determine which forms of religion are acceptable within the dominant orthodoxy of the day and which forms are to be spurned as "heterodox," as well as the bureaucratic impulse to control even authorized religious forms and repress deviancy, is deeply rooted in China's governing tradition. The requirement to register religious groups, an official bureaucracy to monitor religious affairs, and often violent repression of religious groups that fall outside official boundaries have been a feature of every Chinese government for at least a thousand years.

Bays also notes, however, how radically Communist Party rule under Mao Zedong deviated from traditional patterns of religious control and monitoring. Armed with an atheistic ideology that viewed religion as an unscientific "opiate" of the masses and adopting a revolutionary policy agenda that sought to re-create society in its image, China's Communist Party promulgated a policy framework for religion that explicitly sought to isolate it from broader society, with the intention of eradicating it entirely. Extreme measures against religion culminated in a total ban on religious activity during the Cultural Revolution (1966–76).

Mickey Spiegel follows with an overview of religious policy in post-Mao China. In the early 1980s China's Communist Party initiated a policy framework that may be seen as a return to traditional normalcy in religious governance. Spiegel points out that the main thrust of religious policy since 1980 has been to reintegrate religion into the socialist mainstream and to repress those who resist. The fundamental tenets, she observes, are the assertion of government control over religious organizations and the establishment of strict boundaries for "normal" religious activity. Yet the result is official regulation of all aspects of religious life: religious venues, clergy, activities, believers, and even theological doctrines are all subject to government dictates. In addition, religious regulations are vaguely worded, enabling official cadres to interpret them as they wish. In some localities, this arbitrary rule leads to laissez-faire governance; in others, to prohibition and abuse.

Kim-kwong Chan finishes this first section with a discussion of the implications of China's entry into the World Trade Organization for the government's ability to retain control over the church. Chan explains that there are strong reasons to believe that the government's system of religious control is not sustainable. China's policy of economic reform and opening has succeeded spectacularly in some respects, most notably by creating sustained rapid economic growth. Yet it has also created widespread social dislocation, increasing economic inequality, and, for many rural farmers and urban employees of state-owned enterprises, a decline in living standards—all of which have fueled a widespread religious revival throughout Chinese society. Economic marketization and deepening integration into the global economy have also given rise to dense webs of transnational interaction, increased social mobility, and a diffusion of economic power and communications technology. Religious groups in China and abroad have utilized these developments to their own advantage, challenging the government's ability to contain religion's social and political influence. China's entry into the World Trade Organization will accelerate these trends, making it increasingly difficult for the state to sustain its comprehensive system of religious control. Despite these broad-based and irreversible developments, Chan notes, China's leaders have yet to demonstrate a willingness to fundamentally revise their approach to religion. He concludes his chapter with an insightful analysis of an important work conference on religion held by China's top leaders in December 2001, during which President Jiang Zemin insisted that the "Party's leadership in religious work and the government's management of religious affairs must be strengthened and must not be weakened."[32]

The volume's second section examines the internal development of China's Catholic and Protestant churches and their interactions with the state. Jean-Paul Wiest offers a sweeping overview of the church's entry into China in the seventh century and, more specifically, Jesuit Catholics' mission endeavors from the fourteenth century to 1949. Wiest notes the difficulties Christianity has faced over the centuries in sinking roots into China's cultural soil. At least three waves of Christian missionaries came and left—or were wiped out—over a thousand-year period, with few Chinese converts to show for their efforts. Their problems included imperial bans against the religion, following periods of official tolerance, and opposition from China's broader ruling elite, who, charged with maintaining Confucian orthodoxy, despised Christianity's claims of holding the key to universal salvation.

Catholic missions faced particularly formidable challenges. The Jesuits' patiently cultivated inroads to China's ruling elite were abruptly cut off when the Vatican sided with church conservatives in the "rites controversy," which condemned as heretical such traditional Chinese rituals as ancestor worship. The church's close ties to Western imperialist powers and its heavy reliance on them to impose free mission activity under the unequal-treaty system of the early 1840s further alienated China's ruling elites from the Catholics. The church's mission strategy of converting entire communities, rather than individual souls, also hindered its growth, particularly after an imperial ban forced Catholic missionaries to retreat to the rural hinterland. This, Wiest observes, is one reason that China's Catholics today are concentrated in rural strongholds.

Richard Madsen next examines the development of China's Catholic Church under CCP rule, noting patterns of conflict and cooperation between the church and state. Conflict intensified after the Communist takeover. The Vatican under Pope Pius XII adopted an intensely anticommunist stand, issuing an edict that promised excommunication for any collaborators with the communist regime. The Vatican's hostility toward China's Communist Party was matched by the party's determination to assume control over the church. Yet though the CCP eventually convinced a handful of collaborators to establish the official Catholic Patriotic Association, most Chinese Catholic clergy and believers shunned the politically sanctioned organization. Some resisted by worshipping at home, others by organizing underground churches.

In recent decades, however, both the Vatican and the CCP have adopted less confrontational stands. China's rulers allowed China's Catholics to recognize the pope's "spiritual authority," and the Vatican has employed a system of secret ordination that allows bishops and priests within official churches to receive Vatican approval. As Madsen puts it, "A black-and-white conflict between open and underground churches is being replaced by shades of gray." At the same time, continued official repression of the underground church has fostered a culture of martyrdom that strengthens resistance. Although the bitter conflict between the Catholic Church and the CCP of the 1950s may be softening, full reconciliation remains elusive.

Protestant missions similarly increased dramatically under the unequal treaty system, reinforcing negative Chinese perceptions of Christianity. After its strained origins, however, the Protestant enterprise gained a more solid footing in Chinese society, laying the foundations for rapid church growth in the late twentieth century. In his chapter on China's Protestants, Yihua Xu recounts how Chinese Protestants and foreign missionaries alike promoted a variety of measures to promote greater autonomy and indigenization, which became broadly known as the "three-self principles" (self-support, self-propagation, and self-governance). Xu identifies three distinct strains of promoting three-self principles within the church: breakaway churches from mainstream Western denominations; indigenous Protestant movements, which often combined Christian doctrines with elements of traditional Chinese beliefs and practices; and reform measures from within the Sino-foreign Protestant establishment itself.

Ironically, it was the latter category—which was most strongly influenced by Western ideas and values—that produced the Protestant activists who established the Three-Self Patriotic Movement (TSPM) under CCP rule and came to dominate China's Protestant establishment. The key institutional links, Xu points out, were China's YMCA (Young Men's Christian Association), the Anglican Church—particularly its St. John's University in Shanghai—and the Union Theological Seminary in New York. These three institutions groomed a small group of Protestant intellectuals in social activism and liberal theology, aligning them with the international socialist movement and generating support for China's socialist experiment. Nearly all leading Protestant figures after China's communist takeover, continuing down to the present, have emerged from these institutions.

My later chapter discusses Protestantism's development since the communist takeover in 1949. Although there was considerable continuity among Protestant elites in the transition to CCP rule, there was also bitter conflict and turmoil. The party's radical policy agenda resulted in the systematic dismantling of China's network of Protestant institutions, in which the TSPM took a leading role. As the party's denunciation campaigns swept across the country, TSPM officials led attacks against all Protestant churches and movements that did not submit to their control. The result was widespread alienation of China's Protestants.

The church's development during the reform period has been deeply influenced by these earlier events. Political authorities revived the TSPM and rehabilitated the elites that rose within its ranks during the radical Mao Zedong years, yet the state gave grassroots churches more space to conduct religious activities. The spectacular growth rate of Protestantism in China throughout the reform era has placed the forces for change increasingly in the driver's seat and defenders of the established order within the government and the TSPM hierarchy on the defensive. Forces for change have emerged from within the official church, the rapidly growing and increasingly well-organized house-church networks and resurgent indigenous Protestant movements, overseas mission organizations, and, more recently, transnational Chinese Christian networks. Together, they have contributed to the church's bid for greater autonomy from the state.

The book closes with a look at the implications of church-state relations in China for U.S.-China relations. Drawing on their perspectives as former Chinese and U.S. government officials, respectively, the authors of the final two chapters examine the development of the issue of religious freedom in bilateral relations, offering concrete suggestions to the two governments and involved social actors for improving the management of this contentious issue.

Peng Liu, a former official in China's United Front Work Department and current scholar at the Chinese Academy of Social Sciences, explains in his chapter that the starting point on religion in bilateral relations is to recognize the vast gulf that separates American views of religion's proper social status with those of China's ruling Communist Party. Whereas religious freedom is a founding principle of the United States and continues to be embodied in the beliefs of the majority of Americans, China's ruling Communist Party views religion as a form of philosophical idealism that is fundamentally incompatible with Marxist materialism. Religion's foundations in Chinese society are sufficiently broad to prevent the government from eradicating it, yet the party's own ideology prohibits it from endorsing and supporting religion or even just ignoring it. From the party's perspective, the only alternative is to compel religion to "serve the political purpose of building a modern socialist China," Liu explains. Because of its explicitly political and utilitarian approach to religion, he adds, the Communist Party invariably views religious issues, particularly in foreign affairs, "through the filter of its political interests."

The dearth of common ground between these contrasting views, however, should not prevent the two sides from creating a framework for managing their differences, as they have done on other contentious issues, such as Taiwan, the proliferation of nuclear weapons, and trade. For comparative value, he also points to efforts by other Western countries (such as Canada and Norway) to promote greater freedom of religion in China—efforts that rely more on low-key official meetings and technical exchanges and avoid public criticism. Liu proposes several measures both sides can take toward building such a framework, calling on China's government to set up a task force as a counterpart to the U.S. International Religious Freedom Office and on the U.S. government to open channels for input from societal actors. He also encourages Americans to have patience. With the dramatic social changes under way in China and a new generation of leaders seeking a legacy, Liu argues, "the Chinese government's change in religious policies is only a matter of time and opportunity." A constructive approach by the United States can accelerate these changes, whereas a policy based on criticism and contention will redound to the conservatives who oppose change.

Drawing on government experience from the other side of the Atlantic, Carol Lee Hamrin, a former career officer in the U.S. State Department, concludes with her own set of policy prescriptions. Echoing several of Liu's themes, Hamrin suggests that a measure of convergence may be possible after all. Hamrin identifies domestic sources of tensions in both countries as part of the problem. Conflictual church-state relations in China largely reflect problems in the government's broader system of social control. America's response, however, has also been influenced by the culture wars that have raged within this country. Both countries, Hamrin observes, have experienced identity crises in the post–cold war period, giving rise to neoconservative movements in China and the United States. Conservatism in the United States has taken the form of a global crusade to promote market economies, religious and human rights, and political democracies abroad. China's leaders, in turn, faced a worldwide rejection of communist ideology and were cautioned by the Asian financial crisis in 1997. In response, they attempted to shore up domestic support by advancing a strident nationalism. These developments together exacerbated a clash of interests and identities between the two countries.

In the search for policy solutions, Hamrin argues for finding a middle ground between policy frameworks informed by rigid ideologies, either secular or religious. The tragedy of September 11, 2001, upgraded religion's policy salience in both Washington and Beijing, and the war on terror has given the two capitals a new focal point for cooperation. Of a more lasting nature, China's leaders have practical incentives to liberalize religious control, including the need to develop the third sector, to strengthen public morality in an age of corruption and discredited official ideology, and to induce educated Chinese living abroad (many of whom have faith commitments) to return to China.

The United States should respond, Hamrin argues, by building a domestic consensus on international religious freedom policy toward China, which will require revising assumptions and expectations. Policy initiatives should target subnational authorities in China, as well as Beijing, and should encourage participation of commercial interests and nonprofit organizations. Finally, initiatives should be based on international norms, not merely American ones.

Notes

1. Official figures are notoriously unreliable. Publicly available documents usually cite 100 million religious believers; internal reports cite 200 million; informed outside estimates cite higher numbers than both types of official reports. Needless to say, no definitive statistics are available. See Information Office of the State Council of the People's Republic of China, "Freedom of Religious Belief in China," White Paper

(October 1997) (www.china.org.cn/e-white/Freedom/index.htm [November 13, 2003]). An overview of outside estimates is reported in U.S. Department of State, *International Religious Freedom Report 2002: China (Includes Hong Kong and Macau)*, October 7, 2002 (www.state.gov/g/drl/rls/irf/2002/13870.htm [November 13, 2003]).

2. See chapter 6, this volume. Also see Jean Charbonnier, "Guide to the Catholic Church in China," *UCA News*, October 2, 2000, p. 14.

3. For the number of authorized venues, see Bao Jiayuan, "Update on the Church in China," *Chinese Theological Review*, vol. 14 (2000), pp. 116–32. Figures on the total number of Protestants include those who worship in unauthorized "house churches," which are estimated by outside observers and mission organizations that work closely with China's house-church networks to number 40 million to 80 million adherents. See, for example, Open Doors, "Chinese House Church Leader: Huge Need for More Bibles," press release, March 3, 2003 (www.opendoorsusa.org/Display.asp?Page=Chinabibles [November 13, 2003]).

4. Deng Zhaoming, "Recent Millennial Movements on Mainland China: Three Cases," *Inter-Religio*, vol. 34 (Winter 1998), pp. 51–53; Paul Hattaway, "When China's Christians Wish They Were in Prison: An Examination of the Eastern Lightning Cult in China" (April 24, 2001) (www.asiaharvest.org/elreport.htm [November 13, 2003]).

5. For a discussion of varied estimates of Falungong adherents, see James Tong, "An Organizational Analysis of the Falun Gong: Structure, Communications, Financing," *China Quarterly*, no. 171 (September 2002), pp. 636–60.

6. The Religious Affairs Bureau was changed to the State Administration for Religious Affairs in 1998. Because most references to the bureau in the following chapters relate to it before 1998, we use the more familiar "Religious Affairs Bureau" throughout the volume.

7. For a detailed discussion, see Jason Kindopp, "Failed Hegemony: The Theological Construction Campaign," in "The Politics of Protestantism in Contemporary China: State Control, Civil Society, and Social Movement in a Single Party-State" (Ph.D. diss., George Washington University, 2004).

8. Barry Sautman, "Resolving the Tibet Question: Problems and Prospects," *Journal of Contemporary China*, no. 30 (February 2002), pp. 77–107; Dru Gladney, "Xinjiang: China's Future West Bank?" *Current History*, vol. 101 (September 2002), pp. 267–71.

9. See note 3, this chapter.

10. See chapter 6, this volume.

11. For a recent update, see Amnesty International, "China's Anti-Terrorism Legislation and Repression in the Xinjiang Uighur Autonomous Region," *ASA* (March 22, 2002) (web.amnesty.org/library/Index/ENGASA170102002?open&of=ENG-CHN [November 13, 2003]).

12. Author's compilation, based on data from human rights reports.

13. The U.S. State Department's 2001 report on religious freedom begins its discussion of China with the statement, "The situation for religious freedom and spiritual movements worsened in the past year." U.S. Department of State, "International Religious Freedom Report for 2001: Executive Summary" (www.state.gov/g/drl/rls/irf/2001/5531pf.htm [November 13, 2003]), p. 2. The 2002 report notes that "the Government's respect for religious freedom and freedom of conscience remained poor,

especially for members of some unregistered religious groups and spiritual movements such as the Falun Gong." U.S. Department of State, *International Religious Freedom Report 2002*, p. 1.

14. Cited in Murray Scot Tanner, "Cracks in the Wall: China's Eroding Coercive State," *Current History*, vol. 100 (September 2001), pp. 243–49.

15. Figures from Chinese Academy of Sciences economist Hu Angang, cited in Josephine Ma, "Graft-Busters Need Their Own Bureau Economist," *South China Morning Post*, May 16, 2001, p. 1.

16. Chinese economists now estimate China's GINI coefficient for inequality to be approximately 0.45. Kang Xiaoguang, "Weilai 3-5 nian Zhongguo dalu zhengzhi wendingxing fenxi" [An analysis of political stability in mainland China in the next three to five years], *Beijing zhanlue yu guanli* [Beijing strategy and management], June 1, 2002, pp. 1–15.

17. In 2001 the CCP's own Organization Department published a 308-page study detailing the alarming increase in size and frequency of collective protests. *China Investigation Report 2000–2001: Studies of Contradictions among the People under New Conditions* [Zhongguo diaocha baogao: Xin xingshi xia renmin neibu maodun yanjiu, 2000–01], cited in Tanner, "Cracks in the Wall," p. 246.

18. Human Rights Watch, *Dangerous Meditation: China's Campaign against Falungong* (New York, 2002).

19. Li Shixiong and Xiqiu (Bob) Fu, eds. and trans., *Religion and National Security in China: Secret Documents from China's Security Sector* (Bartlesville, Okla.: Voice of the Martyrs, 2002).

20. Elizabeth J. Perry and Mark Selden, "Reform and Resistance in Contemporary China," introduction to *Chinese Society: Change, Conflict, and Resistance* (London: Routledge, 2000), pp. 1–19, 9.

21. Daniel L. Overmyer, "Alternatives: Popular Religious Sects in Chinese Society," *Modern China*, vol. 7 (April 1981), pp. 153–90, 155.

22. C. K. Yang, *Religion in Chinese Society* (University of California Press, 1961), p. 219.

23. Sabrina Petra Ramet, ed., *Protestantism and Politics in Eastern Europe and Russia: The Communist and Post-Communist Eras* (Duke University Press, 1992); Sabrina Petra Ramet, "Adaptation and Transformation of Religious Policy in Communist and Post-Communist Systems," in Sabrina Petra Ramet, ed., *Adaptation and Transformation in Communist and Post-Communist Systems* (Boulder: Westview Press, 1992), pp. 141–84.

24. See, for example, Jozef Tischner, *The Spirit of Solidarity*, trans. Marek B. Zaleski and Benjamin Fiore (San Francisco: Harper and Row, 1982).

25. Niels Nielsen, *Revolutions in Eastern Europe: The Religious Roots* (Maryknoll, N.Y.: Orbis, 1991), chap. 2, citing the work of Ehrhart Neubert.

26. David Martin, *Tongues of Fire: The Explosion of Protestantism in Latin America* (London: Blackwell, 1990); David Stoll, *Is Latin America Turning Protestant? The Politics of Evangelical Growth* (University of California Press, 1990); Won Gue Lee, "A Sociological Study on the Factors of Church Growth and Decline in Korea," *Korea Journal*, vol. 39, no. 4 (1999), pp. 235–69.

27. Samuel P. Huntington, "Religion and the Third Wave," *National Interest*, vol. 24 (Summer 1991), pp. 29–42.

28. For a comparative overview of fundamentalist religion, see Martin E. Marty and R. Scott Appleby, eds., *Accounting for Fundamentalism: The Dynamic Character of Movements* (University of Chicago Press, 1994).

29. Gabriel A. Almond, Emmanuel Sivan, and R. Scott Appleby, "Fundamentalism: Genus and Species," in Martin E. Marty and R. Scott Appleby, eds., *Fundamentalisms Comprehended*, vol. 5 of *The Fundamentalism Project* (University of Chicago Press, 1995), pp. 399–444, 434.

30. Amy Sherman, *The Soul of Development: Biblical Christianity and Economic Transformation in Guatemala* (Oxford University Press, 1996); Daniel H. Levine, "Religious Change, Empowerment, and Power: Reflections on Latin American Experience," in Satya R. Pattnayak, ed., *Organized Religion in the Political Transformation of Latin America* (Lanham, Md.: University Press of America, 1995), pp. 15–40.

31. U.S. Commission on International Religious Freedom, "Annual Report" (May 2002), p. 3 (www.uscirf.gov/reports/02AnnualRpt/2002report.pdf [November 13, 2003]).

32. Sun Chengbin and Yin Hongzhu, "Jiang Zemin, Zhu Rongji Address Religious Work Conference, Other Leaders Take Part," reprinted in Foreign Broadcast Information Service, FBIS-CHI-2001-1212, December 12, 2001.

PART I

*State Policy:
Control of Religion*

2

DANIEL H. BAYS

A Tradition of State Dominance

Looking back over a thousand years of Chinese history, one finds little new about today's pattern of relations between the state and religion in China. Government registration and monitoring of religious activities, although irregularly exercised, has been a constant reality of organized religious life in both traditional and modern times.

Philip Kuhn's insightful 1990 book, *Soulstealers: The Chinese Sorcery Scare of 1768,* describes similar circumstances in China more than 230 years ago.[1] The essentials of the story so engagingly recounted by Kuhn include widespread popular panic in several provinces of central China over rumors of sorcery or witchcraft, the emperor's always-vigilant watchfulness for any signs of sedition or rebellion, and a massive scapegoating of powerless victims and fabrication of evidence against them. In short, the Qianlong emperor mobilized his entire bureaucracy for an extended effort at tracking down and exterminating a nonexistent threat to the dynasty. The main outcomes of this campaign were an eventual tacit imperial acknowledgement that the whole affair was a wild-goose chase, relief on the part of the officials who had been given the onerous responsibility for the investigation and prosecution (but who of course had not dared to point out the farcical nature of the events in midinvestigation), and a large amount of human "collateral damage," or human rights abuses, inflicted upon those hapless victims who had been arrested, interrogated, and tortured, some of whom died in the process.

The interesting point for the purposes of this book is that in this case and in countless others that dot the annals of imperial China, among the main targets for suspicion, arrest, and prosecution were the wandering religious figures—preachers or evangelists—and local lay religious leaders outside the registered mainstream of the religious establishment. Occasionally these included Christians, after Christianity was prohibited in the early eighteenth century.[2] But most cases involved one of two categories. One was the roaming Buddhist or Taoist monks who were not affiliated with a registered temple or monastery and did not have a proper state-issued ordination certificate. The other category of victims, more dangerous in the eyes of the state, was the leaders of organized syncretic sects that were outside the traditions of state-recognized orthodox religions and their designated worship sites.[3] These leaders of heterodox sectarian groups were sometimes priests or monks, sometimes lay persons. Political authorities typically accused the culprits of "deluding the people" with outright antigovernment or "antistate" activities—similar to the Chinese Communist Party's charges against Falungong and some quasi-Christian groups in China today.

The Qianlong emperor's view of these "bad elements" is indicative of a tradition of government attitudes and policies toward grassroots religious movements that goes back at least to the Tang dynasty, thirteen hundred years ago.[4] In the "soul-stealers" case, the emperor fumed that these unregistered religious personnel "steal the name of clergy but lack their discipline" (that is, they do not comply with the state's rules for religious personnel); "engage in depraved and illicit activities" (a frequent charge was, as it is today, illicit sex with gullible female followers); and "are hard to investigate and control" (a classic understatement and a sentiment surely shared today by top party bureaucrats with regard to Falungong).[5] With the central government so quick to suspect them, and lacking the protection of organized, registered religious institutions, these marginal religious elements were, as Kuhn says, "made to order for a nationwide sorcerer-hunt" in 1768 and for comparable witch hunts at other times before and since.[6]

The point here is that in terms of the most fundamental level of assumptions of the state toward religion, there has hardly been a Chinese political regime from the Tang dynasty (618–907) to the present that has not required a form of registration or licensing of religious groups or has not assumed the right to monitor and intervene in religious affairs.[7] For a thousand years there has been a specific institutional apparatus for this purpose. From the Song dynasty until the end of the Qing in 1912, the Board of Rites in the capital supervised a clerical bureaucracy much like today's Religious Affairs Bureau. This body authorized and registered temples and other religious venues and licensed clerics by issuing and renewing ordination certificates. This was done for institutional Buddhism and Taoism. Other religious elements, both the fringe-wandering monks and the lay sectarians, populated the untidy world of unlicensed religious personnel operating outside properly registered religious venues and were thus not part of the system. Thus they were fair game for popular suspicion and rumors and for official harassment, extortion, or more severe persecution. Parallels with the situation of unregistered religious groups in China today are obvious. Moreover, just as today, the behavior of local authorities toward unregistered religious groups often varied from disinterested neglect to violent crackdown, depending on the locality—unless, of course, the emperor or some other top central government official roused himself to identify and condemn a particular religious group or movement as especially noxious or an "evil cult," which would then mobilize the whole national bureaucracy against it.

Why were dynastic governments, like today's government, so insistent on monitoring and intervening in religious matters? One reason, of course, is that the state itself had, and has today, religious pretensions and claims. Now as then, in its mode of public discourse, in its sanctification of the existing political order, and in many other ways the Chinese government behaves as a theocratic organization.[8] Another is that the central government was not just paranoid in its constant suspicion of grassroots religiosity and unregistered movements (that is, it was paranoid, but not without cause). Beginning early in Chinese history, a succession of Taoist- and Buddhist-related sectarian movements evolved into organized syncretic heterodox sects, many with their own scriptures.[9] Eventually, by the late imperial era, these resulted in a whole range of groups, including the White Lotus tradition and other offshoots such as the Eight Trigrams.[10] Some of them did in fact become militant politicized antigovernment forces, a few of which were responsible for weakening and toppling dynasties. These syncretic sects were often characterized by a lively millenarianism.[11] A subset of these groups, distinguished by what one scholar calls a "messianic eschatology," showed a persistent tendency toward political violence and rebellion.[12] Such rebellion was no less threatening to the dynasty for being religiously inspired.

So it is not surprising that imperial bureaucracies developed an instinctive suspicion of any such religious movement that could conceivably evolve into such a dangerous political force. Civic loyalty would always trump spiritual loyalty.[13] Of course the nonpolitical and essentially harmless religious groups and movements were often as much at risk of repression as the politicized and dangerous ones in the eyes of imperial bureaucrats who did not know the difference between them. (Again, despite some differences, parallels with today seem apparent; local officials in China are expected to protect "religion" but suppress "superstition." But as always in such matters, one person's religion can be another's superstition, in particular in the mind-set of a local cadre.)

This, then, was the system as it had evolved to the early modern period, about 1800. During the nineteenth century, the venerable tradition of vigilance toward religious sedition on the part of the central government and its bureaucrats intersected with the modern Protestant missionary movement, which reached China in 1807, almost two hundred years ago. At that time Christianity remained illegal, and, within China, to the extent that it registered at all on the government's radar scope, it was just another potentially seditious sect, one of many on the "monitor and harass at will" list. Christianity at this time was not necessarily even viewed as "foreign" by many government officials in the interior of China. Catholicism, after all, had been around for well over two hundred years and was older than some other illegal homegrown sects on the list of proscribed groups. Protestantism was seen as being in close association with the growing number of foreign traders on the China coast in the early years of the nineteenth century and was typically viewed as foreign. But as late as the 1830s there were still no Chinese Protestants beyond the small coastal enclaves at Macao and Canton (Guangzhou).

At any rate, Chinese Christians, both Catholics and Protestants, remained as subject to government monitoring, prohibition, and suppression as did the adherents of any other illegal sect. There were no exceptions to the rule that civic loyalty outweighed religious loyalty. Those "heretical" sects on the proscribed list were presumed to have put religious loyalty, especially to a sect leader, above loyalty to the state and the throne.[14] And in the view of the Qing state, Christianity certainly belonged on the proscribed list.

Then, for reasons having to do with trade, not religion, conflict between Britain and the Qing government (the Opium War) erupted in 1839. This conflict resulted in a British victory in 1842, and it also resulted in a coercively imposed new framework for China's government-to-government intercourse with the West: the "unequal treaty" system. This was a multilateral system of several treaties signed with various Western powers in succession after the British treaty of 1842. Several features of the treaties were prejudicial to China's economic interests and injurious to her sovereignty (thus the "unequal" label). For purposes of this discussion, the key feature of these new treaties with the Western nations was the end of the prohibition on Christianity. The new treaties, imposed by Western military power ("imperialism," if you will), thus removed Christianity from the well-established official "monitor and harass at will" list of sects and gave it a unique immunity from the Chinese state, a special protected status that no other religion had. Among other results of this development was the removal of Chinese Christians from the full authority and jurisdiction of their own government. Thereby was created the close association between Christianity and Western imperialism in China, which lasted until only about fifty years ago.

One might wonder why the special status given to Chinese Christians would be a problem, assuming that Christians were law-abiding Chinese citizens. The story of the Taiping Rebellion illustrates the problem quite clearly. In the 1830s and 1840s, at the very time that the Opium War occurred and the first treaties were signed, on another historical track a remarkable case of cross-cultural religious transmission was also occurring. Some of the literary products of early Protestant missionary and Chinese converts' Bible translation and tract writing found their way into the hands of a failed government official examinee, Hong Xiuquan. Hong was the sort of fellow who might well have become a sectarian religious leader or founder at any time in Chinese history. A combination of his own visions and guidance from these limited Christian writings convinced Hong that he was "God's Chinese son," as Jonathan Spence puts it, the direct offspring of a monotheistic, basically Judeo-Christian God and thus literally the younger brother of Jesus.[15]

As was typical in the classic pattern of Chinese sect formation and growth in past centuries, Hong's ideas, and his preaching and writings, tapped into social, economic, and ethnic tensions in society at large. Hong's own charisma and the organizing talents of some of his early disciples attracted thousands, then tens of thousands, of followers and in the late 1840s produced in the Far South of China a powerful sectarian movement, the God-Worshippers' Society. Continuing the traditional pattern of behavior for both sectarians and the Chinese government, the increasing scale of the God-Worshippers' activities inevitably prompted government repression. In 1850 the sectarians, faced with the choice between accepting suppression and launching an open political rebellion, chose the latter.

Hong became king of a new political order called the Taiping Heavenly Kingdom, which in fourteen years of one of the bloodiest and most destructive civil wars in human history nearly toppled the Qing dynasty before succumbing in 1864.

The Taipings were hardly "Christian" in anything like an orthodox sense. Yet the influence of the Taiping movement, including both its traditional sectarian context and its Christian components, is grossly underestimated by scholars in assessing the role of Christianity in modern China. Among Western observers in the 1850s, many Protestant missionaries at first thought that the Taipings might be an orthodox Christian movement. These missionaries were about the only ones sufficiently interested to study Taiping ideas seriously. What they found, of course, caused them to condemn Taiping Christianity as blasphemous, even laughable.[16] They did not in the least consider it to be a form of authentic Christianity. However, the Chinese state and the Confucian elite class of the nation (the "gentry," as some call it) certainly viewed the Taipings as Christian, as the Taipings themselves claimed to be. Moreover, the state and the gentry understandably considered the entire Taiping affair to be obvious confirmation of their ingrained suspicions that Christianity, like other sectarian movements, meant subversion and rebellion. Yet (and most frustrating, from the point of view of the Chinese state) this was the very religious movement given special protection by the new treaties forced upon China between 1842 and 1860.[17] Few more powerful historical examples could be found of a cross-cultural communications endeavor (that is, the nineteenth-century Christian missionary movement in China) starting off on the wrong foot.

The decades from 1860 until well after 1900, during the period of expansion of Christianity, saw many outbreaks of local tension and open conflict between foreign missionaries and Chinese converts on the one side and Chinese officials and local elites on the other.[18] There were many reasons for this phenomenon. Although foreign missionaries were only dimly aware of it during these decades, one of the reasons for the turmoil that often accompanied the spread of Christianity was the extent to which the image of Protestant as well as Catholic missions was tainted by Chinese memories of the Christian Taipings. All the instincts of the state were still to demand civic loyalty from all religious groups. The dynasty's impression of Chinese Christians as being disloyal and rebellious, and of foreign missionaries as promoting subversion, remained alive, even while the practical ability of the increasingly enfeebled Chinese state to monitor or suppress any religion declined steadily in the late nineteenth and early twentieth centuries.

After the demise of the Qing state in 1912, and the failure and collapse in 1916 of the republic that succeeded it, there was no national Chinese state to speak of, let alone one with the power to regulate the religious affairs of its people. Yet even at this point, at the lowest ebb of its capability, vestiges of the state at times showed the old instincts of wanting to regulate the practices of popular religion. Paradoxically, even as liberal constitutions created in 1912 and after guaranteed freedom of religious belief, debate erupted over the legitimacy of religious practice. As the republic disintegrated, some individuals, including the respected public intellectual Kang Youwei, advocated a reimposition of orthodoxy, making Confucianism China's official religion. Christians vigorously—and successfully—resisted.[19] Statist-minded modernizers from the first to the fourth decades of the twentieth century denounced both "religion" and "superstition" as vestiges of the past that should be destroyed.[20] For example, when a new national political movement took shape in the 1920s, led by the Nationalist Party, one of its first priorities was to demand a significant degree of regulatory power over religious institutions, especially educational institutions operated by Christian churches and missions.[21] Religious groups, including Christian churches, were required to register their documents, such as bylaws, and names of leaders with the Nationalist government's Ministry of the Interior in the 1930s.[22] Despite these continuing evidences of the compulsion to ensure that civic loyalty outweighed spiritual loyalty, no government during these decades was strong enough to enforce its will over more than a small part of the country; it simply had insufficient control.

Therefore, my own view is that the half century from about 1900 to the founding of the People's Republic of China in 1949 was an anomaly in terms of the historical pattern of state relations with religion, especially Christianity. For the most part the state's monitoring of religion was a moot issue because of the absence of a central state strong enough to do so.

In the meantime, during these same decades Christianity grew and became well rooted in the Chinese landscape, both in its foreign missionary-led and native-led versions. The Chinese Christianity of 1950 was a very different entity from what it had been toward the end of the nineteenth century. This is not the place for a detailed history of Protestant Christianity in China from the mid-1800s to the communist period.[23] But an encapsulated version seems in order. To summarize briefly, I would point out three successive periods of development.

The first, from 1860 to 1900, was the great age of institutional Protestant expansion. The number of Western mission societies represented in China multiplied, and many became highly professionalized. Full of Victorian confidence despite only modest gains in numbers of converts, they built . . . and built: schools, hospitals, churches and chapels, and publishing houses with large translation projects. These decades also involved the unsung but important participation by Chinese Christians in all these endeavors, laying the groundwork for the emergence of a more visible Chinese Protestant community after 1900. The well-developed Protestant school system of the late nineteenth and early twentieth centuries produced both Chinese pastors and leaders and middle-class urban Chinese congregations. Yet in 1900 the Christian presence was tiny (barely a hundred thousand Chinese Protestants) and on the defensive—not because of state regulation (by this time the state was weak) but because of the unresponsiveness of Chinese society.

The second period was from 1900 to the mid-1920s. After the tragic events of the Boxer Uprising in 1900, which seemed such a setback, Protestantism actually enjoyed more than two decades of rapid growth and rise in prestige. Chinese Protestants were active in late Qing reform movements before 1911 and also in the republican revolutionary movement. With the new republic of 1912, Chinese Protestantism seemed to be riding the wave of the future as part of China's modernity.[24] The Chinese Protestant community also became a more visible partner with the foreign missionaries, with its own leaders and priorities. The majority of the delegates at the big 1922 National Christian Conference were Chinese, as were the majority of members of the National Christian Council of China, formed in 1924. Yet the partnership, although real, also remained tilted toward the dominant power of the foreign missionaries, especially in the finances of the Protestant world. Partly for this reason, by the 1920s several Chinese Christian movements had emerged that were wholly independent of the Presbyterian, Baptist, Methodist, or other denominational foreign missions. These included such homegrown Chinese products as the True Jesus Church and the Jesus Family, as well as the "Little Flock" of Watchman Nee (Ni Tuosheng, 1903–72). During these decades, the state was hardly a factor, despite the instincts to reimpose control over religion alluded to earlier. Protestants, indeed Catholics as well, could proceed with their activities without being monitored or regulated by an intrusive Chinese government.

The third and last period of precommunist Protestant history was from about 1925 to 1950. During these years, the Sino-foreign Protestant movement that seemed so promising in the early 1920s suffered heavy blows, though not from actions of a national state so much as from the rise of popular militant nationalism. In the 1920s powerful new political movements mounted effective attacks on the whole structure of the foreign presence and role in China, denouncing Christianity as cultural imperialism, part of the unequal-treaty system. In some ways this was a precursor to much greater pressures to come under communism after 1950. Speaking broadly, the whole Sino-foreign sector of Protestantism was to some extent permanently on the defensive after the late 1920s. Despite Chiang Kai-shek's conversion and baptism (which had the effect of easing the anti-Christian pressures from the Nationalist Party, many of whose leaders were inimical toward all religions as a wasteful obstacle to modernization),[25] the challenges multiplied: the gutting of missions budgets by the Great Depression, the loss of self-confidence and reduction in numbers of the mainline churches' missions effort,[26] the devastation of war with Japan after 1937, and then the Chinese civil war of the late 1940s. The Chinese Protestant mainstream never did manage to shake off its image of being in close collaboration with the foreign presence in China. The new communist government finally, in the early 1950s, as part of reestablishing controls over religion, forced Protestant leaders to publicly renounce their association with foreigners in a way that was humiliating and traumatic for many of them.

Thus the traditional missions-related denominational churches faced one crisis after another from the 1920s on, although interference by a suspicious Chinese state was not one of their major problems. Interestingly, some of the independent Protestant movements that had struggled through their beginnings in the 1920s fared better, in some ways, in the 1930s and 1940s. Unencumbered by the heavy institutional budgetary burden of the missions churches and effective in addressing people in desperation, they grew steadily during these years. By 1950, both the Little Flock and the True Jesus Church were probably larger than any single denomination in the Sino-foreign Protestant sector. The strong evangelical or fundamentalist features of most of these independent groups before 1950 also may have created a resiliency of faith and a core of stubborn believers who later contributed significantly to the survival of Chinese Protestantism when it was in its darkest hour, from the late 1950s to the mid-1970s.

The Sino-foreign Protestant mainstream and the more sectarian independent churches, though different in many ways, were similar in that during the entire first half of the twentieth century they were spared the demands of an intrusive state. However, both sectors of Protestantism, and of course Catholics as well, had to deal with such a state after 1950. Indeed, the demands and pressures that the new government put on the Christian community, now stripped of any vestiges of protection from its links to foreigners, were both powerful and somewhat unexpected. It had been a long time, more than a century, since Christianity had stood nakedly exposed to the actions of any Chinese state and many decades since a Chinese state had existed with both the capability and the inclination to interfere in internal Christian affairs. In the context of this discussion, this development should not have been a surprise. In one sense it was simply the resumption of a long-standing tradition. However, in another sense the new regime, because of its Marxist underpinnings, constituted a more serious threat to the very existence of organized religious life than had any previous regime.

Chinese religious history after 1950 is, of course, tightly intertwined with the theme of state and Communist Party control, interference, and repression. That has been particularly true for Chinese Catholics, as is evident in Richard Madsen's chapter 6 in this volume. Moreover, as Jason Kindopp shows in his essay on Protestantism today (chapter 8), Chinese Protestants also had to function within a much more hostile set of parameters imposed on them by the new state, beginning soon after its inception.[27] Did the restrictions and controls of the new communist regime constitute a difference of degree or of kind when compared with those of previous governments?

One element largely absent from the dynastic motivations for control of religion, though it was increasingly present in the last years of the Qing dynasty and in the republican period after 1912, was nationalism. The new communist regime's intense nationalistic animus against "imperialism" boded ill for those foreign missionaries who remained after 1949. The Korean War in 1950 sealed their fate, and within two years practically all were expelled or jailed. The war also brought Chinese Protestants under suspicion because many had foreign ties.

The state did not overtly attempt to abolish religion, but it did construct a complex and comprehensive apparatus through which to unify, monitor, and control religious groups and organizations and to isolate them from broader society. This apparatus seems to have been rather similar to the control devices used by dynastic governments in the past, but more intense. The new government not only registered and monitored Protestants and other religious believers, as dynastic regimes had done, but also systematically reduced the influence of religion in society (as some premodern regimes had wished to do but had lacked the means).

The "patriotic" religious organizations that were erected under Chinese Communist Party rule operated from a Marxist belief that religion was socially retrograde and doomed to eventual extinction. From their inception, therefore, these organizations not only regulated religious activity but also actively eroded the autonomy of religious groups and communities. In this regard, communist control went significantly beyond pre-1949 levels. As is well known, with the coming of the Cultural Revolution in 1966 all churches, temples, monasteries, and venues for any kind of religious activity were closed for more than a decade. Religion was effectively abolished, a goal of total eradication that went beyond anything attempted by the monitoring devices of dynastic or republican regimes in the pre-1949 era. Organizations such as the Religious Affairs Bureau and the patriotic religious organizations now had no purpose, and they too were dissolved.

In the late 1970s, as part of a general loosening of Maoist controls by the reformist leadership under Deng Xiaoping, the state backed away from a radical stance of eradication of religion and retreated to a more historically familiar policy of registration and monitoring. Both the Religious Affairs Bureau and the patriotic religious organizations were resurrected as the umbrella under which religious life could legitimately occur.[28] The Religious Affairs Bureau, under its directing unit, the United Front Work Department, and the officially authorized religious organizations continue today to constitute what are in many ways the equivalent of the old imperial devices of monitoring and control that existed for many centuries.

Religious monitoring and regulation by the state in the recent past and present is not only a "Chinese communist" phenomenon but also a "Chinese state" one. Attitudes of suspicion and systematic policies of regulation or suppression (or both) toward grassroots religion have characterized the mind-set of all Chinese political regimes. This pattern held until the foreign-imposed treaty system in the nineteenth century removed Christianity from the list of targets of close supervision. The absence of strong central-state power for the first half of the twentieth century also contributed to a somewhat artificial situation, one in which religious movements of all kinds did not have to worry much about state interference, such as demands for registration. Since 1949, however, a more historically "normal" situation has prevailed. All the old instincts of state control have reemerged; bodies such as the Religious Affairs Bureau and the Three-Self Patriotic Movement have been seen by the state as indispensable. In recent years, the extent of the state's control of religion—for example, its ideological dictates and institutional manipulation—has often gone beyond the parameters (and resources) of premodern regimes. But the underlying pattern is familiar. Today's leaders sometimes sound downright archaic—rather like the Qianlong emperor—in denouncing and proscribing certain movements as "evil cults."[29]

This situation will not easily change. This is not to say that it cannot, or will not, change. One might argue that if the present Chinese state is capable of adapting to international regimes such as the World Trade Organization, it is certainly capable of adopting international standards of religious freedom, or at least of easing up on the compulsion to interfere in its citizens' religious lives. Of course it is capable; but it is not inclined to do so. One of the reasons is that the state's suspicion of and interference in religion is not only a short-term policy driven by Marxist ideology and measured in terms of decades. It is also a long-established practice measured in centuries or even millenniums, one rehearsed countless times by emperors and their bureaucrats long before the actions of today's cadres.

Notes

1. Philip Kuhn, *Soulstealers: The Chinese Sorcery Scare of 1768* (Harvard University Press, 1990).

2. After the proscription of (Catholic) Christianity in the early part of the eighteenth century, some local Catholic leaders were arrested and accused of being members of the outlawed White Lotus sect or other allegedly seditious groups. They were generally cleared of these charges of overt sedition, but as followers of an illegal sect they still remained vulnerable to arrest. See Robert Entenmann, "Chinese Catholics and the State during the White Lotus Rebellion, 1796–1805," paper presented at the International Institute for Asian Studies workshop, Contextualization of Christianity in China: An Evaluation in Modern Perspective, University of Leiden, June 6–8, 2002.

3. Religions recognized by the state included Buddhism, Taoism, Islam, and some state-co-opted local deities like Guandi and Mazu. The greatest orthodoxy of all, of course, was the state cult of Confucius and the cult of filial piety and veneration of ancestors.

4. The Chinese state today still routinely refers to holders of unwelcome views, both religious and secular, as "bad elements." See Ian Buruma, *Bad Elements: Chinese Rebels from Los Angeles to Beijing* (Random House, 2001).

5. Kuhn, *Soulstealers,* p. 110.

6. Ibid., p. 111.

7. Kim-kwong Chan, "A Chinese Perspective on the Interpretation of the Chinese Government's Religious Policy," in Alan Hunter and Don Rimmington, eds., *All under Heaven: Chinese Tradition and Christian Life in the People's Republic of China* (Kampen, Netherlands: J. H. Kok, 1992), pp. 45–51; Timothy Brook, "At the Margin of Public Authority: The Ming State and Buddhism," in Theodore Huters, R. Bin Wong, and Pauline Yu, eds., *Culture and State in Chinese History* (Stanford University Press, 1997), pp. 161–81; and Vincent Goossaert, "Counting the Monks: The 1736–1739 Census of the Chinese Clergy," *Late Imperial China,* vol. 21 (December 2000), pp. 40–85. The main themes of this phenomenon were actually laid out clearly forty years ago by the sociologist C. K. Yang in chapter 8 of *Religion in Chinese Society* (University of California Press, 1961), and the situation specifically regarding sectarian religious movements was extensively if tendentiously described almost a century ago in J. J. M. De Groot, *Sectarianism and Religious Persecution in China* (Amsterdam: Johannes Muller, 1903).

8. Alan Hunter and Don Rimmington, "Religion and Social Change in Contemporary China," in Alan Hunter and Don Rimmington, eds., *All under Heaven: Chinese Tradition and Christian Life in the People's Republic of China* (Kampen, Netherlands: J. H. Kok, 1992), pp. 11–37.

9. Daniel Overmyer, *Precious Volumes: An Introduction to Chinese Sectarian Scriptures from the Sixteenth and Seventeenth Centuries* (Harvard University Press, 1999).

10. Stevan Harrell and Elizabeth J. Perry, "Syncretic Sects in Chinese Society: An Introduction," *Modern China,* vol. 8 (July 1982), pp. 283–303 (an introduction to a two-part symposium of eight articles in nos. 8.3 and 8.4 of the journal). For the White Lotus sect, in particular, see B. J. Ter Haar, *The White Lotus Teachings in Chinese Religious History* (Leiden, Netherlands: Brill, 1992).

11. Harrell and Perry, "Syncretic Sects," pp. 290–92.

12. Richard Shek, "Sectarian Eschatology and Violence," in Jonathan N. Lipman and Stevan Harrell, eds., *Violence in China: Essays in Culture and Counterculture* (State University of New York Press, 1990), pp. 87–114.

13. This principle was codified and enshrined in the high Qing period by the "Sacred Edict" of the emperor Kangxi, sixteen hortatory maxims later elaborated upon by his son, the emperor Yongzheng, and put into a colloquial form that could presumably be understood by the common people. Kangxi's maxim 7, "Extirpate heresy to exalt orthodoxy," was expanded considerably by Yongzheng to include a wholesale denunciation of all supernatural beliefs, including the "orthodox" mainstream of Taoism and Buddhism, as superstition or heresy. In a striking parallel to today's Chinese government's tenet that religion will eventually disappear from a sufficiently modernized society, Yongzheng's gloss on maxim 7 confidently predicts that "if none of you believe in heretical sects, they . . . will become extinct naturally." See Pei-kai Cheng and Michael Lestz, with Jonathan D. Spence, *The Search for Modern China: A Documentary Collection* (Norton, 1999), pp. 65–68.

14. For many examples over the past few centuries of the imperial era, standard sources are Susan Naquin, *Millenarian Rebellion in China: The Eight Trigrams Uprising of 1813* (Yale University Press, 1976); Susan Naquin, *Shantung Rebellion: The Wang Lun Uprising of 1774* (Yale University Press, 1981); Daniel Overmyer, *Folk Buddhist Religion* (Harvard University Press, 1976); and De Groot, *Sectarianism.*

15. Jonathan Spence, *God's Chinese Son: The Taiping Heavenly Kingdom of Hong Xiuquan* (Norton, 1996). At least early in his thinking, Hong seems to have conflated the Old Testament Jehovah, the Christian God the Father, and the Lord on High divinity (*Shangdi*) of early China.

16. For example, Hong believed that God had a heavenly wife (that is, the mother of Hong and of Jesus; Hong left the role of Mary fuzzy) and that in fact Jesus had a wife and children in heaven.

17. The second round of treaties between China and the Western nations expanded even more the rights of both foreign Christian missionaries and Chinese Christians throughout the country.

18. See the standard account of Paul Cohen, *China and Christianity: The Missionary Movement and the Growth of Chinese Antiforeignism, 1860–1870* (Harvard University Press, 1963); also several more-recent essays in the first part of Daniel H. Bays, ed., *Christianity in China: From the Eighteenth Century to the Present* (Stanford University Press, 1996).

19. Charles A. Keller, "Nationalism and Chinese Christians: The Religious Freedom Campaign and Movement for Independent Chinese Churches, 1911–1917," *Republican China,* vol. 17 (April 1992), pp. 30–51.

20. See Prasenjit Duara, "Knowledge and Power in the Discourse of Modernity: The Campaigns against Popular Religion in Early-Twentieth-Century China," *Journal of Asian Studies,* vol. 50 (February 1991), pp. 67–83.

21. Jessie G. Lutz, *Chinese Politics and Christian Missions: The Anti-Christian Movements of 1920–1928* (Notre Dame, Ind.: Cross Cultural Publications, 1988).

22. My own observation of materials in the Second Historical Archives in Nanjing; for example, registration files under "Zongjiao" [religion] and subfile "Zhongguo Yesujiao zilihui" [China Christian independent church].

23. For a single source that covers the modern period in broad strokes, see Kenneth Scott Latourette, *A History of Christian Missions in China* (London: SPCK, 1929). Another usable work is Bob Whyte, *Unfinished Encounter: China and Christianity* (London: Collins, 1988). See also my own survey of modern Chinese Protestantism, "China," in Hans Hillerbrand, ed., *Encyclopedia of Protestantism* (New York: Routledge, 2003), and contributions by several scholars in R. G. Tiedemann, ed., *Handbook of Christianity in China,* vol. 2, *1800 to the Present* (Leiden, Netherlands: Brill, 2004, forthcoming).

24. A fine study of influential reformist Chinese Christians early in the twentieth century is Ryan Dunch, *Fuzhou Protestants and the Making of a Modern China, 1857–1927* (Yale University Press, 2001).

25. See Duara, "Knowledge and Power in the Discourse of Modernity."

26. For this point, see the fine study by Lian Xi, *The Conversion of Missionaries: Liberalism in American Protestant Missions in China, 1907–1932* (Pennsylvania State University Press, 1997).

27. For Protestants, useful histories of the 1950s to the 1970s, from varying political points of view, can be found in Whyte, *Unfinished Encounter;* Richard C. Bush Jr., *Religion in Communist China* (New York: Abingdon, 1970); Francis P. Jones, *The Church in Communist China: A Protestant Appraisal* (New York: Friendship, 1962); Philip L. Wickeri, *Seeking the Common Ground: Protestant Christianity, the Three-Self Movement, and China's United Front* (Maryknoll, N.Y.: Orbis, 1988); and Thomas A. Harvey, *Acquainted with Grief: Wang Mingdao's Stand for the Persecuted Church in China* (Grand Rapids, Mich.: Brazos, 2002).

28. Actually, some of the problems of having such an overtly political organization as the Three-Self Patriotic Movement monitoring matters of faith were acknowledged within a year, in fall 1980, when the third National Christian Conference created a new body, the China Christian Council, to pair with the Three-Self Patriotic Movement. The China Christian Council is supposed to concern itself with matters of faith, church order, theological education, and the like. Its personnel and leadership overlap so much with that of the Three-Self Patriotic Movement, however, that the two are virtually indistinguishable and are in fact referred to as the *lianghui* (two committees). With Wu Yaozong's death in 1979, Ding Guangxun was elevated to top Protestant leadership and was made head of both organizations.

29. This label, indicating extreme illegality, marks the sect as the target of vigorous extermination efforts by the police power of the state. It is used not only for the Falungong but also for quasi-Christian groups such as Eastern Lightning, the Disciples' Sect, the Established King, and several others. In considering parallels in this general area of analysis, I am indebted to the insights of Daniel J. Nietering, "Grounds for Suspicion: China's Totalitarian Regimes Encounter Heterodoxy" (unpublished seminar paper, Calvin College, Department of History, Spring 2003).

3

MICKEY SPIEGEL

Control and Containment in the Reform Era

On March 31, 1982, four years after the new leadership under Deng Xiaoping set China on a path of economic reform, the Central Committee of the Chinese Communist Party promulgated a fresh religious policy. Just as economic reform countered Mao's "continuous revolution" strategy of mobilizing the masses against class enemies, so the new religious policy cast aside the radical attempts to eradicate religion that prevailed during the Cultural Revolution (1966–76). Embodied in "The Basic Viewpoint and Policy on the Religious Question during Our Country's Socialist Period" (hereafter referred to as Document 19),[1] the new policy sought to harness the productive capacity of religious adherents in the interest of building a strong, modern state without fostering the emergence of centers of loyalty to compete with or even threaten the party's primacy.

It had become clear that a total ban on religion served neither economic modernization nor social stability. China's leaders discovered during the Cultural Revolution that outlawing religious practice; destroying churches, temples, mosques, and religious artifacts; and imprisoning, deporting, and executing clergy only drove believers further underground, deepened their faith, and furthered the culture of martyrdom embedded in some faith-based communities. Rather than limiting religious belief, the Cultural Revolution policies might have deepened commitment.

As Marxists, the leadership could not renounce atheism—to this day no party member may be a religious believer. But the leadership could concede that as "old thinking and habits cannot be thoroughly wiped out in a short period," Chinese citizens could expect a long interim stage during which religion would be tolerated, if not welcomed.[2] Thus party leaders repudiated the total ban on all religious belief and expression and the harsh measures of enforcement they had adopted and opted instead for a strategy of strict party-state control of religion centered on co-optation. In exchange for permission to worship their gods, believers would have to abide by a regulatory structure designed to limit religious group autonomy and stifle congregational growth.

The new policy promised "respect for and protection of the freedom of religious belief."[3] Less than a year later this assurance was codified in article 36 of China's 1982 constitution.[4] The authors of this document chose their wording carefully, revealing just how little religious freedom the leaders were actually willing to confer. By limiting the protections to religious belief and to normal religious activities, Document 19 and the constitution restricted the realm of religious freedom to individual conviction and government-sanctioned normality. In reality, all aspects of religious expression and practice were subject to regulation. Document 19 and article 36 of the constitution laid the foundation for Chinese acceptance of an international regulatory framework that narrowed opportunities for believers to practice as they chose and with whom they chose and to communicate their beliefs to others.[5]

Article 36 of the 1982 constitution offers protection for normal religious activities, but it does not define the meaning of "normal," other than to declare that religion must not be used to disrupt public order, impair health, or interfere with education.[6] In a circular fashion typical of Chinese Communist Party rule, this vagueness has come to mean that anything the authorities deem illegal is ipso facto abnormal and, therefore, illegal. Interpretation is subject to the political whims of political authorities because no independent judiciary exists to counter their judgments. Sometimes Beijing sets the general line. Sometimes the local cadres decide. For example, Document 19 requires that China's religious communities be self-governing, self-supporting, self-propagating, and free from foreign domination. Before 1989, that meant that Catholics in China could not acknowledge the pope; consequently, bishops loyal to the Vatican were subject to constant harassment and repeated detention. In recent times, China's Catholics have been able to acknowledge the pope's "spiritual authority," and many "official" bishops (those ordained by Chinese authorities rather than by the pope) have quietly and without interference from Beijing sought and obtained the pope's blessing.

In addition, the government severely compromises the promise of "freedom of religious belief" by reserving to itself the right to decide what is and what is not a religion. Only Buddhism, Taoism, Protestantism (labeled "Christianity" in Chinese), Catholicism, and Islam qualify as legitimate religions. Other world-class systems with few believers in China—Hinduism, Judaism, and Eastern Orthodoxy—are not recognized. The government has acknowledged popular folk religion, which is central to the lives of millions of Chinese, only to the extent that some of the beliefs associated with it have been labeled superstitious and, therefore, discouraged.

Even recognized religions are compromised by official edicts. For example, much of the diversity within Chinese Protestantism has been squelched by the government's elimination of the ritual, theological, and doctrinal differences among its denominations and its declaration of Christianity as a postdenominational one-size-fits-all faith. Chinese authorities have refused to recognize many conservative Protestant belief systems as true religions, in part because adherents have held onto their theological differences and thus to their independence. Chinese officials have labeled such independents as heterodox, at times with compliance from more mainstream Protestant groups, and have found reasons to ban and persecute them. The group called the Local Church, referred to by nonmembers as the Shouters (*huhanpai*), is a case in point. Since the 1980s, the government has targeted groups of Shouters for their independence and evangelism and for their strict interpretation of the divide between church and state.[7]

In addition to official and inconsistent interpretation of what is normal or abnormal and what is orthodox or heterodox, China's leaders have quietly condoned extralegal methods in the fight to prevent exponential growth in the number of believers and to undermine the strength and autonomy of religious communities. Influential religious leaders who have in any way defied the government are separated from their followers. Some have been detained; others are sent on long journeys; some are subjected to mandatory reeducation sessions. Prohibitive fines levied on families and the destruction of property shatter community solidarity. At the same time, government officials offer obedient religious leaders some space for congregational growth and a measure of recognition and influence at home and abroad if they join or cooperate with the government's religious bureaucracy and with the party's policy goals.

The Control Apparatus

A nationwide bureaucracy, made up of bureaus within the party, the state, and the police and augmented by nominally autonomous "patriotic" religious organizations, has the task of keeping religious organization and practice within acceptable bounds. The members of the Standing Committee of the Politburo, the country's top leaders, set broad policy direction. The party's United Front Work Department, as part of its mission to weld nonparty constituencies to party policies, assists in formulating policy and directing its implementation.[8] The state's Religious Affairs Bureau issues its own regulations and conducts much of the day-to-day supervision of religious bodies.[9] Both the United Front Work Department and the Religious Affairs Bureau are hierarchically organized according to administrative levels, from the national down to the county level. In addition, each of the religions recognized by the government has a corresponding "patriotic" organization with sole representative authority. The organizations purportedly function as conduits between the religious communities and the party and state. The Three-Self Patriotic Movement oversees Protestant affairs, the Catholic Patriotic Association oversees Catholic affairs, and so on. These associations, also organized hierarchically by administrative level, are not voluntary organizations, and their members are not necessarily believers, given the dictum that party members must be atheists. The organizations must "accept the leadership of the Party and the government" and "defend the interests of the state."[10]

The Ministry of Public Security, together with local police agencies, works closely with the Religious Affairs Bureau and officials from the patriotic religious organizations to break up unauthorized religious meetings, detain practitioners, and levy fines. Implementation of central or provincial regulations has been at the discretion of the local authorities, and what has been construed as normal religious practice has varied over space and time.

Establishing a "Rule of Law"

Having established a broad policy framework for restricting and controlling religion and having crafted an intrusive bureaucracy to enforce it, China's leaders set about turning Chinese Communist Party policy guidelines into government regulations. This effort to build a so-called rule of law was intended to provide greater regularity in dealing with matters requiring permanent supervision and control. The leadership was motivated in part by public relations problems that arose following the promulgation of Document 19. Instances of the abuse of clergy and influential lay religionists had surfaced. Publicity about prolonged disappearances, long sentences, restriction on movement, mandatory study sessions under enforced detention, and substantial fines damaged China's international image and brought into question the party's claim of instituting a long-term, consistent solution to the problem of controlling religious affairs.

For government leaders, a "rule of law" had several advantages. Most notably, it allowed them to claim that people were being detained or otherwise punished not for religious belief or practice but rather for breaking the law. This fiction made it easier to isolate the die-hard religious elements while "reeducating" the bulk of believers and reintegrating them into the social mainstream. In addition, it was hoped that a rule of law, deemed more acceptable to the international community than a crude crackdown on religious belief and practice, would weaken condemnation from overseas.

This "rule of law," however, was in fact "rule by law," a scheme whereby those in power used the law for their own purposes. In addition, it was not based on law at all, that is, on formal legislation enacted by the National People's Congress; rather, it was grounded in regulations to which there was no legal recourse.

These rule-of-law issues came to the forefront in 1991 with the promulgation of the "Circular on Some Problems Concerning the Further Improvement of Work on Religion" (hereafter referred to as Document 6).[11] According to the circular, the nine-year-old Document 19 policies were by and large accomplishing their goals, but "foreign hostile forces" and renegade elements within China's borders were still using religion to undermine China's socialist system and to turn the "hearts and minds" of the young against Marxist doctrine. The cure for this, according to Document 6, was more rule by law. "Regulating religious affairs according to the law" could eliminate such unwanted influences and at the same time protect the rights of believers.[12] To accomplish these goals, believers and the security and judicial forces responsible for compliance had to accept the developing legal structure. The heart of the matter was mandatory registration for every congregation, church, monastery, mosque, and temple.

Thereafter, a series of regulations emanating from the central and local governments clarified and strengthened the broadly worded directives of

Document 6, and the State Council (China's executive branch) promulgated detailed rules for its implementation. Two sets were issued in 1994, regulations governing the management of and registration procedures for venues for religious activities.[13] The "Method for the Annual Inspection of Places of Religious Activities" followed in 1996.[14] Taken together, the new regulations clarify the process of registration itself, set out a string of requirements without which it is futile even to consider applying, and quietly make known what facets of congregational organization and activity come under bureaucratic oversight, if not outright control, once registration has been approved.

These central government policies and regulations only began the process of crafting a regulatory structure. Using the central policies as guidelines, municipalities, provinces, counties, and other jurisdictions turned principles into practice and drafted their own sets of specific implementing rules, many of which are severely restrictive. The municipal and provincial regulations encompass personnel, publications, religious activities other than worship, appropriate sites for activities, foreign contacts, seminary education, and so-called legal responsibilities—issues that affect and compromise the expression of religious belief. The remarkable similarity among the rules from the various localities attests to the fact that they were all drafted according to a national template, a standard procedure in Chinese regulatory systems.[15] The two newest sets of rules—one for Jiangsu Province, effective June 1, 2002, the other for the municipality of Beijing, effective November 1, 2002—do not significantly differ from the regulations going back ten years. A careful comparison of local regulations, such as the "1998 Ordinance on the Management of Religious Affairs of Guangzhou Municipality" and the 1995 "Regulations from the Shanghai Religious Affairs Bureau," suggests, however, that certain jurisdictions are more concerned with some issues than with others, the most likely reason being variations in local conditions.[16]

The patriotic religious organizations at virtually every administrative level, fulfilling their task to "guide" congregants in policy implementation, have issued directives for specific compliance as well as doctrinal interpretation.[17] For example, documents from the Three-Self Patriotic Movement, in addition to reinforcing the policies spelled out in national and local regulations, give guidance on what is or is not a proper sermon, remind local churches that children under the age of eighteen should not receive religious instruction nor be baptized or admitted to the church, admonish congregants not to listen to overseas religious broadcasts, inveigh against denominational separatism and unorthodox beliefs, and prohibit local churches from practicing "freelance" religion.[18] The "Church Order for Chinese Protestant Christian Churches," issued December 28, 1996, lays out model rules for churches as to who may be a congregant, how a church must be organized and managed, and how sacraments are to be administered. The models also speak to the qualifications, duties, and titles of clergy; ordination procedures and ceremonies; and admonishments and punishments for clergy. The order specifically states that "local church constitution[s] may not contradict this Church Order."[19]

Targeted Areas for Regulation

Taken together, official regulations touch on virtually every aspect of religious existence. Several prominent issue areas relate to religious sites, clerical qualifications, permissible religious activities, religious literature, and foreign contacts.

Mandatory Registration of Religious Venues

The key issue in China's religious policy is mandatory registration of all venues for religious activity. Failure to register a congregation (or its equivalent) with the proper authorities renders it and all its activities illegal and vulnerable to closure. As Ye Xiaowen, head of the Religious Affairs Bureau, explained in 1996, "Our aim is not registration for its own sake, but . . . control over places for religious activities as well as over all religious activities themselves."[20]

To be considered for registration, a site must comply with two somewhat differing sets of national and local requirements, the first broadly and loosely worded, the second reasonably straightforward, if stringent. The most important national stipulation makes it clear that there can be nothing ad hoc about a religious gathering. The applicant group must have a fixed name and meeting place, believers who meet regularly, professional clergy (a requirement that eliminates the many congregations relying on lay leaders), a legal source of income, and an independent management body composed of believers.[21] It is this management body that is in charge. Its members, although supposedly democratically chosen, can be considered for their posts only after careful vetting by government cadres in the Religious Affairs Bureau. For example, the "Regulations for the Management of Religious Activities in Qinghai Province" states that successful applicants for membership in a religious group "must uphold the leadership of the Chinese Communist Party, uphold socialism, be patriotic"; impart such values to religious teachers, personnel, and citizens; and assume responsibility for finances, activities, production and service activities, and property.[22]

The second set of national registration requirements lists criteria that are sufficiently subjective to allow no recourse to religious believers should their applications be disapproved. Included among them are "obedience to national law, regulations and policies," "income and expenditures . . . in accordance with relevant national regulations," and "operating seriously in accordance with democratic procedures."[23] As interpretation of the rules lies with the rule makers themselves, subjectivity is reinforced. A further, if unstated, registration criterion appears to be size. Large congregations—there is no specific size limit—are at greater risk of rejection. So too is a congregation with an outspoken leader and a very public presence. Sites can be in compliance but still be refused legitimacy for any number of extralegal reasons, including personal vendettas, turf battles, overzealousness on the part of cadres anxious to impress their superiors and earn bonuses, and failed attempts at extorting payoffs.

Sites choosing not to register are, by definition, illegal and subject to immediate closure, at best, and criminal persecution of the congregants, at worst. Even so, many groups make this choice. The divisions within China's Catholic and Protestant churches are well known and complex. In both cases, a rough divide can be made between groups that are willing to come under the control of religious authorities and those that reject the idea completely.

At one extreme are the many Catholic congregations known colloquially as "official," or "open," churches. Their members and leaders are willing to give up a certain amount of independence, including the power to choose their bishops, in exchange for permission to worship in peace. At the other end of the spectrum are the so-called underground Catholic churches—a misnomer, given that their existence is well known. These congregations reject any state or party interference with doctrine, theology, or rites. Loyalty to the pope and a desire to remain in close communion with the universal church account for much of their unwillingness to conform to official regulations. Many underground churches are led by elderly bishops who endured extraordinary hardship and lengthy prison terms after the 1949 establishment of the People's Republic of China and again during the

Cultural Revolution. The Holy See cannot afford to forsake those bishops or to denigrate the sacrifice of those who died.

The issue for Protestants is similar. The divide, however, is based more on theological grounds. Many mainstream Protestants (Anglicans, Lutherans, and Methodists) are willing to tolerate official control, which leaves much of their ritual and canon intact. For so-called house-church members, the issue stems from doctrinal beliefs or practices that are anathema to Chinese authorities. For example, government religious officials forbid belief in the Second Coming on the grounds it interferes with the people's dedication to production. In addition, the government requires a "three-designates" policy: a fixed location for worship, a permanent responsible leader, and activities restricted to a given geographic area—policies that fly in the face of itinerant evangelism and the use of an impermanent set of lay leaders who cannot be held responsible for overall congregational behavior to the same degree as professional clergy.

There are other reasons to avoid registration. The very act opens a congregation's membership list to official scrutiny. By registering, a congregation implicitly concedes to government supervision of its finances, business enterprises, building and welfare programs, ongoing religious activities, and choice of religious literature. A rejected application opens the door to a greater degree of surveillance, harassment, or even persecution of members than prevailed before the attempt, particularly if local religious authorities have reason to suspect the group has retained a degree of cohesiveness.

The situation for evangelical congregations became even more complicated after July 1999, when the Chinese government launched a nationwide campaign to eradicate the Falungong, an exercise and meditation organization claiming more than 70 million practitioners in China at the time.[24] In October 1999 the government created a stronger legal basis for prosecuting those who organize or make use of "evil religious organizations." Reverting to the game of definitions, the government defined "heretical cults" as "illegal organizations that have been established under the guise of religion, . . . deifying their leading members, enchanting and deceiving others by concocting and spreading superstitious fallacies, recruiting and controlling their members and endangering the society."[25] In the year that followed, Chinese officials made use of the new definition to further control Protestant groups that fell outside the mainstream. An April 2000 Ministry of Public Security document characterized fourteen Protestant organizations and their offshoots as "cults."[26]

Control over Clergy

Document 19 explicitly requires that clerical leaders be both patriotic and committed to socialism. But the shortage of trained clerics—a result of deaths and expulsions and of the hiatus in religious education during most of the Mao era—brought the government both challenges and opportunities in this regard. The challenge came from the rise of the "nonprofessionals," including many part-timers, whom the government had difficulty identifying, tracking, and ultimately holding accountable for the activities of a congregation. The opportunity came from the prospect of training a new generation of would-be religious professionals in socialist religious principles. Officials felt that they would be able to contain freelance preachers in due time and that congregations committed to a system of lay leaders could be forced to change.

Many subnational regulations, such as those issued by Shanghai and Guangzhou municipalities, stipulate that religious personnel must be vetted and certified by the applicable branch of the relevant patriotic association. Without case-by-case approval to do otherwise, leaders can perform their duties only in "lawfully registered places for religious worship." The regulations also specify that such leaders cannot "conduct and preside over religious activities outside [the relevant] municipality" without permission, nor can an outside religious leader come to Guangzhou or Shanghai in a religious capacity without consent.[27]

Local authorities oversee the training of religious professionals. For example, the city of Shanghai is home to a major religious training center. The Shanghai regulations speak forcefully on the issue of religious training and make it clear that seminaries are not independent entities and that personnel, curriculum, and admissions are subject to official approval. They go so far as to specifically mandate overall government supervision and direction of training centers and to require recommendation from a local religious community before an applicant can be considered for admission.[28] In contrast, Guangzhou does not have a major religious training center, and its regulations barely mention the issue.

Authorities have used a variety of methods to ensure that clergy put the state above personal faith. Although the number of clergy imprisoned has diminished over the past decade, the threat still remains. After a clandestine Conference of Catholic Bishops in 1989, for example, officials targeted Catholic bishops, sentencing many, holding others incommunicado for years, limiting the movement and access to visitors of those permitted to return home, and demanding participation in "reeducation" sessions. The advanced age of these "underground" bishops made the task of diminishing their influence easier. As they died, many of those who replaced them made some degree of accommodation with the official Chinese church.

Authorities also attempted, with considerable success, to neutralize outspoken and uncompromising priests. Priests are subject to constant surveillance, harassment, repeated detentions, confiscation of their books and equipment, and judicially or administratively imposed incarceration. Father Lu Xiaozhou from Wenzhou, Zhejiang Province, was placed in the custody of the Religious Affairs Bureau in June 2003. Officials there hoped to force him to agree in writing to become part of the official Catholic Patriotic Association.[29] Furthermore, a government-mandated merger of Catholic dioceses makes it easier to control influential clergy. Short-term detention before and during major religious holidays is yet another tactic for circumventing clerical influence.

Tactics used to discredit leaders of the less tightly organized but nevertheless hierarchical Protestant house churches are even more rigorous. Prison terms tend to be longer for senior leaders, multiple arrests are common, and fines are steep. However, torture and ill treatment, reports of which surface repeatedly, appear to be directed against local leaders. Several leaders of groups considered orthodox by Christian standards but identified as cults by Chinese authorities have received life sentences. Charges against such senior figures often include allegations of rape, fraud, engaging in feudal superstition, undermining the law, and disturbing the social order.

Attempts to train clergy outside government-vetted institutions, either in "underground" seminaries or, more informally, through secret training sessions sometimes organized with the help of foreign missionaries, are frequently interrupted by public security officers. Such seminaries are closed, and its participants fined and detained. Government functionaries periodically reassess officially sanctioned seminaries. As a result, "patriotic education" may replace theology classes, and the content of the latter may be adjusted to meet government criteria for religious adaptation to socialism.

Restricting Religious Activities

The regulations seek to constrain religious activities. Almost all activities that would be held outside of monasteries, nunneries, temples, mosques, and churches are prohibited. Within the approved sites, however, believers may, for example, worship Buddha, pray, fast, hold services, celebrate Mass, and anoint the sick.[30] Only certified clergy may preside over communal worship. Once registered, a group must still obtain special permission before starting a business enterprise or a public welfare program, raising funds, or holding an exhibition of any kind. Under no circumstances may a site publicize or host religious debates on a religion or faith other than its own. "Superstitious" activities, such as fortune-telling, divination, exorcism, and healing, are expressly forbidden. The regulations prohibit religious activities from hindering production, endangering social order, or "affect[ing] the work, studies, and life of residents."[31] The vagueness of these prohibitions gives political authorities virtual carte blanche to pronounce adverse judgments on religious activities they dislike.

Publication and Distribution of Religious Materials

Document 19 forbids the circulation of reading materials that have not been "approved for publication by the responsible government department." Many local regulations now stipulate that the "publishing, printing, reproduction and distribution" of religious scriptures, books, and audiovisual and electronic materials cannot take place without the consent of a religious affairs bureau at the provincial level or higher.[32] Printing units themselves must first be approved, and distribution is limited both by quantity and by geographic area.

It is unclear whether there are sufficient Bibles available in China to meet demand. Those who argue that the supply is insufficient also point to the cost and to the trepidation felt by those who belong to unregistered groups who must buy from official sources, usually registered churches. Bibles may not be ordered directly from publication houses, bookstore supplies are limited, and foreigners may only import religious materials sufficient for personal use. It has also been reported that clergy on the mainland often do not receive religious publications mailed from Hong Kong.[33] Most such material was not returned to the sender.

Moreover, distribution of any religious texts or tapes without explicit official permission to do so may be harshly punished. The most blatant recent example of so-called Bible smuggling came to light in May 2001, after three men carried thousands of Bibles to unregistered church groups in mainland China. Not only did they lack permission to distribute the books, but the annotated version they smuggled did not adhere to officially sanctioned text. The court levied steep fines on the three and sentenced them to prison. Chinese citizens distributing other unauthorized religious materials, such as audio or videotapes, are also subject to punishment. In addition, authorities routinely confiscate privately owned unauthorized religious materials, including Bibles and reference books, belonging to citizens.

Foreign Contacts

Government leaders have insisted on an independent, self-governing church in China, and Document 19 imposes stringent controls on relations between Chinese congregations and international religious groups. The rationale is relatively simple. China's leaders have believed—or have professed to believe—that organized Christianity has been invasive and disruptive for generations and is intent on compromising China's independence. The leaders have been cognizant of the church's role in the overthrow of communism in Eastern Europe, and they have witnessed the significant participation of monks and nuns in the independence movement in Tibet. They have few doubts that in Xinjiang some ethnic nationalists use Islam as a rallying point for independence.

Since the issuance of Document 19, three national documents—each more stringent than the last—have addressed the relation between Chinese and foreign religious communities. According to the 1991 Document 6, overseas religious organizations or personnel are forbidden to build monasteries, temples, or churches or engage in missionary work.[34] The State Council's 1994 regulations regarding the religious activities of foreign nationals in China limits foreigners to attendance at religious activities at approved sites and forbids their lecturing or sermonizing without permission from religious leaders at the provincial, autonomous region, or municipality level.[35] Foreigners are banned from conducting missionary work or distributing religious materials, and the solicitation and acceptance of foreign funds are strictly regulated. The Religious Affairs Bureau issued a follow-up set of rules in 2000 that exhaustively details the prohibitions related to the missionary activity of foreigners.[36]

Local regulations have followed this theme. Regulations from Jingxian County, in Hebei Province, show how stringent local regulations can be regarding religious visitors from abroad or even those from within China. A visitor must apply to the Public Security Bureau for temporary registration and provide duplicate information to the Religious Affairs Bureau. The unit that invited the visitor also must submit a report to both units at the conclusion of the visit. The flow of money from visiting outsiders is strictly regulated. Visitors must register the value and planned use of gifts with both bureaus. Follow-up reports on implemented projects are required semiannually.[37] The province of Fujian has regulations that expressly forbid the reproduction, sale, or distribution of "religious publications, recordings, videos, or other evangelical materials from outside the borders of China."[38]

In many isolated areas of China, foreigners often conduct Bible education for house-church congregants or assist in training lay leaders in matters of doctrine and liturgy. However, the presence of foreigners increases the danger for local participants, as it is they who are usually jailed or fined and sometimes beaten. It is their property that is destroyed, and their livelihoods that are adversely affected. In August 2000, for example, after three American missionaries were caught in Henan Province with members of the China Fangcheng Church, 130 members of the congregation were detained for questioning. The missionaries were deported.

Conclusion

Chinese authorities have been debating possible changes in the way religion is regulated. Recent reports have implied that, on the surface at least, a new policy would lift some of the current restrictions. Predictions are dangerous, but it is highly likely that China's leaders will still manage to keep religious congregations small, highly localized, and divorced from a meaningful role within a vibrant civil society. The "cult" policy, summarized in article 300 of the 1997 revision of the Criminal Law and further enhanced by the October 1999 "explanations," has provided the leadership with its newest weapon. The article—applicable to those who "organize or utilize superstitious sects, secret societies and evil religious organizations" or those who "sabotage the implementation of the state's laws and executive regulations by utilizing superstition"—has already been tested and, in combination with extrajudicial means, found effective against Christian groups that have tried to push beyond legal limits.[39] The point has not been lost on other marginal groups. Until a pluralistic Chinese society comes into being, religion in China will be unable to develop organically. Its growth, its meaning, and its influence will be constrained by political decisions made by China's leaders.

Two decades after the promulgation of Document 19, the number of Chinese worshipers and religious venues in China is at an all-time high. Yet there is less and less room for religious beliefs, religious organizations, and religious activities that challenge the view of China's leaders regarding the place of religion in a modernizing socialist society. The point may seem counterintuitive, and it may be that the Chinese government will discover it has, in fact, let the genie out of the bottle. Policymakers do not want to antagonize millions of China's citizens. Instead, they gamble that so long as limited expressions of faith are tolerated, and so long as the threat of punishment for transgression is occasionally validated, the faithful will not challenge the government's insistence that religious belief is a societal sideshow. This policy framework rests, however, on questionable assumptions: that individuals may come together to worship but may not form an autonomous community; that no community of believers may decide for itself on measures to alleviate economic stress, which is the sole prerogative of the government; that no community of believers may interpret the cultural canon or challenge prevailing social mores; and so forth.

Worshippers willing to play by rules they have little say in setting, and to organize in a way that continually reaffirms the primacy and the power of the Chinese government and the Chinese Communist Party, have much to gain. Primarily, they are afforded a relaxation of vigilance, an easing of tension that opens a space for turning inward, for the repeated reaffirmations of faith that sustain and invigorate believers but do not challenge the state. The number of worshippers hardly matters to the ruling elite so long as believers respect the boundary markers it sets. For a time, at least, stasis is achieved.

China's leaders may not yet fully comprehend the power of religious belief, however. The willingness, even the desire, to sacrifice for one's faith may push some believers to demand ever more space and recognition as a societal force. As Mao wrote in another context, when a critical mass is achieved under such conditions, "a single spark can light a prairie fire."[40]

Notes

1. "Document No. 19: The Basic Viewpoint and Policy on the Religious Question during Our Country's Socialist Period," *Chinese Law and Government*, vol. 33 (March–April 2000), pp. 17–34.
2. Ibid., p. 19.
3. Ibid., p. 22.
4. Constitution of the People's Republic of China, adopted at the Fifth Session of the Fifth National People's Congress and promulgated for implementation by the

proclamation of the National People's Congress on December 4, 1982, reprinted in Donald E. MacInnis, *Religion in China Today: Policy and Practice* (Maryknoll, N.Y.: Orbis, 1989), pp. 34–35.

5. UN General Assembly, *International Covenant on Civil and Political Rights*, adopted December 16, 1966, General Assembly Resolution 2200A (XXI), entered into force March 23, 1976, signed by China in October 1998, not yet ratified, article 18.

6. Constitution of the People's Republic, article 36.

7. "China: Persecution of a Protestant Sect," *Human Rights Watch/Asia*, vol. 6 (June 1994).

8. The United Front Work Department is a Chinese Communist Party organ responsible for organizing support for party policies among Chinese who are not party members. According to its own report, it is an alliance led by the party for accomplishing its historical mission. As such it must "consolidate the will, wisdom, and strength of various social strata, nationalities, political parties, groups, and circles." "The New Situation in the United Front," *Beijing liaowang* [Beijing perspectives], no. 34 (August 19, 2002), p. 6, reprinted in Foreign Broadcast Information Service, FBIS-CHI-2002-0828, August 28, 2002.

9. The bureau's official title is now the State Administration for Religious Affairs.

10. "Document No. 6: Circular on Some Problems Concerning the Further Improvement of Work on Religion," *Chinese Law and Government*, vol. 33 (March–April 2000), pp. 56–63.

11. Ibid.

12. Ibid., p. 59.

13. "Regulations Regarding the Management of Places of Religious Activities," Order 145, *Chinese Law and Government*, vol. 33 (March–April 2000), pp. 66–68; "Registration Procedures for Venues for Religious Activities," *Chinese Law and Government*, vol. 33 (March–April 2000), pp. 69–70.

14. "Method for the Annual Inspection of Places of Religious Activities," *Chinese Law and Government*, vol. 33 (March–April 2000), pp. 71–74.

15. Richard Madsen, editor's introduction to *Chinese Law and Government*, vol. 33 (May–June 2000), pp. 5–11.

16. "1998 Ordinance on the Management of Religious Affairs of Guangzhou Municipality," *Chinese Law and Government*, vol. 33 (May–June 2000), pp. 17–26; "Regulations from the Shanghai Religious Affairs Bureau," article 17, in *China: State Control of Religion*, pp. 90–99 (New York: Human Rights Watch/Asia, 1997).

17. For examples, see the documents in Wing-ning Pang, Pik-wan Wong, and James Tong, eds., "The Three-Self Churches and 'Freedom' of Religion in China, 1980–1997," special issue, *Chinese Law and Government*, vol. 33 (November–December 2000).

18. See, for example, "Nine Rules of the Lianghui in Shanxi Province on Adherence to Normal Religious Activities," *Chinese Law and Government*, vol. 33 (November–December 2000), pp. 26–28; "Patriotic Covenant of Protestant Christians in Henan Province; Second Session of the Third Plenary Meeting and Second Session of the First Plenary Meeting of the Protestant Churches in Henan Province," *Chinese Law and Government*, vol. 33 (November–December 2000), pp. 17–18; "Regulations Concerning the Protection of Normal Religious Activities in the Hunan Christian

Church," *Chinese Law and Government*, vol. 33 (November–December 2000), pp. 34–36.

19. "Church Order for Chinese Protestant Christian Churches," *Chinese Law and Government*, vol. 33 (November–December 2000), pp. 43–51, 44.

20. The remark was made during a special report on religion to a Religious Affairs Bureau meeting in early 1996. The *People's Consultative Conference News* published the final segment on February 1, 1996, in its Religion and the Nation section, as "Stress Three Matters," *Tripod*, vol. 16 (March–April 1996), pp. 45–50.

21. "Registration Procedures for Venues for Religious Activities," p. 69.

22. "Regulations for the Management of Religious Activities in Qinghai Province," *Chinese Law and Government*, vol. 33 (May–June 2000), articles 6 and 7.

23. "Method for the Annual Inspection of Places of Religious Activities," p. 71.

24. *Dangerous Meditation: China's Campaign against Falungong* (New York: Human Rights Watch, 2002), p. 12.

25. "Chinese Agency on Use of Criminal Law to Deal with Cults," BBC Worldwide Monitoring, October 30, 1999.

26. Ministry of Public Security of the People's Republic of China, "Notice on Various Issues Regarding Identifying and Banning of Cultic Organizations," no. 39 (2000), in Li Shixiong and Xiqiu (Bob) Fu, eds. and trans., *Religion and National Security in China: Secret Documents from China's Security Sector* (Bartlesville, Okla.: Voice of the Martyrs, 2002), pp. 19–39.

27. "Regulations from the Shanghai Religious Affairs Bureau," article 17, p. 54.

28. Ibid., articles 35–39.

29. "China: Catholic Priest, Protestants Reportedly Arrested," *UCA News,* June 23, 2003.

30. "Regulations from the Shanghai Religious Affairs Bureau," article 30.

31. "Regulations for the Management of Religious Activities in Qinghai Province," article 10, p. 85; see also "Provisional Regulations for the Registration and Management of Places of Religious Activity in Fujian," *Chinese Law and Government*, vol. 33 (May–June 2000), pp. 30–33.

32. "1998 Ordinance on the Management of Religious Affairs of Guangzhou Municipality," articles 41–46, p. 22.

33. "China: UCAN Feature—Religious Publications to China Not Always Received," *UCA News*, October 18, 2002.

34. "Document No. 6," p. 59.

35. "Regulations on the Supervision of the Religious Activities of Foreigners in China," Order 144, *Chinese Law and Government*, vol. 33 (March–April 2000), pp. 64–65.

36. China, State Administration for Religious Affairs, "Full Text on Rules of Religious Activities of Aliens within China," reprinted in Foreign Broadcast Information Service, FBIS-CHI-2000-0926, September 26, 2000.

37. "Regulations Concerning Outside Personnel Who Come to Jingxian (Hebei Province) for Activities, or Bearing Donations or Gifts," *Tripod*, vol. 16 (March–April 1996), p. 38.

38. "Provisional Regulations for the Registration and Management of Places of Religious Activity in Fujian," article 18.

39. Beijing Xinhua Domestic Service, "China: Text of Criminal Law," March 17, 1997, reprinted in Foreign Broadcast Information Service, FBIS-CHI-97-056, March 25, 1997.

40. "A Single Spark Can Light a Prairie Fire," in *Selected Works of Mao Tse-tung* (Peking: Foreign Languages Press, 1967), vol. 1, pp. 117–28.

4 KIM-KWONG CHAN

Accession to the World Trade Organization and State Adaptation

In autumn 2001, most of the world's media attention was on the September 11 terrorist attacks on the Pentagon and New York's World Trade Center towers and the antiterrorist aftermath. The attention of China's media, by contrast, was focused on three events: China's accession to the World Trade Organization (WTO), the entry of China's soccer team into World Cup competition for the first time, and Beijing's successful bid to host the 2008 Olympics. For China's official media, and indeed for many Chinese, these events signified China's coming of age in the twenty-first century and the emergence of China as an important player in the international community. President George W. Bush confirmed these sentiments at the Asia-Pacific Economic Cooperation forum in Shanghai in October 2001, when he recognized China as a great nation with whom the United States must work closely in the campaign against terrorism.

Of these three seminal events, the Olympics and the World Cup are temporary nationalistic boosters. Accession to the WTO, however, serves as a landmark for a new phase in China's progressive transformation from a planned socialist economy to free market capitalism, for it will require a much wider opening up of the economy. This new phase will affect China in many ways, including changes in religion's role in Chinese society, as well as in official policy on the governance of religion and a consequent shift in church-state relations.

Entry into the World Trade Organization and Social Change

Two decades of economic development under the Reform and Opening Policy have transformed the face of China from a massive state-owned collective corporation to the largest potential market in the world. Today, not only do China's leaders encourage capitalism, but the erstwhile "proletarian" Chinese Communist Party is actively recruiting China's budding class of entrepreneurs to join the ranks of ruling elites. The regime also welcomes Western capitalists to invest in large-scale economic and infrastructure projects, from banking to railways. Accession to the WTO will significantly accelerate these trends by imposing a timetable on China's regulatory structure to reduce trade barriers and to open the domestic market, further deepening China's integration into the global economic order.[1]

The socioeconomic changes catalyzed by China's economic integration will be no less sweeping than its 1949 adoption of socialism. Whereas in the nineteenth century China was forced to open up for international commercial activities, and in the 1950s through the 1970s it chose isolationism, this time China is voluntarily joining the global economic order, opening up its once jealously guarded domestic market to foreign investors.

The terms of China's WTO accession require China to deal with foreign merchants through mutual market access and minimum trade barriers. As a result, economic sectors in China will meet with their competitors on fair and open ground in the global marketplace, relying mainly on their own strength rather than state assistance. Furthermore, China's state-owned enterprises will privatize into independent corporations, responding to market demands rather than political decisions. Such structural changes carry significant social implications. For example, workers in state-owned enterprises will no longer enjoy lifetime-guaranteed jobs. Those firms that prove themselves unable to compete will be permitted to go bankrupt. Workers will have a greater choice of jobs to select from and will be able to move to places where there is greater opportunity. The cradle-to-grave social welfare formerly provided by state-owned enterprises will no longer be available; instead, the local community and individuals will gradually assume this responsibility.

These changes will further accelerate ongoing social stratification and pluralization of life-styles in China. China's population is already well into a transformation from a work force segmented into traditional socialist categories of worker, peasant, soldier, and cadre—all within a relatively narrow range of income—to one that is highly stratified. A recent study commissioned by the Chinese Academy of Social Sciences to analyze the nation's changing social structure has reclassified the population into ten different occupational categories. Examples in the report include a self-made billionaire entrepreneur, a CEO of a joint-venture corporation with a monthly salary of US$12,000, workers employed by state-owned enterprises with wages of US$200 a month, and a peasant in rural Gansu Province earning less than US$10 a month.[2] With such a diverse range of income and multiple types of social classification, China is becoming not only a diverse society but one with a polarization of wealth. There are many life-style options for those with the means to afford them; the growing "underclass," however, is losing out.

Accession to the WTO will reshape many economic sectors. The most devastated will be the agricultural sector. Almost three-quarters of Chinese are farmers, and the grain price in China is about 25 to 30 percent higher than the world market price. China's terms of entry into the WTO require imported grain to be allowed to compete in the domestic market with a relatively low tariff—good news for China's food-processing industries but bad news for its farmers. The hardest hit will be the central and western regions, which have the highest per capita concentration of farmers and the largest number of low-yield plots. Many farmers will go bankrupt, spurring a massive migration of job seekers from rural to urban areas. It is estimated that as many as 100 million bankrupt farmers, along with the current 100 million surplus farm laborers, will flood the labor market. These surplus laborers will compete in the cities for jobs currently taken up by an estimated 120 million migrant workers, which will add to the intensive competition for the limited new jobs provided by the economic boom in major cities. Such a massive population migration is sure to reshape the demographic profile of China.[3]

Heavy industry in China is made up mostly of state-owned enterprises. These firms are, in general, inefficient and have survived only because of politically determined loans from China's state-owned banks. They are also vastly overstaffed, at one time having employed almost 100 million workers. From 1997 to 2000, however, state-owned enterprises eliminated 43 million jobs, and more job cuts are on the horizon as China's leaders remain determined to shake up inefficient firms through competition in the global market.[4] Many of these unemployed workers (most of whom are in their forties or fifties) have little hope of getting jobs in the private sector, which recruits more skillful and younger workers, such as fresh graduates from schools. The highest concentration of such firms is in the northeastern region—dubbed China's Rust Belt—as well as some areas in central and western regions. In general, the economic prospects for these areas are grim.

Reform policies were initially launched in China's coastal region, and with the aggregation of wealth and commercial experience, this region has led the nation in attracting foreign investment. Manufacturing and export facilities are also well established there. As a result, the area continues to be a magnet for talented people as well as resources. Membership in the WTO will further enhance the prosperity of the coastal region, as most of the nation's internationally competitive light industries and finance, high-tech, and service sectors are concentrated there. Millions of new jobs will be created; business people from all over the world will converge at the new international business mecca, Shanghai; and the coastal region more broadly will continue to be the wealthiest part of China and one of the most prosperous regions in the Pacific Rim.

All these changes—economic polarization, countervailing regional dynamics, massive population flows, new social classes, and diverse opportunities—will radically reshape China into a society full of paradox and contradictions. The new China will be a society with an open market under autocratic rule, the coexistence of rich and poor, a job market filled with opportunities and devastation, a ruling party that welcomes capitalists but tries to stem labor unrest, and a market policy based on survival of the fittest in a socialist society with deeply rooted norms of egalitarianism. As a result, WTO accession is generating an atmosphere of euphoria, optimism, and opportunity together with uncertainty, instability, and insecurity.

Implications for Religion

In such times of radical social transformation, people tend to search for some form of permanency. With the demise of the Chinese Communist Party's ideology as a source of popular inspiration, religion has returned as an attractive source of meaning for many facing often-traumatic social change. This phenomenon is especially evident in both economically depressed areas (such as the northeastern city of Shengyang, which has a large number of unemployed workers) and economic boom areas (such as the southern coastal city of Wenzhou, which boasts the highest number of merchants per capita in China), where religion is growing the fastest.[5] It is also apparent in the growth of unauthorized "new" religions, such as the Falungong and the quasi-Christian Eastern Lightning sect.[6] Several factors seem particularly salient in catalyzing future religious change and revival; prominent among them are transnational interaction, resurgent regionalism, and internal mobility.

Transnational Interaction

Accession to the WTO will usher in a new wave of foreign influence as multinational corporations compete for market share in China's newly liberalized domestic market. The Chinese will also pay more attention to the international scene, as their economic, political, and cultural interests increasingly mesh with global developments. As a result, the Chinese will have more contact with multiple value systems, including religions such as Christianity. With more access across borders through commercial and cultural interaction, average Chinese citizens who hitherto may have had limited knowledge of Christianity will have more contact with it. Many mission organizations are already using this opportunity to launch mission campaigns, whether to empower already-existing Chinese religious organizations, to proselytize in frontier areas, or to target Chinese citizens living outside of China. Their efforts will continue to increase the overall influence of religion in China, as religion's status shifts from a taboo subject and outdated ideology, as it was under the Chinese Communist Party, to a part of the heritage of world civilization, as defined by current party policy. International standards for religious freedom will become widely known.

As the tempo of foreign investment increases, a growing number of foreigners will come to live and work in China. They will not only cluster in the major trading cities, such as Shanghai and Beijing, but will increasingly spread out to smaller cities in China's interior, bringing with them new lifestyles, values, and religious faiths. There are already well-established expatriate religious activities in major cities, from Jewish Sabbath to Russian Orthodox services, and new religious communities will sprout up wherever groups of foreigners take up residence. For example, at least eleven different expatriate Protestant groups currently operate in Beijing, where just ten years ago there was only one, the Beijing International Christian Fellowship. They will most likely demand more international chaplain services, placing new pressures on China's government. The current religious policy of separating foreign and national religious services is also likely to face new challenges as the incidence of intermarriage between foreigners and Chinese nationals continues to increase.

The new religious faiths brought to China from overseas may also include some not currently sanctioned by China's government. (China's government currently recognizes only five religions: Catholicism, Protestantism, Buddhism, Taoism, and Islam.) For example, some Chinese may have accepted the Mormon faith while studying or doing business in the United States. When they return to China, they will most likely introduce this new religion to their friends and neighbors. Some Chinese may have come to embrace Greek Orthodoxy, Hinduism, the Baha'i faith, or even Shintoism while stationed overseas for commercial activities. Although these faiths are generally accepted by the international community as legitimate religions, they remain unauthorized by the Chinese government, especially for Chinese nationals. As these religions find their way into China and develop a critical mass of adherents, they will eventually confront China's existing regulatory framework, placing pressure on the Chinese government to adapt to the new social realities.

Deepening integration into the global economy affects Chinese religious believers not only within China but in other countries as well. Accession to the WTO creates opportunities for Chinese business to compete on the global market. Chinese merchants have already made their presence felt in newly emerging markets in Central Asia, Eastern Europe, Southeast Asia, and the Middle East, especially in commodity goods, such as electric household appliances, clothing, and motorcycles. Many of these merchants are religious believers who spread their faith along their trading routes—somewhat similar to their Middle East counterparts fifteen centuries ago, who spread Nestorianism and Manichaeism while traveling to China along the Silk Route. Mainland Chinese Christian merchants have already established their own churches or fellowships in most major cities in Europe, from Barcelona to Bucharest. Moreover, in many places the church is the only organized Chinese community that provides social support and services. The contribution that religion is making to the Chinese diasporas is spilling over into local populations, as Chinese migrants integrate into their new communities. These developments have enormous missiological significance, considering that China has diplomatic and commercial relations with virtually every country, even such hard-to-access nations as North Korea, Libya, and Iraq.[7]

Regionalism

As in other parts of the developing world, the forces of globalization have revived local identities and cultural practices as communities search for continuity and stability amid tumultuous change. Folk religions have revived in force across the Chinese countryside; in many locales, village temples have regained the status they enjoyed before the communist revolution. China's government remains ambivalent toward indigenous folk religion. Although variations of syncretic folk religion are not, strictly speaking, part of authorized Buddhism or Taoism, political authorities do not usually forcibly eliminate them. The regional diversification that WTO entry accelerates will also reinforce regionalism. One of the markings of Chinese regionalism is regional culture, including local legends and deities. For example, in Fujian Province the cult of Mazu has reemerged and has become the center of local festivals. The local government de facto treats this Mazu worship as a legitimate religion, alongside the five authorized religions. Unable to ignore such popular folk religion, local governments are beginning to adopt measures to "legitimate" it as one of the sanctioned religions by trying to have it included within the central government's regulatory framework.[8]

Such developments may produce a new focal point in local community life, helping to shape new local identities to address the identity crisis that has appeared with the demise of communist ideology and of the official nationwide social categories. The wealth generated from commercial activities, especially in coastal provinces, will add fuel to these religious phenomena and strengthen local identities. Even in poverty-stricken places, such as the northern yellow-earth plains in Shaanxi Province, farmers appear to have more confidence in petitioning for help from local deities than from the local government in times of crisis, such as a drought. The general loss of confidence in secular authority prompts them to seek assistance from the transcendent world, a part of the daily reality in traditional China, as is evident in the increased popularity of local temples and deities.

Internal Mobility

Finally, the staggering acceleration in the number of internal migrants and transients resulting from WTO accession will continue to change the religious dynamic in China. Historically, mass internal migration has often been followed by equally dramatic changes in the religious landscape, both in China and in other parts of the world. In China today, for example, many uprooted farmers making a living in coastal factories find themselves longing for a support structure. Growing numbers among them are finding faith, hope, and caring in a local religious group, be it a church or a mosque, to sustain them during this transition. Many then bring their newly acquired faith back to their home villages, which may have had no previous exposure to the religion.

A similar type of religious transmission is occurring alongside the quest for market opportunities within China. Market competition compels merchants to seek out opportunities in ever more obscure and hard-to-reach places. Many of these entrepreneurs, especially those from Wenzhou, are religious believers, and they may spread their faith along with their merchandise. For example, Wenzhou merchants established the first Christian meeting point in Lhasa, Tibet. Soon, there will be small clusters of religious believers in places where no one would have anticipated.

Government Policy Response

Accession to the WTO ushers in a wide range of new social challenges for the Chinese government to manage—from labor unrest to the tensions caused by economic polarization to mass internal migration. China's leaders face unprecedented challenges in fully integrating China into the international community while preserving the Chinese Communist Party's grip on power. To address these issues, the Chinese government has in the past few years conducted a series of assessments of post-WTO social conditions and has formulated new policies to address them to meet its political objectives.

Religion policy has unprecedented salience in these assessments. China's ruling elites long ignored religion as a secondary social issue, mainly relevant to small ethnic minorities; but the rapid resurgence of religious activity and the government's troubled campaign against the Falungong drew the attention of the nation's top leaders. The evidence came in December 2001, when President Jiang Zemin convened a work conference on religion in Beijing. The entire Politburo as well as the top national leaders from all branches of the government, the party, and the military attended Jiang's conference—a rare assemblage of top political authorities for the purpose of discussing policy on religious affairs in China.[9]

The conference signaled an adjustment in religious policy to better address China's anticipated religious growth in a restless society. Jiang emphasized his 1993 "Three Sentences" on religious work: fully implementing the party's policy on freedom of religious belief, governing religious affairs by law, and guiding religious groups to adapt into the socialist society.[10] Jiang also added a fourth element: affirming the principle of independence and autonomy of the Chinese religious organizations. All four elements of the policy were heavily coded in political jargon. In the months after this conference, the government launched a series of study sessions for Religious Affairs Bureau cadres and various leaders to decode this policy. In November 2002 Wang Zuo'an, the deputy director-general of the bureau, published a thick volume, entitled *Religious Issues and Religious Policy in China*, that expands on this new policy framework.[11] In January 2003 Premier Zhu Rongji visited the bureau's new office and summarized the new policy in a speech published later.[12]

This policy framework was the product of a long debate within the party as to what the religious policy should be after China's entry into the WTO. Progressives called for liberalization of control over religion, as in economic matters, to merge into the global world order, while conservatives wanted to suppress the growth of religion as an essential component of maintaining party orthodoxy, which considers religion an unscientific worldview hindering the progress of the society as well as a breeding ground for social unrest. The new policy framework adopted by the government may be seen as a compromise between these two positions with a pragmatic objective: to manage religion so as to ensure social stability in the face of the social challenges created by WTO accession. In summary, the policy contains five major components: recognition, containment, guidance, nationalism, and suppression.

Recognition

At the conference, the Chinese Communist Party openly acknowledged that religion has always existed and will continue to exist as a fundamental component of human civilization. This admission, coupled with the conference's avoidance of the thorny and embarrassing theoretical question of whether religion is in essence the "opiate of the people," implied that communist ideology may not be the exclusive means through which to interpret religion, as the party has always asserted in the past. Party leaders thus adopted a pragmatic stance on religion, somewhat similar to their position on economic matters, adopting reforms by baptizing them as "socialism with Chinese characteristics."

Having recognized the permanence of religion, the party must now find means to coexist with religion—formerly an ideological enemy to be eradicated by force if necessary. However, political leaders, adhering to the government's long-standing prohibition against encouraging religion's development, preserved the fundamental ideological difference—theism versus atheism—between religious believers and party members by affirming that religious believers may not become party members and party members may not take on religious beliefs. The contradictory result is that the party can take in capitalists as party members, but no religious believer can join the party.[13] They also urged the officials to increase propaganda supporting a scientific worldview and atheism, especially among the youth, to combat the encroachment of religious influences among teenagers.[14]

Containment

The conference reaffirmed the government's long-standing policy of containing religion through government fiat, both in definition and in the area of operation. The government retained its authority to define the legitimacy of various religions, and old definitions were not updated. Only those religions legitimated by the government are allowed to exist legally in China and enjoy the limited freedom conferred by official regulations. By contrast, the government labels as "evil cults" those religious groups, such as the Falungong, that do not fall within its definition of "normal religion," and these groups are subject to prosecution under China's criminal code. "Normal" religious groups must continue to register with the government if they are to claim their legal protection; otherwise they are considered illegal and will be prosecuted. In short, the government preserved regulatory means of confining religious groups to a manageable social space.

Currently, government agencies are actively drafting national regulations on religion, in addition to many local regulations, and the Religious Affairs Bureau is being expanded and upgraded to meet the increasing demand created by the government's involvement, anticipating the growth of religion in China. Clearly, China's leaders will feel secure only to the extent that religion does not get out of hand and remains under government control.

Guidance

The third major theme to emerge from the conference was official guidance over the development of religion. Officials' speeches frequently repeated the refrain (uttered first by Jiang Zemin in a 1992 speech) that religion must adapt to socialist society. A precise translation of the phrase suggests that the adaptation is reciprocal: religion must be made to fit the Chinese society, and society must adjust to the presence of religion. Within China's political context, however, there is no real mutuality in the process. The government defines what kind of adaptation is required by what religion, to the point of changing its teachings as well as its practices to suit the party's political objectives. In other words, the party provides guidance to the religious groups, directing them toward a particular orientation and role in Chinese society, and these groups are expected to follow its leadership if they hope to be "adopted" into the socialist Chinese "family."

The main sociopolitical focus of China since its accession to the WTO is economic development and social stability. Jiang called upon the religious organizations to assist the nation in economic development, such as channeling foreign investment or helping in relief and development projects, as the means of furthering the interests of its socialist society. Contrary to many observers' speculation, the government has not acknowledged the contribution that religious groups can make in shaping society's system of moral values, which is universally seen as the main contribution of religion in any civilization and is especially needed in the dehumanized market-oriented society in China. This element is conspicuously absent from the government's list of ways religion can help in nation building. The government still seems to regard the development of moral values as the sole responsibility of the Chinese Communist Party. Since religious groups are to have no role in shaping the value system of Chinese society, government "guidance" for religious groups in this area is notable by its absence.

Nationalism

Because WTO accession links China with the global economic order, and the Internet links the Chinese with a virtual global village, one could easily assume that the religions in China will soon affiliate more closely with their respective overseas counterparts and ecumenical bodies. However, the December conference and subsequent statements shattered any such expectation. Chinese authorities have long stressed the centrality of "patriotism" for religious organizations, especially those that have linkages with the West, such as Catholicism and Protestantism. The government once again has emphasized the principles of independence and autonomy for all religions in China—meaning independence from any foreign religious bodies, not independence from the Chinese civil authorities. So while the rest of Chinese society enjoys a closer connection with the global community as a benefit from WTO accession, religious groups in China will remain distant from their international counterparts. The Sino-Vatican relationship can expect no positive contribution from WTO accession.

Furthermore, the government has warned religious groups of possible infiltration by zealous mission groups cashing in on the window of opportunity created by WTO accession. Religious Affairs Bureau director-general Ye Xiaowen's opening remarks at the National Chinese Christian Conference in Beijing in May 2002 stressed that the Chinese church must confront the possibility that many hostile foreign mission groups may use opportunities opened up by WTO accession to gain a foothold in China. He instructed official church leaders to step up anti-infiltration measures to block this foreign intrusion while at the same time cultivating positive relationships with friendly foreign religious bodies to promote China's policies and achievements.[15] Following this conference, the China Christian Council called upon the various provincial council leaders to increase their anti-infiltration capacity and brace for possible new waves of foreign missionary invasion while continuing to develop relationships with those groups willing to support the stance of the China Christian Council.[16]

Suppression

Finally, China's leaders have demonstrated continued willingness to use force to suppress autonomous religious groups. The government is aware of the emergence and expansion of various new religious groups in China. Some of these groups have been introduced by foreigners, such as the Jehovah's Witnesses, but most are indigenous groups, such as the Falungong and Eastern Lightning. Despite their illegal status, many of these groups are attracting increasing numbers of followers. They draw on the huge pool of dissatisfied unemployed workers or poor farmers, who may cling to anything that gives them hope, however exotic the teaching may appear. Furthermore, grievances against the established order that such religious groups often embody may echo the antigovernment sentiments harbored by other Chinese groups who think that the government has given them a raw deal, especially after WTO accession.

Newly developed religious groups may prove a destabilizing influence by undermining government authority through religious teaching of eschatological messages. Fully aware of these dangers, the government justifies suppression of these groups on grounds of protecting national security. The government has already established special units within the Ministry of Public Security that wage police campaigns to suppress these "evil cults," and the government will very likely increase the suppression, particularly if the groups continue to draw large numbers of people losing out in China's economic transition.

Implications for Future Political Change

As Daniel Bays details in chapter 2 of this volume, China's rulers have always exercised control over religion.[17] Moreover, in China's governing tradition, political authority has usually embraced a nonreligious official ideology, be it Confucianism or Communism. Moreover, China has always been a multireligious society, in which no one single religion has been dominant over others. Therefore, religious groups have always been a minority within a society under the state's civic control. Control over religion is regarded as a sacred mandate that any responsible government must maintain if it hopes to preserve a harmonious society. No group, including religious groups, is permitted to challenge the political authority; nor is socially destabilizing disharmony allowed among religious groups. So long as religious groups support the current regime and remain within the state-defined role, political authorities will tolerate them. If they do not, the government retains the prerogative to suppress them. This model of governance has been in practice, with relatively few exceptions, for almost two thousand years, and there is little evidence to suggest that the current regime will forsake this time-honored method of control over religion.

China's entry into the WTO, however, will spur increasing flows of capital, people, and ideas. Many Chinese will experience different forms of church-state relationships as they travel or read and are exposed to societies in other countries. They will become aware of the robust role religious groups can play, in sharp contrast with the traditional subservient model currently exercised in China. Religious groups in China may well seek more influence in society, similar to that enjoyed by their counterparts in other countries. The influence of religious values can easily go beyond current government-imposed boundaries, especially in the noninstitutional areas of social values and morality that elude government regulation. Consequently, religion in China will begin to seek a new church-state relationship, shifting from the subservient model envisioned by the Chinese authorities to something yet to be defined.

In addition to religious groups, many nongovernmental civic groups are emerging in China in such diverse areas as charitable services, consumer rights, and environmental protection. Religious groups and faith-based or value-based organizations already are joining this emerging "third sector." Given the need and the opportunity for religion to play a more participatory part in Chinese society, especially in social services and economic development, religious groups will become more popular and will have more influence among the population. Undertaking nonreligious activities will also enable them to strengthen their foothold in society. Some religious groups—such as Protestants and Catholics—are already well organized and possess a network of authority beyond the regional level, unlike most current third-sector groups. By further cultivating national networks and international linkages, religious groups can become an important element in societal change, both nationally and internationally. New alliances between environmentalist groups, religious groups, and development groups may be established, for example, to promote environmental issues. Once such a potential is reached, the third sector could play a decisive role in the future political arena in China.

Yet religion will also most likely continue to be a receptacle for popular frustration and disenfranchisement, offering China's have-nots ways to escape their desperate situation. Although the love, care, patience, and hope offered by religious groups can empower such people to confront daily hardships with grace and dignity, the groups may also channel popular dissatisfaction and anger into a powerful political force trying to transform the society, perhaps even by violent means.[18] Alternatively, adherents may be encouraged to escape reality by focusing exclusively on the spiritual realm, such as in some of the more extreme eschatological teachings. In short, religion can be a two-edged sword, capable of either stabilizing or destabilizing society in times of dramatic change. It will be a challenge to China's leaders to handle this powerful sword.

Conclusion

Religion is one of the many emerging issues facing the Chinese government as China enters into the new socioeconomic order of the WTO. On the one hand, the Chinese authorities want to tackle religion through the traditional policies of containment and control; on the other hand, the society is changing so radically and dynamically that there is little hope of containing religion and its influences by force or regulatory means. The more the government tries to control and suppress religion, the more religion can turn into a destabilizing force by going underground and using discontented social elements to turn against the regime. However, if the government allows more freedom and tolerance for various religions to develop in China—possibly beyond the current limit of five—then religious groups may easily become a stabilizing factor that will help absorb many social shocks. The flourishing of various religions, a truly diverse expression of faith and conviction, can facilitate the development of a more pluralistic and democratic society with sound moral foundations, a widely recognized criterion of a developed and civilized society.

It will take a lot of courage for the Chinese authorities to restructure the administrative systems that regulate religion, some of which date back to the Soviet era, for the authorities probably feel that letting go of their current control over religion would open a Pandora's box of issues they hitherto have not encountered. As China integrates into the international economic order, Chinese society will merge closer to the international community in other realms as well—culture, trends, life-styles, and knowledge—and religion will be no exception. Religion in China may take on a more international role as religious groups seek closer ties with their counterparts beyond the national boundaries. Tension will inevitably arise between the religious issues springing from WTO accession and the government's response to these issues based on current policies. If the Chinese government realizes the importance of religious liberty to a stable social environment and becomes willing to loosen its control over religion, such a move will be a decisive factor in the coming of age of China as it joins the global international community.

Notes

1. The WTO website (www.wto.org) is full of useful information. For the Chinese government's position on the WTO, see "China WTO Updates" (www.china.org.cn/

english/21693.htm [November 13, 2003]). For a balanced view of China's WTO accession, see Supachai Panitchpakdi and Mark L. Clifford, *China and the WTO: Changing China, Changing World Trade* (Singapore: John Wiley and Sons [Asia], 2002).

2. Lu Xueyi, ed., "Dangdai Zhongguo shehui jiecheng yanjiu baogao" [Research report on social strata in contemporary China], February 2002 (available in Chinese at www.china.org.cn/chinese/PI-c/105530.htm [November 13, 2003]).

3. The Chinese Academy of Social Sciences has published population projections in a report entitled "Zhongguo shehui xingshe fenshi yu yuqie zongbaogao, 2002–2003" [Analysis and projection of Chinese society, 2002–2003] (www.china.org.cn/chinese/zhuanti/250780.htm [November 13, 2003]). A section of this report discusses the number of internal migrants.

4. See Matthew Forney, "Workers' Wasteland," *Time* (Asian ed.), June 17, 2002, pp. 40–47.

5. Wenzhou is a coastal city in Zhejiang Province with its own dialect, incomprehensible to others. Its people are famous for their independent spirit and entrepreneurship. It was the first region to take advantage of the Reform and Opening Policy to establish private enterprises. Wenzhou merchants can be found not only all over China but also scattered in most of the emerging markets in the world. Ninety-eight percent of Wenzhou's gross domestic product in the year 2000 came from private enterprises, the highest percentage among all municipalities in China. See "Intellectual Property: Charge of the Lighter Brigade," *Far East Economic Review*, August 23, 2001, pp. 46–47.

6. Eastern Lightning is one of the many pseudo-Christian sects developing in China; the Chinese authorities regard these groups as evil cults. The Chinese government's lists and descriptions of these groups are available in General Office of Ministry of Public Security, "Information Regarding the Organizations Already Identified as Cults," in Li Shixiong and Xiqiu (Bob) Fu, eds. and trans., *Religion and National Security in China: Secret Documents from China's Security Sector* (Bartlesville, Okla.: Voice of the Martyrs, 2002), pp. 24–39. The Eastern Lightning sect has its own website (www.godword.org [November 13, 2003]). Christian circles generally regard these sects as "cults"; see, for example, the China for Jesus website (www.chinaforjesus.com [November 13, 2003]).

7. Kim-kwong Chan and Tetsunao Yamamori, *Holistic Entrepreneurs in China: A Handbook on the World Trade Organization and New Opportunities for Christians* (Pasadena, Calif.: William Carey International University Press, 2002), focuses on the missiological dimension of Chinese business people.

8. Chinese folk religion has had no official status until recently, when some of the regional offices of the Religious Affairs Bureau issued provisional regulations to govern folk religion such as Mazu. See Regional News Editor, "Nanping shi guanyu jiaqiang guanli minjian xinyan huodong de zhanxin guiding" [Nanping City provisional regulation regarding the strengthening of management of folk religion activities], in *Fujian zongjiao* [Fujian religion], no. 34 (Spring 2003), p. 47.

9. See the full report of this conference, as well as Jiang Zemin, "Zai quanguo zongjiao gongzuo huiyi shang de jianghua" [Speech delivered at the National Religious Work Conference], in *Renmin ribao* [People's daily], December 13, 2001, p. 1. Subsequent commentary was published in the party's internal bulletin, *Tongxin* [Communication], January 2002, pp. 1–20.

10. Jiang Zemin, "Gaodu zhongshi minzu gongzuo he zongjiao gong zuo" [Highly emphasizing nationality and religious work], a speech delivered at the National United Front Work Department on November 7, 1993, Beijing, in Documentation Research Office of the Chinese Communist Party, ed., *Jiang Zemin lun yu Zhongguo teshi shehui zhuyi* [Selected readings on Jiang Zemin's comments on socialism with Chinese characteristics] (Beijing: Central Document Press, 2002), p. 357.

11. Wang Zuo'an, *Zhongguo de zongjiao wenti he zongjiao zhengce* [Religious issues and religious policy in China] (Beijing: Religious Culture Press, 2002).

12. "Zhu Rongji jianghua" [Zhu Rongji's address], *Lilun dongtai* [Trends in theory], no. 1,590 (February 20, 2003), pp. 1–7.

13. In fact, some prominent Chinese religious leaders, such as the Reverend Li Chuwen of Shanghai International Church, have been secret members of the Chinese Communist Party. During this conference, the party theoretician Pan Yue published in an obscure newspaper an article suggesting the possibility of openly including patriotic religious leaders in the party by citing examples of the October Revolution in the Soviet Union. Many observers speculated that the Chinese Communist Party might head in such a direction. However, this conference clearly rejected the idea. Confidential sources suggested that Pan's article had been circulated among national leaders before the start of the conference and that some factions within the party had accepted this position on religious affairs. It was alleged that Jiang had read the article and later rejected the idea after consulting with some top religious leaders in China. Apparently, they worried that religious believers in China might have a hard time accepting the idea of their leaders' holding membership in a party that upholds atheism. See Pan Yue, "Women ying you zenyang de zongjiao guan? Lun Makesi zhuyi bixu yu shi ju jin" [What kind of view should we have on religion? A discussion on the need for Marxism to progress with the times], *Shenzhen tequ bao* [Shenzhen Special Economic Zone daily], February 16, 2001, p. 2.

14. "Zhu Rongji jianghua," p. 4.

15. The new president of the China Christian Council, the Reverend Cao Shengjie, reiterated Ye's sentiments by including strongly worded remarks on the "foreign infiltration" issue in a work report concerning the direction of the China Christian Council's future relations with foreign religious groups. See "Summary of the Work Report Delivered to the Seventh National Chinese Christian Conference," *Amity News Service*, vol. 11 (June 2002) (www.amityfoundation.org/ANS/Articles/ans2002/ and2002.6/2002_6_8.htm [November 13, 2003]).

16. See, for example, the remarks by Chen Meilin at the Hainan Christian Council Conference in September 2002, in the council's newsletter, *Huixun* [Council news], no. 3 (October 2002), pp. 3–7.

17. For further analysis, see Kim-kwong Chan, "A Chinese Perspective on the Interpretation of the Chinese Government's Religious Policy," in Alan Hunter and Don Rimmington, eds., *All under Heaven: Chinese Tradition and Christian Life in the People's Republic of China* (Kampen, Netherlands: J. H. Kok, 1992), pp. 38–44.

18. For examples of the benefits that derive from religious involvement, see the cases discussed in Tetsunao Yamamori and Kim-kwong Chan, *Witness to Power: Stories of God's Quiet Work in a Changing China* (Carlisle, Scotland: Paternoster, 2000), chaps. 5 and 8.

PART II

*Church-State
Interaction*

5

JEAN-PAUL WIEST

Setting Roots: The Catholic Church in China to 1949

The Christian presence in China has a long but broken history, shrouded by the mystery of time. Legend has it that St. Thomas traveled to China from India, converted some Chinese, and then returned to Meliapur on the coast of southeast India, where he died. Studies claiming that Jewish communities were already prospering in China during the first century raise the possibility that Christian merchants of Jewish and Syrian extraction traveling to the Far East brought the Christian message to communities along the Silk Road. Legends are only legends, however, and possibilities do not make history, unless solid evidence can be found to substantiate their claims.[1]

What is beyond dispute is that missionaries brought the Christian message to China on more than one occasion. They came in four major successive waves. Monks of the Syro-Persian Church of the East—often referred to as Nestorians by other Christian churches—arrived in the seventh century and left in the mid-ninth century. Monks from the same church returned in the thirteenth century, together with Franciscan friars, but were gone by the end of the following century. The Jesuits and other Roman Catholic societies arrived in the late sixteenth century and retained an institutional presence until the first half of the eighteenth century. With the dawn of the nineteenth century, Protestant missionaries appeared and Catholic groups returned, but by the early 1950s, few of either group remained on Chinese soil.

A simple explanation would be that religious motives led to the arrival of missionaries and religious persecutions resulted in their departure and expulsion. Yet a closer look at the facts reveals a more complex story. Other factors—economic, social, cultural, and political—played an important part in the ups and downs of relations between Christianity and China. The why and the how of present church-state relations within China derive from a complex historical and political context.

Christianity during the Tang Dynasty

The arrival in the capital city of Chang'an (modern Xi'an) of the Persian bishop Aluoben in 635 is the first known record of the presence of missionaries from the Church of the East, also known as the East Syrian Church. The Taizong emperor of the Tang dynasty welcomed the missionaries and ordered a translation of their works; three years later, he issued an edict of toleration. Christianity became known in Chinese as the "Luminous Religion" (*jing jiao*) and benefited from the protection of the court with little interruption for more than two hundred years, until 845. In that year, an imperial decree ordered the closure of a large number of monasteries belonging to non-Chinese religions and the return of their monks to secular life. Although the persecution was influenced by a Taoist reaction against encroachments by foreign religions, and by Buddhism in particular, political motives and economic expedients seem to have played a much more important part. Indeed, as a result of the loss of control over large areas corresponding to modern Gansu and Shaanxi Provinces, China had become less receptive to foreign influence and more inward looking. The edict not only transferred all monks of foreign religions from the Office of Religion to the Department of Foreign Affairs but also withdrew the tax-exempt status they had enjoyed for themselves and their temples. This allowed for the confiscation of their goods and properties, a boon to the imperial coffers depleted by years of wars and rebellions.

Although the decree was rescinded one year later, it drastically altered the religious climate in China. Buddhism, which had already deeply permeated Chinese society, rebounded rapidly after the ban was lifted but did not regain its economic and political influence. The Luminous Religion, on the other hand, never recovered from the blow and for all practical purposes gradually disappeared.

The first collapse of Christianity has often been blamed on the so-called heretical tenets of the Church of the East and an out-of-control syncretic propensity. In fact, economic and political factors were the main causes of its success as well as its demise. As a result of the military consolidation of the western borders by the first Tang emperor, the Silk Road had been reopened to merchants, which allowed also the flow of new forms of music, dance, arts, and religions. Most Tang rulers followed a tolerant policy toward foreigners, and Tang China became a cosmopolitan society. Monks of the Church of the East were welcomed not only because they preached "a religion beneficial to the human race"[2] but also because they posed no political threat. This is the only case in the entire history of relations between the state and Christianity in China in which Christianity was free of any association with military and political expansionism.

Yet at the same time, all the available evidence suggests that it remained mostly the religion of foreigners and failed to set down solid indigenous roots. Unlike Buddhism, which from the beginning developed a large native missionary constituency and a Chinese leadership, the Luminous Religion seems to have reserved to its foreign missionaries all major positions of authority. So when it lost the support of the Tang court in 845, most of its monks left the country. Although the ban lasted for only one year, the church lacked a Christian presence that could act as a springboard for reentry into China and a reservoir of missionary enterprise. Troubles along the Silk Road made the return of these monks and the sending of new ones especially difficult. Samarkand, the nearest position of strength in the Church of the East, lay sixteen hundred miles away. Cut from its Persian base and lacking sufficient internal resources to sustain its life, the Luminous Religion withered away.

The Return of the Church of the East

The Nestorians continued to flourish in Central Asia among the Uighur, Naiman, and Ongut tribes and gradually spread among the Keraits and the Mongols. In thirteenth-century China, the advent of the Mongol Yuan dynasty marked the beginning of a strong comeback for Christianity in China. Researchers have identified at least twenty-two cities with substantial groups of believers in the Luminous Religion during the Yuan. Perhaps the most compelling sign of the vitality of the Christian church in China during this period is the fact that in 1280 Mar Mark, a monk of Uighur descent, born and raised in Shaanxi Province, was elected patriarch of Baghdad to rule over the entire Church of the East.

The Luminous Religion of the thirteenth and fourteenth centuries repeated its earlier mistakes by catering mostly to Mongols and other foreign communities and concentrating authority in foreign hands. With the overthrow of the foreign Mongol Yuan dynasty in 1368, the church lost the protection and favors it had enjoyed for some one hundred years. In addition, it could no longer count on the support of its mother church because the Church of the East in its Persian and Mesopotamian heartland had begun to weaken under violent campaigns from Mongol khans who had embraced Islam. With the ascent of Tamerlane in 1369, the situation got even worse. What followed were thirty-five years of ruthless executions of Christians and the systematic destruction of church properties aimed at eradicating Christianity from Tamerlane's empire. Its vast multiethnic network in ruin, the surviving Syro-Persian church was never again able to reach out to China. Without contact with its distant spiritual and magisterial center, the Luminous Religion once more disappeared from the public scene, because it lacked the native leadership and the Chinese following necessary for survival.

Faced with such difficulties of communication, one wonders why the Church of the East remained oblivious of the need to bring native Chinese monks into leadership positions. This attitude is in striking contrast with its profound attempts to sink roots in Chinese culture. None of the documents available mentions Chinese-born Nestorians of any importance. Buddhism, by contrast, produced illustrious Chinese monks, such as Fa Xian in the fifth century and Xuan Zang in the seventh.

The Franciscan Mission

The first arrival of Roman Catholic missionaries in China also occurred under Mongol rule during the thirteenth century. In 1245 Pope Innocent IV sent a Franciscan friar to the Mongol court at Karakorum to convince the Great Khan, Kublai, to stop his advance into Europe. Although the retreat of the Mongol horsemen had no connection with the diplomatic skills of the friar, the papacy continued to dispatch Franciscan-led missions to Persia, Mongolia, and China in an attempt to convert the tribes of the vast Mongol Empire and to enlist their help against Islam. Again no political alliance was achieved by these envoys, but their missionary efforts led to the establishment of a Roman Catholic outpost in Mongol-occupied China, where the Great Khan had founded the Yuan dynasty in 1271. In 1294 the Franciscan Giovanni da Montecorvino became the first Roman Catholic missionary to set foot on Chinese soil, and soon thereafter he built a church in the capital, Beijing (Marco Polo's Cambalic). Like the earlier Syro-Persian monks, the Franciscan friars enjoyed the protection of the emperor and received a substantial state salary that enabled them to found churches in other major cities such as Hangzhou, Yangzhou, and Quanzhou (Marco Polo's Zaitong). Their efforts were aimed mainly at converting the emperor and the so-called Nestorian princes and high officials of the cosmopolitan non-Chinese court. Outside the court, most of their followers appear to have belonged to the rich foreign merchant community of the large cities of that time. For most Chinese, the religion brought by the Franciscans, like Islam and Nestorianism, was a religion of foreigners.

The Franciscan presence in China was small and short lived. The perils and privations of the long voyage from Europe to the Far East inflicted heavy casualties, cutting missionary reinforcement to a trickle. Montecorvino had to wait eleven years for the arrival of another friar to help him. After the turn of the century, moreover, the rapid spread of Islam throughout Central Asia further compounded the pope's difficulty in staffing the Chinese missions.

In China, meanwhile, hostility toward the foreign Mongol Yuan dynasty and those associated with it became more widespread and violent after 1340. Like their Syro-Persian counterparts, Roman Catholic communities were persecuted and their churches destroyed by Chinese patriots. When the Franciscan bishop of Quanzhou was slain in 1362, he was one of the last Catholic missionaries still in Chinese territory. At the time of the establishment of the Chinese Ming dynasty in 1368, Catholics in China may have numbered as many as thirty thousand, but the majority was probably non-Han Chinese.

Under such circumstances, the Holy See eventually lost all contact with its Chinese missions. Although it continued to send out missionaries from time to time, none seem to have reached China until the sixteenth century, when the Portuguese concession-port of Macao was opened for mission work. Within China proper, the Catholic Church, for lack of native leadership and a strong Chinese following, disappeared almost without a trace. All that remained were a few Chinese Catholics who persevered and handed down their faith in an unbroken tradition until missionaries discovered their descendants at the turn of the twentieth century.

The Late Ming to the Mid-Qing Dynasties

At least seven entities with political clout were involved in the return of Christianity at different times, in different combinations, and with different results. They were the Western powers of Portugal, Spain, France, and Russia; Chinese emperors; Chinese officials and literati; the Jesuits; other Roman Catholic orders and congregations; the Russian Orthodox Church; and the Holy See. Of these elements, the Jesuits are the only one found in all combinations of events.

Portugal, the Holy See, and the Jesuits

Through a series of papal bulls, the popes of the last decades of the fifteenth century divided recently discovered territories into spheres of influence between Spain and Portugal. Through the 1494 Treaty of Tordesillas, Spain received most of the Americas and the territories west of them. Portugal got Brazil, Africa, and the Far East. In 1565, in violation of the treaty, Spain conquered the Philippines and thereby gained a foothold in the Far East. The two kingdoms had within their respective spheres the exclusive rights of navigation, conquest, and commerce, but at the same time they were entrusted with the responsibility of spreading the gospel and administering the new churches. This system was known as the right of royal patronage, *padroado real* for the Portuguese king and *patronado real* for the Spanish monarch. The Holy See was to regret the decision.

The Vatican's first attempt to reposition Christian missionary activity under its authority was the creation of the Society of Jesus. Founded in 1534, the Jesuits were organized specifically as a religious group at the exclusive service of the pope, free from political interference and not bound by traditional ecclesiastical structures.[3] The appointment of the Italian Alessandro Valignano as Jesuit Visitor to the East in 1573 signaled a movement to assert Jesuit spiritual authority above the political control of the Portuguese *padroado* and the Spanish *patronado* and, by the same process, to achieve a measure of independence for the Jesuits in China.

From the start, Valignano's insistence on recruiting Italian Jesuits for his missions indicated a commitment to find missionaries not deeply affected by the conquistador understanding of Christianity and the world. From experience, he knew that the Italians of the period were free from this infection. Indeed, all the key figures in the initial period of the Jesuit presence in China were Italians who, like Matteo Ricci, were imbued with the ideas of the Italian Renaissance and were intellectually prepared in the Roman College of the Society of Jesus, the future Gregorian University. As the person in charge, Valignano was the one whose insight and determination set the tone and held the course of the Jesuit missions in China for more than thirty years until his death in Macao in 1606. Convinced that Chinese culture contained elements that serve as a foundation for the building of an indigenous Christian church and a new Chinese Christian culture, Valignano entrusted the task to the Italian Matteo Ricci, and every new initiative of Ricci's was taken with his full agreement.

The Jesuits' Plan to Convert China

When the Jesuits Michele Ruggieri and Matteo Ricci entered China in 1583, they were the first Christians to reestablish a permanent missionary presence in more than two hundred years. They and the Jesuits that followed them were only vaguely aware that Franciscan friars and monks of the Church of the East had preceded them. Unhampered by the past, the Jesuits searched for ways to adapt Christianity within the context of Chinese literature, philosophy, and social institutions. Accommodation, respect, and friendship characterized this approach. The archetype of this attitude was Matteo Ricci, whose goal was to create a favorable climate that would lead toward an expanding movement of conversion. Their intellectual and moral qualities had considerable positive influence on China's cultivated society and on its emperor.

That the missionaries were successful to a certain extent is beyond doubt. From just a statistical standpoint, the number of Chinese Christians swelled from less than 1,000 in 1600 to 217,000 in 1815,[4] with important communities in Jiangsu, Zhejiang, Fujian, Guizhou, Sichuan, Shanxi, and Shaanxi. Until Rome issued its first ban against Confucian ceremonials in 1704, a good number of converts were high officials, degree holders of various ranks, and members of the local elite. They were found in the capital as well as in Christian communities in the provinces. Most famous among them are Xu Guangqi, Li Zhizao, and Yang Tingyun, often referred to as the three pillars of the Chinese church.

Above all, the Jesuits aimed at the conversion of the emperor, which, in their eyes, would facilitate the conversion of the whole of China. Although they never achieved this aim with the Ming or the Qing emperors, they did succeed in converting important figures within the imperial court, including members of the imperial family, eunuchs, and court women. The closest the Jesuits came to converting an emperor was in the late 1640s, when they baptized most of the retinue and family of the emperor Yongli, the last monarch of the Southern Ming dynasty, including his mother, his wife, and his child. This was a court in disarray, however, that was soon to be slaughtered by the troops of the new Qing dynasty. Under the first two Qing monarchs, the situation of Christianity remained precarious until the Kangxi emperor in 1692 issued the Edict of Toleration, which protected existing church buildings and allowed the propagation of Christianity among the Chinese as a harmless activity that did not endanger China. The edict did not turn out to be a sign that the emperor was soon to convert, as some Jesuits believed. In fact, it was drastically amended fifteen years later and was finally revoked in 1724.

Confucian Orthodoxy in Opposition to Christianity

If some officials and members of the local elite looked favorably on Christianity, the majority seem to have been neutral or to have ignored it. A substantial number, however, remained highly suspicious of its tenets and of the intentions of missionaries and converts. Although there were various reasons for their dislike of Christianity, the accusation of contravening the Confucian orthodoxy, and therefore of being heretical, was at the core of all their opposition. The origin of this dual notion can be traced back to China's most revered philosophers, Confucius and Mencius. As Confucianism became the state ideology and the standard of personal ethics, orthodoxy came to refer to the "correct" social, political, and ritual order realized by the "correct" administration, at the apex of which stood the emperor. The label of heterodoxy could therefore be applied to almost any teaching or practice that departed from the Confucian path, and it is within this context that religions were deemed acceptable or not in Chinese society. As long as they did not interfere in the political realm or question Confucian moral standards, they could develop alongside Confucianism, though not on the same hierarchical level, and under strict administrative control of the state. When they were perceived as a threat to the existing local order, local authorities persecuted them as heterodox.

During the seventeenth and eighteenth centuries, officials and literati often leveled accusations against Christianity. When trouble flared up it was often fanned by anti-Christian literature. The tensions and diatribes never developed into widespread lasting persecutions, however. Although personal antipathy against individual missionaries and xenophobic reaction were present, the key ingredient in most incidents seems to have been the perception of Christianity as a threat to the existing order. The Confucians not only considered aspects of Christian doctrine as dangerous, they also frowned on Christianity's superiority over other religions and, at the least, equality with Confucianism. This was viewed as a challenge to Confucian orthodoxy and ultimately to the authority of the emperor, who at the summit of society, was the supreme ruler and religious leader all in one.

The Rites Controversy

The Catholic missionary presence in China remained in the hands of the Jesuits until 1633, when the Roman Office of Propaganda Fide decided to permit other missionary groups to join in.[5] Prompted by Portugal's inability to provide missionaries in sufficient number and its excessive control over the missions, this office also created new ecclesiastical divisions, called vicariates apostolic, that were headed by bishops directly dependent on the Holy See and independent of the Portuguese crown. Although early signs seemed to point to a successful cooperative effort, the reality turned out to be entirely different: the newcomers rejected the Jesuits' accommodation to Chinese culture as excessive and inadmissible. By the time the Kangxi emperor issued his Edict of Toleration, the dispute was already undermining the hope surrounding that ruling. The difference of opinion worsened into a bitter conflict known as the Chinese rites controversy, which drew the involvement of the papacy and the Qing dynasty.

The core of the controversy revolved around three questions: the use of the Chinese terms *tian* and *Shangdi* rather than a Latin transliteration in designating the Christian God, rituals for ancestors, and ceremonies in honor of Confucius. The Jesuits contended that the concepts of heaven (*tian*) and the Lord on High (*Shangdi*) of the Chinese classics did not taint the Christian God with pagan associations. Moreover, they regarded the cult of ancestors as simply a way of practicing the basic Christian virtues of honoring parents, and they argued that Confucian ceremonies were nonsuperstitious civil ceremonials to signify respect for the legitimate authority. The other missionaries contended that ancestral and Confucian rituals were idolatrous, and they rejected the use of terms from the Chinese classics for key theological terms. In 1700 the Kangxi emperor subscribed to the Jesuits' interpretation. Rome, on the other hand, vacillated for a time but finally decided against the Jesuits' position. Repeatedly in 1704, 1710, 1715, and 1742, the Holy See condemned their approach and in 1773 disbanded the order. In response to Rome's condemnations, the Kangxi emperor in 1706 and 1720 deported missionaries who refused to follow the "Ricci" views on the Chinese rites. His successor, the Yongzheng emperor, banned Christianity in 1724. Qing rulers allowed only missionaries with secular skills and scientific expertise to remain legally.

Although it was never strictly enforced, the ban signaled the start of more than a century of intermittent persecutions of China's Christians, who numbered 200,000 at the time. The total number of foreign missionaries working outside the Qing court peaked at around 140 in 1701. That number fell by nearly half following the 1706 expulsion but then rose again to between 80 and 90 men, proving that missionaries had managed to hide in the countryside and new ones had been able to slip into China. Their number did not steadily decline until the second half of the eighteenth century, and this resulted primarily from the poor state of the religious situation in Europe. By 1800, no more than 26 missionaries operated illegally within China. The Qing emperor retained the services of 10 to 15 more for their artistic and technical skills.

The ban of 1724 made missionaries realize the urgency of training Chinese for the priesthood. At the beginning of the eighteenth century, there were only 6 Chinese priests for the whole of China. Yet by the dawn of the nineteenth century they numbered about two-thirds of the 75 priests at work in the country. Moreover, despite the persecutions, most Christian communities were able to sustain themselves so that the number of Christians remained steady and even slightly increased, reaching 217,000 in 1815. In Sichuan alone the number of Christians grew from roughly 4,000 in 1756 to 60,000 by 1815, while the number of Chinese priests increased from 2 to about 20.[6]

The argument that Christianity failed in China during the eighteenth century as a result of the rites controversy is therefore much too simplistic. What is certain is that the condemnation of Ricci's approach changed the status and the membership enrollment of the church. The interdiction of performing Confucian rites closed the door to any possibility of conversion among officials, and any support the church may have had among them disappeared. More than ever Christianity became a heterodox religion despised by China's literati and persecuted by its officialdom and the gentry. The missionaries had no choice but to hide in the countryside and to work among the uneducated farmers, which explains the mostly rural situation of the Catholic Church in nineteenth-century China.

At the heart of the controversy was the question of how much Christianity could adapt to Chinese culture and traditions and still maintain the integrity of its faith—or, more appropriately, how the Chinese could adopt Christianity without abandoning their own culture. The outcome of the controversy shows that the Western theology of that time "lacked the inner resources necessary to an encounter with the spirit of the ancient culture of China."[7] But in fact, this was a question that only Chinese Christians, even as uneducated as they might have been—and not foreign missionaries—could answer appropriately. Their continuous existence into the present proves that they have found a way.

Christianity in the Late Qing and Republican Periods

At the beginning of the nineteenth century, foreign missionaries continued to enter the country incognito and to minister in secret to mostly rural communities. When apprehended by the local authorities, they were usually escorted back to Macao. A few, however, lingered in Chinese jails or were even put to death. Christian communities in Guizhou and Sichuan, in particular, were targets of severe repression. Among the 120 saints canonized by Pope John Paul II on October 1, 2000, nine were martyred in those two provinces between 1815 and 1839, including one foreign bishop, four Chinese priests, and four catechists.

The authorization for foreign missionaries to reenter the country legally came only in the mid-nineteenth century as a result of the aggression of Western powers against China. In striking contrast to the Jesuits who had preceded them, these newcomers, whether Catholic or Protestant, had for the most part little appreciation for Chinese society. They viewed it as a hostile pagan environment and as a dying and decadent culture that needed to be replaced by a Christian—meaning Western—civilization. So when the Western powers, through a series of "unequal treaties," forced China to accept foreign influences, including Christianity, many missionaries were jubilant at the prospect of converting China's millions.

The Treaty of Nanking (modern Nanjing) in 1842 was the first step of several that forced China to open up to foreign trade and to let foreigners enter China for religious as well as commercial reasons. In 1846, at the insistence of the French plenipotentiary Théodore de Lagrené, the Daoguang emperor issued a decree permitting the Chinese to profess the Catholic faith. The decree also ordered the restitution of previously confiscated church properties and the punishment of local officials who persecuted Catholics. The decree was never published, however, and thus remained largely ineffective. With the execution of the French missionary Auguste Chapdelaine in 1856, France stepped up its role as protector of Catholic missions and joined Great Britain in the Second Opium War, the so called Arrow War. In the Sino-French treaties of 1858 and 1860, religious liberty for all Christians was reaffirmed and extended to the interior of China. The treaties also guaranteed the protection of missionaries traveling to the interior, provided they carried valid passports. All anti-Christian legislation was revoked. Although these measures were directed at the Chinese Catholic community, they also greatly benefited Protestants. Meanwhile, as the sole Catholic power among the signatories, France assumed the protection of all Catholic missionaries regardless of nationality. The Peking (Beijing) Convention of 1860 gave missionaries the right to buy property for religious purposes. With the tacit consent of the Holy See, France effectively exercised for sixty years an almost exclusive protection over all Chinese converts, Catholic missionaries, and church properties in China.

The coercive measures taken by Western imperial powers intensified the already existing opposition to Christianity among members of Chinese officialdom and the gentry. They began to view it as an external force transmitted by outsiders with political and military backing that was aimed at revolutionizing the entire spiritual foundation of China. Diatribes against Christianity as a heterodox doctrine grew more vitriolic. The most influential of the anti-Christian tracts and books of the nineteenth century was the *Bixie jishi* [Record of facts to ward off heterodoxy]. It accused Christians of sorcery and sexual perversion and of indulging in a series of revolting practices, which only further confirmed the utterly heterodox nature of their religion. As China's economic and social situation deteriorated, officials and local notables repeatedly diverted the anger and frustration of the Chinese masses away from themselves and the Qing dynasty by blaming foreigners and making missionaries and converts the targets.

The decrees and treaties guaranteeing religious freedom signed during the second half of the nineteenth century did little to stem anti-Christian sentiment. Missionary involvement in legal cases on behalf of Christians further irked the non-Christian population. When incidents occurred, Western powers used them as justifications for launching military actions that forced China into making more concessions, further fueling Chinese resentment against Christianity. Occasionally violence turned deadly, as in the massacre of the French consul at Tianjin in 1870, during which two priests, ten Sisters of Charity, and eight lay persons were slaughtered. Anti-Christian violence reached a climax when "the anti-Christian tradition fed by xenophobia, by personal humiliations experienced in hundreds of missionary cases, and by a desperate desire to keep China whole, exploded" into the Boxer Uprising of 1900.[8] The stinging defeat of the Qing army by the International Expeditionary Force and the humiliation felt by many Chinese further boosted the growing nationalist movement and hastened the demise of the Manchu dynasty.

Although the fall of the dynasty in 1911 brought an end to Confucianism as the state ideology, the anti-Christian tradition did not disappear; it was merely transmuted into nationalism. In their efforts to bring an end to the humiliating unequal treaties that kept China in a semicolonial state, nationalist Chinese often turned their anger toward Christian missions, which they associated with Western expansion and dubbed the cultural arm of Western imperialism. Although the unequal treaties were not abolished until 1943, the nationalist campaign against Christianity quickly subsided under the ruling Nationalist Party in the late 1920s. The conversions to Christianity of Chiang Kai-shek and some high-ranking Nationalist Party officials offer some explanation, but the main reasons were matters of national security that needed urgent attention. As the communist challenge and the Japanese aggression in Manchuria turned into an all-out protracted war, anti-Christian opposition did not surface again in a noticeable way until the establishment of a new government in 1949.

The Roman Catholic Church to 1949

Compelled by the growing negative political repercussions emanating from the French protectorate, the Holy See began to put more distance between missionary interests and France after 1881. France repeatedly thwarted Rome's attempts to establish direct diplomatic relations with the Chinese government until 1922, when Bishop Celso Costantini was appointed the first apostolic delegate to China. Although not officially a member of the diplomatic corps, Costantini became the de facto religious representative of the pope in supervising the entire Catholic Church in China, effectively ending the French protectorate over Catholic missions in China. In 1943 the Chinese government dispatched an ambassador to the Vatican, and three years later Rome sent an internuncio to China.

In the first half of the twentieth century, changes began to appear, indicating that a truly Chinese Christianity might finally emerge. The Protestants were the first to initiate a large-scale process of devolution of authority to Chinese pastors. They also targeted the educated class of Chinese society, creating thirteen Protestant universities and converting high-ranking officials, including President Chiang Kai-shek.

On the Catholic side, a small group of priests led by Father Vincent Lebbe, probably the missionary most sensitive to Chinese culture since Ricci, jolted the missionary community by calling for the church to relinquish the protection of foreign powers and to put in place an indigenous leadership. Lebbe's stand began a process that, combined with other factors, led the Holy See to condemn imperialistic attitudes among missionaries and to ask them to be more appreciative of the local culture. The pope also affirmed the rights of the Chinese to govern their own church and acted on it by ordaining six Chinese bishops in 1926. In 1939 the Vatican went even further by recognizing its own mistakes and revoking the condemnation of the Chinese rites. The veneration of Confucius, ceremonies in honor of deceased ancestors, and other Chinese national customs were declared to be purely civil in character and therefore permissible to Catholics. In 1946 Pope Pius XII appointed Thomas Tian Gengxin as China's first cardinal. The same year, the pope elevated the China mission to the rank of local church with twenty archdioceses and seventy-nine dioceses. By the early 1950s, however, changes had not yet pervaded deeply into the Chinese Catholic Church, which, for the most part, remained largely controlled by foreign bishops.

Despite the appalling imperialistic or culturally insensitive character of many Catholic and Protestant missions during the first part of the twentieth century, the contributions of both to China should also be acknowledged. They provided modern education, medical care, and social and relief services, all in conformity with national governmental regulations. The Japanese invasion of 1937, more than anything else, caused many missionaries to ally themselves with the Chinese people's drive for national development and liberation. This attitude helped alleviate Chinese suspicions toward the church and brought in many converts.

The victory of Mao Zedong's communist forces in 1949 resulted in the complete rejection of Western imperialism. The communist government accused the Protestant and Catholic churches, which had strongly backed the Nationalist Party regime, of having sold out to the Western nations in order to exploit the Chinese people. It gradually expelled or forced out all foreign missionaries, who left behind 3.5 million Chinese Catholics and 1 million Protestants. Once more, the hope for a strong Chinese Christianity grew dim.

Conclusion

With its organization, finances, and leadership largely in the hands of missionaries, the Chinese Catholic Church at the time of the communist takeover in 1949 remained, for all practical purposes, a foreign institution. When the communist ax fell on the missionaries, Chinese Catholics were also suspected of being traitors and spies who could not be trusted and who should be punished unless they could prove their patriotism. The advent of the communist regime forced China's Catholics to pass suddenly from a state of infancy and almost total dependence on Western churches to a state of selfhood and self-determination. Since then the church has charted a difficult and courageous course through seas of suffering and oppression.

In many ways, Christianity has persevered until today because of its missionary heritage. In spite of its many imperfections, the missionaries' catechetical programs and training of local priests and sisters gave the native church a solid foundation. Yet it was the expulsion of the mission churches that opened the way for a truly local church to emerge. Today, as Richard Madsen notes in the next chapter, the Chinese Catholic Church is alive and well, though confronted with thorny internal and external problems.

Notes

1. For a bird's-eye view of the legend of St. Thomas, see Iris Columba Cary-Elwes, *China and the Cross: A Survey of Missionary History* (New York: P. J. Kenedy and Sons, 1957), pp. 9–11, and Jürgen Tubach, "Der Apostel Thomas in China: Die Herkunft einer Tradition" [The apostle Thomas in China: The origin of a tradition], *Zeitschrift für Kirchengeschichte* [Magazine for church history], vol. 108 (1997), pp. 58–74.

2. Antonino Forte, "The Edict of 638 Allowing the Diffusion of Christianity in China," in Paul Pelliot, *L'inscription nestorienne de Si-ngan-fou* [The Nestorian inscription of Si-ngan-fou], edited by Antonino Forte (Kyoto, Japan: Scuola di Studi sull'Asia Orientale, 1996), pp. 353–54.

3. In addition to the three regular vows of chastity, poverty, and obedience to their superiors, the Jesuits take a fourth vow of service to the pope in whatever form he sees fit.

4. Nicolas Standaert, ed., *Handbook of Christianity in China*, vol. 1, *635–1800* (Leiden, Netherlands: Brill, 2001), pp. 382–83.

5. In 1622 the Holy See, tired of abuses perpetrated by the *padroado* and *patronado* system, created the Office of Propaganda Fide to regain direct control of the evangelization of mission territories.

6. Pierre Jeanne, "The Early Church in Sichuan Province: A Study of the Conditions Leading to the Synod of 1803," *Tripod*, no. 15 (June 1983), pp. 52–53.

7. Bob Whyte, *Unfinished Encounter: China and Christianity* (London: Fount Paperbacks, 1988), p. 92.

8. Jessie Gregory Lutz, *Chinese Politics and Christian Missions: The Anti-Christian Movements of 1920–1928* (Notre Dame, Ind.: Cross Cultural Publications, 1988), p. 26.

6

RICHARD MADSEN

Catholic Conflict and Cooperation in the People's Republic of China

As it consolidated its power after victory in the Chinese civil war, the Maoist regime established tight control over all Chinese religious communities and steadily attempted to stifle all forms of religious expression. The attack on the Catholic Church was especially harsh, for reasons that are understandable if seen from the perspective of the new Chinese government at that time. Although it claimed the allegiance of only a tiny part of the Chinese population (roughly 3 million followers, about 1 percent of the population), the Catholic Church was well organized, staunchly anticommunist, and intimately connected with foreign powers that wanted to undo the Chinese communist regime. One of its leading prelates, Archbishop (later Cardinal) Yu Bin of Nanjing, was a major international advocate of Chiang Kai-shek and the Nationalist Party and a close friend of New York's Francis Cardinal Spellman, who was an inspiration to those American Catholics who passionately argued for the "rollback" of communism in Asia.[1] Pope Pius XII was staunchly anticommunist, and the Vatican tried to mobilize China's Catholics to take an uncompromising stand against the communist regime. Archbishop Antonio Riberi, the Vatican's internuncio (ambassador) to China, forbade Catholics, under pain of excommunication, to join any communist-controlled organization or to "publish, to read, to write, or to propagate any communist literature."[2]

As it did with the other major religions, the government of the People's Republic of China quickly established "mass organizations" to serve as a transmission belt from the party-state to the church. These organizations were formally under the authority of religious leaders deemed "reliable" by the government, but they were really under control of the Chinese Communist Party's United Front Work Department, whose policies were implemented by the state Religious Affairs Bureau. In 1950 the government began to set up local "Catholic reform committees," the first building blocks of what eventually became the Chinese Catholic Patriotic Association. The Vatican denounced these committees and excommunicated all participants. The communist government quickly expelled the Vatican internuncio, together with all foreign missionaries. In 1952 Pope Pius XII issued an encyclical defending the missionaries and condemning the communists. The Chinese government stepped up imprisonment of clergy and laity whom it considered subversive. In 1954 the pope issued another encyclical denouncing the "three autonomies" or "three selfs" (self-governance, self-support, and self-propagation) insisted upon by the Chinese government. In 1955 the most influential Catholic leader remaining in China (leading prelates like Archbishop Yu Bin having long since fled to Taiwan), Shanghai's bishop Gong Pinmei, was imprisoned and would remain so for more than thirty years.

What sustained such church leaders was the faith that they would be rewarded in heaven for their martyrdom. This belief in the holiness of their martyrs also inspired ordinary Catholic lay people and provided a standard by which they would judge the authenticity of their clergy. Meanwhile, progovernment Catholics carried out elections of bishops to fill vacancies in dioceses where the bishop had been imprisoned. Such progovernment Catholics acted out of a mix of motives, ranging from opportunism to a sincere desire to help the church survive. In 1956, during the liberal period of the Hundred Flowers movement, the government relaxed some of its pressure on the church and even admitted to mistakes in its policies toward Catholics. This began to attract more Catholics to a wary progovernment position.[3]

In 1957, in line with the antirightist movement's attack on all political disloyalty, the government established the national Catholic Patriotic Association (CPA), which centralized control over all local Catholic patriotic associations. The Vatican responded with an appeal to Chinese Catholics to "resist any patriotic movement even to the point of bleeding and death."[4] The Chinese government, in turn, branded all recalcitrant Catholics as rightists. The leadership of the CPA then moved to consecrate several new bishops without Vatican approval. Pope Pius XII issued a third encyclical, denouncing the CPA and condemning the episcopal consecrations.[5]

In 1958 Pope John XXIII used the word *schism* to refer to the progovernment portion of the Chinese church. He later retracted the term and made some overtures to Chinese Catholic leaders, which were, however, rejected at the direction of the Chinese government.[6] Meanwhile, most ordinary lay people shunned the bishops and priests who collaborated with the CPA and remained united in at least passive opposition to government control. Any active opposition would have been extremely difficult, because besides being under the control of the CPA they were subjected to surveillance in their villages, neighborhoods, and workplaces by a vast, interlocking network of party-controlled organizations.

The CPA-controlled churches that remained publicly open were few in number, and their services were sparsely attended. Most Catholics fulfilled their spiritual needs in secret, either by carrying out private devotions at home or through clandestine services conducted by "underground" priests. Mothers and grandmothers secretly baptized their children and taught them prayers, devotions, and basic doctrine. Sometimes, local communities continued to receive the quiet guidance of the lay leaders who had customarily been appointed by their priests to help run the congregation.

Despite these difficult circumstances, an indigenous Catholic devotional life continued to evolve, although not necessarily in directions that would have been fully encouraged by guardians of Vatican orthodoxy. Stories of miraculous healings and deliverances from enemies were passed from generation to generation, perhaps embellished in the telling and inadvertently commingled with folk religious beliefs. Rumors of apparitions by the Virgin Mary sometimes mobilized large numbers of people to defy government prohibitions against unauthorized travel and assembly. At least one such assembly in Shanxi Province provoked a military crackdown in the late 1950s.

During the Cultural Revolution (1966–76), Catholics suffered even more calamities. Religion was attacked by Red Guard zealots as part of their assault on the "four olds"—old ideas, old culture, old customs, and old habits. All public worship was forbidden, even that under the CPA. Church buildings were destroyed or converted to secular use. Most bishops and priests—even those who had joined the CPA—were subjected to "struggle sessions" and sent to labor camps.

In spite of the harsh repression, Catholics remained in the church. By the 1980s, there were an estimated 10 million Chinese Catholics—the Catholic population having kept pace with overall population growth in China.[7] How had Catholics been able to withstand persecution, when even their missionaries had often considered them poorly educated "rice Christians"?

Simply put, the reason Chinese Catholics remained in the church was that it was difficult for them to leave. Most Catholics were concentrated in villages or segments of villages in which everyone else was Catholic. In some places, like Hebei Province, whole counties were Catholic. (Catholic missionary policy had been aimed at converting whole communities rather than individuals. Church policy forbade baptism of an individual who would be unable to live in an extended Catholic family or neighborhood, for fear that such a person might easily backslide and thereby be in more danger of damnation than if he or she had never accepted the faith at all.) Religious practice in these villages was woven into the entire familistic fabric of community life. In such communities, even a person who had little personal faith would probably have to marry a Catholic and, even more important, be buried as a Catholic, for there was no other way that people could be properly mourned by their communities and properly connected with their ancestors in the afterlife. For a rural person—and for residents of such "urban villages" as the all-Catholic Xujiawei neighborhood in Shanghai—it was virtually impossible to completely shed a Catholic identity. The government only increased the social solidarity of Catholic communities by its household registration system, which tightly restricted mobility out of villages and urban work units. The government perhaps even deepened the commitment of Catholics to their faith when it discriminated against them for having an identity that they could not have shed even if they had wanted to.

A Partial Opening

The reform era, launched by Deng Xiaoping after the death of Mao Zedong, brought an end to the harshest forms of religious repression. Chinese leaders faced the fact that Maoist repression had not destroyed religion but had only driven much of it underground. In 1982 Document 19 laid out the framework for the new regulations. The new regulations led to the reopening of previously existing churches and to the building of some new ones. The regulations also gave Catholic bishops and priests more autonomy than they had had in thirty years to make decisions about basic church doctrine and ritual. They could even claim loyalty to the pope's "spiritual authority," although they were not supposed to accept Vatican authority over the practical organization of the church.

Organizational authority was to be exercised by the CPA, which was now revived after having been dismantled during the Cultural Revolution. Under the supervision of the United Front Work Department and the Religious Affairs Bureau, the CPA (together with a related organization called the National Catholic Administrative Committee) controlled economic and political aspects of the church. The CPA claimed authority to decide who could be appointed bishop and who could be given authorization to practice ministry, when and where new church buildings could be constructed, how church monies could be spent, and what kinds of connections could be established with foreign church members. Most Chinese Catholics probably agree that these matters are not for a quasi-governmental association to decide—especially one controlled by atheistic communist officials—but should rather be decided by the Catholic hierarchy in accord with directives issued from the Vatican. However, the Chinese government had relaxed its regulatory framework enough that many Catholics found it acceptable to worship publicly in officially approved "open churches."

The open churches filled up. The enthusiasm of worshipers in such churches was sometimes far greater than one might expect to find in most American Catholic parishes. The eagerness of Chinese Catholics to return to public worship is understandable in view of their beliefs about the importance of the sacraments in religious life. In Catholic theology, the sacraments are indispensable channels for God's grace. No matter how devoutly one may pray in private, one's spiritual needs can never be fully met without receiving the sacraments, and the efficacy of the sacraments depends on their being administered by a priest who has been validly ordained. (These doctrines were emphasized even more by the Counter-Reformation theology that held sway before the Second Vatican Council—a theology that guided the thinking of most Chinese Catholics in the 1980s, because they had been unable to learn about the reforms of Vatican II.)

The policies of the Maoist era cut most Chinese Catholics off from regular sacramental ministry by priests. They were starved for such ministry and perhaps even willing to accept the sacraments from priests who had compromised themselves partially by collaborating with the CPA. Catholic theology, after all, holds that the sacraments work *ex opere operato*; that is, they are effective irrespective of the holiness of the priest who administers them, as long as that priest has been validly ordained and is in communion with Rome. Many of the priests who now emerged to work in the officially opened churches fit this standard. Although all had to give some lip service to the CPA, many did not even join that government-controlled organization. Although many Catholics were willing to receive the sacraments from such priests, far fewer were willing to receive them from those priests and bishops who were most closely associated with the CPA.

A visitor to the Catholic cathedral in Tianjin in the 1980s recounts an incident that illustrates the kinds of distinctions that Catholics made. He attended an early morning mass celebrated by a priest who had never accepted the Chinese Catholic Patriotic Association and had suffered for his resistance, but was now being allowed by the government to resume his priestly functions. The mass was crowded. After the first priest finished, another priest came out to begin a second mass. All at once, with almost military precision, the whole congregation stood up, turned their backs to the altar, and with a loud stamping sound walked out of the church. The second priest, the visitor later learned, was called "Father Unbeliever" by the Tianjin Catholics and was widely despised because of his collaboration with the government.

Although the CPA was officially supposed to oversee the Tianjin Cathedral, it was obviously not able to exercise tight control over the religious practice—and even political practice—of its congregants. The reach of the CPA was even further limited by the growth of a vigorous "underground" church whose members defied government regulations.

Growth in the number of underground believers had been facilitated by secret instructions issued to the underground by the Vatican in 1978.[8] In line with similar instructions given to persecuted Catholics in Eastern Europe, the document aimed to help the underground church to grow in spite of its inability to communicate through regular channels with Rome. Underground bishops were given permission to choose and consecrate other bishops without going through the normal vetting by the Vatican bureaucracy and to ordain priests who had not had the normal Vatican-approved seminary training. The result was that aging underground bishops consecrated many new bishops to be their successors. In fact, they created a surplus of bishops in the expectation that many of these would end up in prison. Some of these bishops had weak qualifications for their role, and a number of priests were ordained with sketchy theological training. As if to make up for weak formal qualifications, some of these new bishops and priests emphasized their zeal for risking martyrdom in defense of the faith.

Many got their martyrdom. In the fall of 1989, the underground church held a national bishops' conference in Shanxi Province. This meeting was raided by the police and its participants arrested. The arrests, however, only increased the willingness of the underground to defy the government. Underground Catholics were further emboldened by the role of the church in the collapse of communism in Eastern Europe. Frightened by those same Eastern European events, the government was even more determined to keep Chinese Catholics under control.

The government lacked control mechanisms, however, that could easily stifle unwanted religious practices. The Maoist era's strict restrictions on mobility had been relaxed to allow for the emergence of a market economy. No longer were people completely dependent on state-controlled institutions for their livelihood. China's borders had become more porous, allowing for more contact with outside sources of support.

Under these circumstances, underground priests could circulate around a region, slipping in and out of villages to administer the sacraments and to offer spiritual counsel. Such priests could be supported by contributions from disposable income made possible in China's market economy. (They could also use money to buy freedom of operation for themselves by bribing local officials.) They received additional funds from overseas—much of it from Hong Kong and Taiwan but some from the United States and Europe. Communication with the Vatican and overseas church authorities was made possible by visitors who passed in and out of China on tourist visas.

Without the help of comprehensive networks for control and surveillance, the only way for the police to control the underground church has been through periodic "strike hard" campaigns to intimidate underground Catholics by harshly punishing some high-profile victims. Given the devotion to martyrdom among the underground, however, these campaigns can be counterproductive.

The anger of the underground church toward repression has not usually led to direct attacks on government officials. Although there undoubtedly are some underground Catholics who would like to see the Chinese Communist Party swept into the dustbin of history, the primary concerns of most Catholics, underground as well as official, have been religious. Their anger has been mainly directed at fellow church members whom they believe have betrayed the faith. Sometimes members of the underground church issue bitter verbal denunciations against bishops, priests, and even laity closely associated with the official church. An especial cause for bitterness would be any suspicion that an official church member might have informed police about underground activities. On some occasions, the anger has led to physical violence. The most grisly case thus far involved the murder of an open-church priest by an underground-church member in 1992 by poisoning the wine in his chalice at mass. On Good Friday in 2001, someone cut off the ear of an open-church priest in Heilongjiang Province—presumably in imitation of Saint Peter's cutting off the ear of the high priest's servant who came to arrest Jesus in the Garden of Gethsemane.[9]

A Blurring of Divisions

Such bitter divisions are most common when there are irresolvable disputes between underground- and open-church bishops over who should be the head of a diocese. Such disputes have actually been diminishing, however, because the Vatican has been quietly giving its "apostolic mandate," or official approval, to bishops in the open church. By 2002, Rome had given more than two-thirds of such bishops its official approval, often conveyed through special delegates traveling on tourist visas.[10] As more bishops receive legitimation from the Vatican, a snowball effect takes place: those who have not been legitimated have difficulty gaining the respect of their congregants and all the more eagerly seek papal approval. Most new bishops now seek an apostolic mandate and insist on having at least one Vatican-approved bishop take part in their consecration ritual. If an open-church bishop is known to have such an apostolic mandate, the main basis for an antagonistic relationship with a local underground bishop disappears.

This complicated ecclesiastical and political situation has begun to collapse the Maoist-era boundaries between an underground church loyal to the pope and a "patriotic" church loyal to the Communist Party-state. In the name of loyalty to the pope, some members of the underground church are acting in ways that the Vatican might not have approved had it been able to supervise them more closely. Some of the new underground bishops and priests may not be adequately trained. Without sufficient guidance, grassroots underground communities sometimes develop religious practices that do not conform to Catholic orthodoxy. Some Vatican officials are concerned about lack of fiscal accountability among underground communities. On the other hand, the open church is not necessarily out of communion with the Vatican.

A black-and-white conflict between open and underground churches is being replaced by shades of gray. Although they remain in wide use among Catholics in China, perhaps the terms *open* and *underground* no longer represent the sociological divisions of the Chinese Catholic community. A better pair of Chinese contrast terms might be *official (guanfang)* and *unofficial (wuguanfang)*. As used in modern Chinese parlance, official refers to the realm of activity that is publicly recognized and controlled by the state. Unofficial refers to a realm of private transactions at least partly independent of state control. In ordinary Chinese speech, unofficial has a connotation of unorthodox or deviant, reflecting a political system that denies the legitimacy of any forms of association not under state supervision. But official and unofficial are not neatly separated. They form a continuum. Most people have to live and work under the supervision of state-controlled organizations, but within those organizations (sometimes in complicity with the organization's leaders) they carry out a great deal of unofficial activity that sometimes contradicts and subverts the stated purposes of the organization.

Within the unofficial realm, relations among various factions of Catholics have been undergoing an evolution toward convergence. In many places, priests who have not been recognized by the officially approved part of the church no longer have to carry out their ministry clandestinely. In some places, these unofficial priests actually live in the same rectories with officially approved priests, and sometimes they even say mass in the same church building. Unofficial Catholic communities have built their own church buildings, without formal permission from the government but with tacit approval from local officials. Catholics will sometimes choose to attend services in an open or unregistered church on the basis of convenience rather than on any ideological principle. A younger generation of Catholics, in particular, seems less committed to the old divisions. Meanwhile, the CPA has been losing much of its influence. Although official bishops have to "give face" (as one Chinese Catholic put it to me) to the CPA, of course, they do not need to pay close attention to its policies. In many places, local branches of the CPA, which are needed to carry out policies of the national association, have disappeared.

Conflict and Cooperation

The evolution, however, is not steady. In the absence of a stable legal framework guaranteeing religious freedom and in the absence of normal diplomatic relations with the Vatican, relations between church and state have gone through cycles of relaxation and repression. The latest round of repression began in 1999. In the first half of that year, the Chinese government engaged in serious negotiations with the Vatican on normalization of relations. In July of that year, however, having been shaken in April by the Falungong demonstration in front of the leadership compound in Beijing, the government launched a massive campaign not only against the Falungong but against other dissident religious groups as well. Concerned that it was losing its grip on unofficial Catholics, the government moved to rebuild local branches of the CPA and tried to make bishops and priests declare their unambiguous loyalty to CPA authority. Public security officials demolished unregistered church buildings in Fujian and Wenzhou.

These moves provoked underground Catholics to appoint more of their own new bishops and to expand their control over the church. By the end of the year, negotiations with the Vatican had broken down. Then, as if to put its seal on the breakdown, on January 6, 2000, the Feast of the Epiphany, the CPA staged a consecration of five new bishops who had not been approved by the Vatican—and were unacceptable to most Chinese Catholics.

The consecration of the patriotic bishops, however, revealed more weakness than strength. The CPA had intended to consecrate twelve bishops (symbolizing the twelve apostles), but it could find only five priests willing to defy the Vatican. In contrast to the norm for such ceremonies in China, which are held in churches packed with joyous people, the Epiphany consecrations were held in a half-empty cathedral and were attended mostly by government officials (though, for the first time ever, they were broadcast on state television). The seminarians at the National Seminary in Beijing refused to board the bus sent to bring them to the ceremony. (Because of this, their rector was dismissed.) Catholic resistance, though passive, was effective, and by 2000 the government began to retreat and allowed the consecration of several new bishops who were known to have apostolic mandates.

However, on October 1, 2000, the Vatican antagonized the Chinese authorities by canonizing as saints 120 Chinese martyrs (mostly from the nineteenth century)—an event that was secretly celebrated by many ordinary Catholics but denounced by the Chinese government. (The denunciations were duly echoed by leaders of the CPA.) The timing of the event, on China's National Day, was especially provocative. Vatican officials said that the date had been chosen because it was the feast day of Saint Theresa of Lisieux, the patroness of missions. If its relations with the Chinese government had been better, however, the Vatican probably could have changed the date once Chinese sensitivities had become apparent.

Since this low point, there have been gradual improvements in Sino-Vatican relations, helped along by a conciliatory speech by Pope John Paul II in October 2001, on the occasion of the four-hundred-year anniversary of the arrival of the great Jesuit missionary Matteo Ricci in Beijing. By the middle of 2002, there were rumors of tentative new moves on both sides toward rapprochement, but so far these have produced no visible results.

A basis for rapprochement is that both sides have developed common interests in the post–cold war era. From the Vatican's perspective, the greatest threat to the church is no longer militant communism but endemic social disorder—the same disorder that threatens the Chinese government. In spite of some continued repression, Chinese Catholics have been gaining a good deal of practical freedom to practice their religion, but it has been gained through lawlessness rather than the rule of law.

The church has freedom because the central government can no longer control much of anything that goes on at the grass roots. However, the secular corruption that comes with this anarchy also affects the church. When, for example, local church leaders get into the business of bribing local officials to maintain their freedom, they become vulnerable to extortion and, even worse, to dishonesty with church finances. Moreover, the practices of evading central political control also can be used to evade central ecclesiastical control. Because Catholics generally distrust the central leadership of the CPA, they carry on by following their own local rules. From the Vatican's point of view, however, this can lead to an erosion of orthodoxy and a breakdown in ecclesiastical discipline. The Vatican would like to regularize hierarchical authority within the Chinese church. If it could normalize diplomatic relations with China and post an internuncio in Beijing, it might be able to accomplish some of this goal.

Allowing the Vatican to establish centralized control over local congregations could help the Chinese government assert some control over its grass roots, if the government could sufficiently keep the central ecclesiastical authorities in subordination. The Vatican has been willing to make some important concessions in this regard. It has been willing to adopt the

"Vietnam model" in which the Vatican appoints bishops from a list approved by the government. However, the Vatican insists on having the final say in the selection of bishops, and so far the Chinese government refuses to accept this. As has been the case since the founding of the People's Republic of China, the state calculates that it cannot tolerate the risk of a unified, well-organized Catholic Church led by ecclesiastical authorities whose complete cooperation cannot be absolutely guaranteed.

Challenges to Stability

Although the Chinese Catholic Church is restless and somewhat turbulent, it is not, in its present form at least, a serious threat to the stability of the Chinese government. Its believers are concerned more with religious than with political matters. Catholics still constitute no more than 1 percent of the population, and they are mostly poor. In those areas where they are concentrated in countywide enclaves, they might form a unified force against outside control. But under present circumstances, they are not well enough organized to conduct widespread coordinated action. China's Catholics are less a potential cause of instability than a reflection of the general disorganization of China as a whole.

As this general disorganization invites outside economic entrepreneurs who hope to profit from an unregulated environment, so it also beckons religious entrepreneurs. A number of religious orders, mission societies, and advocacy associations have made the Chinese Catholic Church part of their cause. In their variety, they reflect basic divisions in the universal Catholic Church, and they sometimes bring these divisions to China.

In the United States, for example, a major proponent of the underground church is the Cardinal Kung Foundation, run by the nephew of Gong Pinmei, who came to the United States in 1988 after he was released for "humanitarian" reasons, having spent thirty years in prison and three years under house arrest. (The pope had secretly elevated him to cardinal in 1979.) Well funded and adept at public outreach, the Cardinal Kung Foundation is connected with prominent right-wing religious groups in the United States. The foundation channels money to the underground church, gathers important information on Catholics imprisoned for their faith in China, and provides arguments for those who advocate confronting China for human rights violations. It also denounces the alleged accommodationist stance of the less well funded U.S. Catholic China

Bureau (in the interests of full disclosure: I am a member of this group's board of directors), which tries to help the Chinese church by maintaining contacts through the open church.

In the stridency of the rhetorical "culture wars" within the American Catholic Church, the difference in approach between these two groups can sometimes become magnified into a polarized opposition between an imagined underground and official Chinese church that does not really correspond to the blurred boundaries that exist in China. Meanwhile, the various religious orders—Jesuits, Dominicans, Benedictines, Franciscans, Vincentians, and so forth—are each developing their own "China programs." The disorganization of the church in China makes it vulnerable to being pulled in different directions by the efforts of these outside groups. Moreover, the ambiguities and lack of transparency accompanying such disorganization make it easy for groups within the American church to imaginatively project their own divisions onto China.

A healthier relationship between the worldwide church and China would probably depend on a healthier relationship between the Chinese church and the Chinese state. If China had a stable rule of law that bestowed clear rights and responsibilities on religious groups, and if the government normalized diplomatic relations with the Vatican, the Chinese church could organize itself in a more open and consistent manner. Tensions between church and state would remain, but they could be confronted in a more systematic, principled way than they are now. The worldwide church could provide needed assistance to China without getting caught up in the intrigues that the current disorganized situation encourages. Finally, the view of the worldwide church—and especially the American church—toward China would be clearer, more sensitive to ambiguities, and less prone to hyperbole.

Notes

The first two sections of this chapter are a synthesis of material in my earlier *China's Catholics: Tragedy and Hope in an Emerging Civil Society* (University of California Press, 1998). The last three sections are drawn from my "Saints and the State: Religious Evolution and Problems of Governance in China," *Asian Perspective,* 2001.

1. Eric O. Hanson, *Catholic Politics in China and Korea* (Maryknoll, N.Y.: Orbis, 1980), pp. 87–89.

2. Kim-kwong Chan, *Struggling for Survival: The Catholic Church in China* (Hong Kong: Christian Study Centre on Religion and Culture, 1992), pp. 22–23.

3. Ibid., pp. 43–44.
4. Ibid., p. 52.
5. Ibid., p. 55.
6. Ibid., p. 56.
7. The Chinese government claims that there are only about 4 million Catholics in China, a figure that would not include underground Catholics. In the early 1990s informed outside observers estimated the total Catholic population at about 10 million. See Anthony Lam, "How Many Catholics Are There in China?" *Tripod*, vol. 71 (September–October 1992), pp. 51–57. Recently, many journalists have been using the figure of 12 million.

8. Holy See, Propaganda Fide, "Faculties and Privileges Granted to Clergy and Laymen Who Reside in China under Difficult Circumstances," Latin text provided in Kim-kwong Chan, *Towards a Contextual Ecclesiology: The Catholic Church in the People's Republic of China (1979–1983)—Its Life and Theological Implications* (Hong Kong: Photech Systems, 1987), pp. 438–42.

9. The murder case is discussed in Madsen, *China's Catholics*, p. 156. The case of the severed ear was reported in *UCA News*, April 23, 2001, and May 30, 2001.

10. The figure of two-thirds was reported by Jeroom Heyndrickx, "Epiphany 2000: The Beijing-Rome Confrontation," *Tablet*, January 13, 2000.

7

YIHUA XU

"Patriotic" Protestants: The Making of an Official Church

More than half a century has passed since the Protestant Three-Self Patriotic Movement (TSPM) was established and quickly rose to monopolize institutionalized Protestantism in China. The TSPM's origin remains poorly understood, however, both at home and abroad. On the mainland, it has long been regarded as a sensitive subject for research, and a typical book about the history of the Chinese Christian church either stops at 1949, the year of the communist takeover, or contains only a tiny section on the whole history after 1949. Overseas observers, on the other hand, usually emphasize external factors in analyzing the TSPM and regard it as a movement planned and controlled by the new communist regime and forced upon the Chinese Protestant church by regime activists.

These external factors are indeed crucial, but they are still inadequate as an explanation of the origins of the TSPM. The movement drew on a legacy of efforts begun in the 1920s to promote the "three-self" principles—self-governance, self-support, and self-propagation—among China's Protestants.[1] The TSPM's early activists initially emerged from Protestant institutions with strong ties to the West, most notably the Chinese YMCA (Young Men's Christian Association), the Episcopal Church in China, St. Johns University in Shanghai, and even Union Theological Seminary in New York City. After the communist takeover, however, the original ideals of the three-self movement were harnessed to serve the state, resulting in a dramatic reduction in the number of Protestant institutions and a rollback of the church's role in society.

Early Three-Self Efforts

From Protestantism's initial entry into China in 1807 to the TSPM's establishment in 1950, numerous efforts were made by Western missionaries and Chinese Christians alike to make churches in China more independent or indigenous. Although varied, these efforts all intended to make Christianity more acceptable to the Chinese people and more adaptable to Chinese society. The parties responsible for the reforms can be roughly divided into three groups: autonomous independent churches, indigenous broad-based movements, and mainstream denominations.

Independent Churches

The first efforts emerged in the form of independent or separatist churches and movements. Most of these officially separated from the denominational churches and institutions established and supported by Western missionary societies, or what has been called the "Sino-foreign Protestant establishment."[2] They became financially independent and were managed by Chinese Christians themselves. As early as the late nineteenth century, attempts to build independent churches appeared in places like Guangzhou (Canton), Shanghai, and Shandong. Larger independent churches emerged after the turn of the twentieth century, inspired by the various nationalist and revolutionary movements in the country during these years. In 1920 the National Conference of Chinese Independent Churches was organized, with 120 delegates representing 189 churches. Of these independent churches the most well known was Pastor Yu Guozhen's Chinese Independent Church (*Zhongguo Yesujiao zhilihui*), established in 1906, which at its peak reached more than 150 churches and thirty thousand members nationwide.

Although these churches broke free from established denominations, they retained much of their denominational identities and practices.[3] Their relationship with Western mission societies was complicated, varying from confrontational to friendly. Most of them were loosely organized and short lived, producing few church institutions, such as publishing houses, schools, hospitals, and theological seminaries. They drew their members mainly from middle-class urban dwellers. After 1927, with the establishment and consolidation of the Nationalist Party government and the increasing indigenization of mainstream denominations in China, these independent churches became even more marginalized, and most of them either dissolved or returned to the old denominational churches. By 1935, the number of independent churches had dwindled from more than six hundred in the mid-1920s to about two hundred. Even at their peak, they were not large enough to have a strong impact on the Protestant church in China, and they aimed more at institutional independence than at theological reflection and contextualization.

As the first Chinese-led independence movement, however, the independent churches became a visible and inspiring part of early efforts to promote three-self principles among China's Protestants. They were also the forerunners of the conservative evangelical Protestants, who resisted the TSPM's hegemony after 1949.

Indigenous Movements

Indigenous movements without a mission background also emerged during Protestantism's high tide in the early twentieth century, with more enduring results. Founded by charismatic and often authoritarian Chinese Christian personalities, these churches or sectarian movements represented a more radical break with the Western tradition, integrating more deeply with Chinese customs and religiosity. They emphasized autonomy and independence in their institutions and often established ecclesiastical traditions of their own. Their attitudes toward foreign missions also varied from contentious to amicable, but most had little contact with mission societies. Their theology was an amalgam of Western imports—most notably the charismatic Pentecostal and Holiness traditions—and elements of Chinese folk religion. They emphasized personal evangelism but had little interest in social involvement and welfare or politics. Most were based in rural areas, and some, like the Jesus Family (*Yesu jiating*) in Shandong, were characterized by an isolated communal style of living.

Most of these indigenous movements emerged in the first three decades of the twentieth century and rapidly became a formidable force in the Protestant church in China. The True Jesus Church, for instance, had as many as 120,000 followers and seven hundred churches throughout the country by 1949. Despite their popular appeal and homegrown credentials, however, these indigenous groups came under attack by the TSPM in the early 1950s and were forced to merge with the TSPM. Several groups, such as the True Jesus Church and the Little Flock (or Local Assemblies), managed to relocate their headquarters overseas. Despite repression, these groups retained their popular appeal, and they have become once again among the fastest-growing churches in China and in Chinese-speaking communities all over the world.

Mainstream Denominations

Finally, many mainstream denominations and mission societies advocated indigenization. With the notable exceptions of the Baptist churches and the China Inland Mission, these churches cooperated with the National Christian Council of China, the only national coordinating and liaison agency of the Protestant church in China before 1950. These institutions promoted an indigenization movement aimed at de-Westernizing Christian doctrines and encouraging the integration of Christianity and Chinese culture. They opposed the unequal treaties imposed upon China by Western powers, but most of them still worked with foreign missionaries and did not regard them as imperialists or the agents of imperialist countries. Indigenization efforts within the Sino-foreign Protestant establishment picked up in the first two decades of the twentieth century, producing a number of large union and ecumenical churches. For example, the Church of Christ in China combined Presbyterian, Congregational, Methodist, and Baptist elements and became the largest denomination in China, with a membership of more than 120,000 (about one-third of all Protestants in 1927, when it was formally established). The names of these union and ecumenical churches all included the word *Chinese* (*Zhonghua*) or *China* (*Zhongguo*).

Chinese Christians also assumed leadership positions, even if Western missionaries retained considerable power. Finances were an enduring source of dependence on Western missions. In spite of considerable efforts to encourage greater Chinese contributions, the numerous church institutions, such as schools and hospitals, consumed a large proportion of church funds and personnel, making the devolution of power from Western missionaries to Chinese Christians more difficult. Theologically, some of these churches, especially the various Baptist churches and the China Inland Mission, were more conservative than others, like the Episcopal Church. In addition, all were divided internally, primarily between liberal clergy in urban areas and conservative congregations in rural areas.

Despite their limitations and internal disputes, these denominational churches played a constructive role in introducing and interpreting Western religious and theological thought and in creating indigenous forms of religious expression in the areas of Christian literature, art, rituals, and hymns. They enhanced the social image and acceptability of Christianity in China and produced capable Chinese Protestant leaders, who later became active in the worldwide ecumenical movement. It was from the mainstream churches and institutions in the National Christian Council that the TSPM recruited most of its early activists.

The TSPM and Protestant Institutions

To a large extent, the TSPM grew out of the Protestant churches in China, though ironically, its roots are primarily in the mainstream denominational churches and institutions with mission ties rather than the independent church movement—as TSPM leaders often claim. A full understanding of the TSPM could be achieved by an examination of the relationship between the TSPM and three of these older institutions: the Chinese YMCA, the Chinese Episcopal Church (the Holy Anglican Church), and Union Theological Seminary in New York City.

Shanghai and the YMCA

Since its arrival in China in 1885, the YMCA has been an urban phenomenon, developing alongside the growing mission presence, especially in the area of education. Most of its core members were well-educated urban professionals, entrepreneurs, returned students, and mission school graduates. The Shanghai YMCA, one of China's first, was founded in 1905 by a few alumni of St. John's University, established by the American Church Mission (the Episcopal Church in the United States) in Shanghai. The Shanghai YMCA was able to construct its own building only seven years after its founding, with donations from U.S. churches. William H. Taft, secretary of war at the time and the future president of the United States, attended the dedication ceremony of the new building.

When the Sino-Japanese War broke out in 1937, many Western missionaries either returned home or retreated to the interior with the Chinese. The Japanese army detained around twelve hundred missionaries immediately after the bombing of Pearl Harbor, bringing the activities of Western missions in coastal areas to a halt. Because of its high degree of localization, the Chinese YMCA was able to remain in operation, filling part of the vacuum left by the withdrawal of Western missionaries. China's newly formed Communist Party even used the legal status of church-related institutions like the YMCA and student Christian fellowships to carry out its underground activities.

One of the YMCA's most important programs during this period was educational training, particularly of its own secretaries. The Shanghai YMCA's training program began with a class of four students in 1943 and by 1949 had trained a total of sixty-nine students. Many of its graduates later became top leaders of the TSPM and its sister organization after 1979, the China Christian Council.

It was not a coincidence that the YMCA became the cradle of TSPM leaders. The YMCA was one of the first Christian institutions in China to be staffed chiefly by Chinese, and it achieved a great deal of independence long before the mainstream denominations. Most of its secretaries were theologically liberal and less sectarian or denomination oriented. The many who were college graduates had much wider social contacts than local pastors. Not surprisingly, the YMCA was one of the most radical Christian organizations during various nationalist movements. All of these factors made it much easier for its young and energetic "social reformers" to adapt to the new regime and to play a crucial role in the formation of the TSPM.

Episcopal Roots and St. John's University

A large majority of the Shanghai YMCA trainees came from the Baptist Church, the Church of Christ, the Methodist Church, and, most notably, the Episcopal Church. The Episcopal Church in China was a typical institution of the Sino-foreign Protestant establishment. Introduced by American Episcopalian missionaries in 1845, it had thirteen dioceses in China by 1949. Most had been established by mission societies based in Britain, the United States, and Canada. Although it attracted fewer converts than other missions, the Episcopal Church was one of the most influential denominational churches in China, producing a number of leading Chinese theologians, such as Zhao Zichen (T. C. Chao), Wu Leichuan, and Wei Zhuomin (Francis Wei). A number of them became high-level officials within the TSPM, though the church itself did not offer strong support for the movement. For example, all three of the TSPM's leading figures in the post-Mao period—Bishop Ding Guangxun, Dr. Han Wenzao, and Bishop Shen Yifan—were affiliated with the Episcopal Church.

A key link between the Episcopal Church and the TSPM is St. John's University. When the Sino-Japanese War broke out, St. John's had not yet registered with the Chinese government, and as a result it became the only major institution of higher learning that continued to operate in occupied Shanghai after the other colleges and universities, both public and private, had moved to the interior. One of the chief organizers of the Shanghai YMCA training program was Ding Guangxun, a St. John's graduate, who naturally focused his recruiting efforts at his alma mater.

There were other links as well. The Episcopal Church's emphasis on education produced better-educated ministers than other denominations. It was the only mission society in China with two Christian institutions of higher learning that used English as the medium of instruction—St. John's University in Shanghai and Boone University in Wuchang. Like the YMCA secretaries, Episcopalian ministers and church workers trained at St. John's or Boone had extensive social contacts and relatively liberal views of theology, and their foreign-language skills made them more visible to the outside world.

Moreover, the Episcopal Church, like most of the major denominational churches, concentrated its efforts on major cities, where many Episcopalian ministers became involved in a variety of nationalist and revolutionary movements. The Daily Knowledge Society, one of the best-known anti-Qing revolutionary societies before the 1911 revolution, was founded by a group of Episcopalian ministers in Wuchang who had trained at St. John's and Boone. The church also had important friends in both the ruling Nationalist Party and the Chinese Communist Party. The Right Reverend Logan H. Roots, the bishop of the Episcopal Church's Hankou Diocese, was a personal friend of Zhou Enlai, who became China's premier after the communist takeover. A few St. John's–trained Episcopalian ministers even left the Christian ministry to join the Communist Party. The Reverend Pu Huaren (Paul Pu) had served as an English interpreter for the Central Committee of the Chinese Communist Party and as the director of the New China News Agency before the communists took power. The Reverend Dong Jianwu (H. C. Tung), Pu's classmate at St. John's, became a top secret agent for the party while still serving as rector of St. Peter's Church in Shanghai.[4]

Union Theological Seminary

Quite a few of these YMCA secretaries and Episcopalian church workers had been to the United States for advanced studies, most notably at Union Theological Seminary in New York City. Before 1949, almost all the major theological seminaries in China were founded and supported by Western missionary societies, and theological education was regarded as the "last castle" of Western control.⁵ Because some churches and church organizations, notably the Episcopal Church and the YMCA, had a policy of sending their workers to study abroad for a period of time, many Chinese Christian leaders received theological education outside China. Altogether, thirty-nine scholars from China studied at Union Theological Seminary for a year or more before the TSPM was founded, and some of them became influential Christian leaders after returning to their homeland. These Union-trained leaders included Cheng Jingyi (the first secretary general of the National Christian Council of China), Liu Tingfang (the first Chinese dean of the Yenching University School of Religion), Wu Yaozong (the founder of the TSPM), and Ding Guangxun (the leading Protestant figure in China since 1980). Many Chinese who studied at Union also had a YMCA background, owing in part to Union's theologically liberal reputation and in part to its high admission standards, for which the well-educated YMCA secretaries were more qualified candidates.⁶

Union Theological Seminary therefore strengthened the liberal wing of Chinese Protestantism, which was primarily responsible for founding the TSPM after the communist takeover. Several distinguished Union professors, such as Harry Emerson Fosdick, Harry F. Ward, Henry Pitney Van Dusen, and Harrison S. Elliot, either visited China or worked in China as missionaries. Their Chinese students translated their writings into Chinese and used them in China's seminary education. Union's influence was particularly visible in Beijing's Yenching University School of Religion, the most prestigious and liberal theological school in the country. Indeed, with at least fifteen Union alumni among its faculty members and former students, Yenching essentially modeled itself after the American seminary. It was liberal theological strongholds such as Yenching that became the TSPM's primary source of personnel and ideology.

It must be pointed out that the theological liberals of Chinese Protestantism, including the three groups mentioned above, did not blindly follow the Western theological trends. The Christian messages from the West were interpreted by them through the double lenses of their national experience and their cultural heritage. Along with theological conservatives, they stressed national salvation and social reconstruction, two major themes of Chinese theology in the first half of the twentieth century. But they differed from their conservative counterparts in their emphasis on applying rationalism and science to theological issues and taking a reformist or even radical approach to social issues. In these contexts, Western liberalism did provide them with a strong foundation. By making their theology more relevant and adaptable to the revolutionary social environment of the time, they also brought themselves closer to the communist ideology and were thereby more acceptable to the new regime.

Institutionalization of the TSPM

On July 28, 1950, ten months after founding the PRC, forty Protestant Christian leaders in China jointly signed a document entitled "Direction of Endeavor for Chinese Christianity in the Construction of New China" (which became widely known as the Christian Manifesto). Following the party's directives, TSPM leaders called on Christians all over the country to support the common political platform of the new government and demanded that the church purge itself of imperialist influences. Churches and organizations relying on foreign personnel and financial aid were singled out, in particular, and were required to sever overseas ties as soon as possible and work toward self-reliance. On September 23, 1950, the *People's Daily*—the official newspaper of the Chinese Communist Party—published the manifesto on its front page, together with a list of 1,525 signatories. (According to TSPM leaders, some 400,000 Protestants ultimately signed the manifesto.) The TSPM was thus born.

One of the TSPM's chief goals was to "unify" the Protestant churches in China under the party's leadership. Because the TSPM's core activists lacked strong church connections and did not occupy high positions in either denominational churches or the National Christian Council, their strategy initially focused on assuming control of these institutions. For example, with the government's strong backing, Wu Yaozong was elected the vice chairman of the National Christian Council and the moderator of the Church of Christ in China, although he had been merely the secretary of the Shanghai YMCA before the communist takeover.

Neither the party nor TSPM leaders were satisfied, however, with taking over existing institutions. Only a thorough institutional transformation would suffice. On April 21, 1951, TSPM activists formed the Preparatory Committee of the Chinese Protestant Resist America and Aid Korea Three-Self Reform Movement Committee (the TSPM's prototype organization) to edge out and replace existing Protestant institutions. In an important conference of the Protestant churches held in Beijing from July 22 to August 5, 1954, the National Committee of the Three-Self Patriotic

Movement was formally established, with Wu Yaozong as its first chairman. The newly established TSPM appointed some leaders of mainstream denominations and the National Christian Council to senior positions, but the real power and key posts were held by the young activists from the YMCA and St. John's University. Indeed, each of the seven full-time officials of the National Committee of the TSPM in the early years was a former YMCA secretary.

Once established, the TSPM systematically dismantled most Protestant institutions. Their demise was accelerated by the Chinese Communist Party's decision to cut off overseas funding for all church organizations. Most schools, hospitals, and welfare institutions had low levels of domestic support. It was reported that some were not able to pay their own postage after the U.S. government seized Chinese properties in the United States in December 1950. Cut off from overseas funding, they were obliged to obtain support from the new regime. The communist regime was not inclined to support most of these institutions, however, and either disbanded or assumed control over them. Other institutions, such as theological seminaries and publishing houses, were turned over to the TSPM, only to be thoroughly reconstructed and, in most cases, eliminated.

For example, forty-three Protestant seminaries and Bible schools operated on the mainland in 1950. When the funds from abroad were cut off, some of these institutions were forced to close. Others, such as the Yenching University School of Religion, struggled to continue by cutting costs and asking support from local congregations. Zhao Zichen, the dean of this school—the most liberal in the country—even tried to raise funds from China's ultraconservative indigenous Protestant movements, such as the Jesus Family. In 1952 the TSPM merged twelve theological seminaries and Bible schools into the Nanjing Union Theological Seminary. A similar merger in 1953 folded eleven theological seminaries and Bible schools into the Yenching Union Theological Seminary in Beijing. These consolidations left only four independent theological and Bible schools in the country; and by 1961, all but the seminary in Nanjing had ceased to operate. Even the Nanjing Seminary stopped offering regular courses after 1958, and after 1966 it ceased operations entirely. No theological training was offered again until 1982, when the Nanjing Union Theological Seminary reopened after the Cultural Revolution.

China's Protestant publishing enterprises faced a similar fate. On the eve of the communist victory, the number of Protestant publishing houses had already dropped from several dozen before the Sino-Japanese War to only ten, eight of which were based in Shanghai. Most closed after foreign funding stopped. In March 1950 a conference in Beijing, convened by the new government to address the issue of Christian publications, produced a resolution regarding the merger and government censorship of Christian publications. In 1953 four Christian publishing houses formed a united editorial committee, which later established the United Christian Publishing House in China. The other remaining Christian presses could maintain only a nominal existence, and by 1958, all of them, including the newly formed institution, had ceased to function.

Of the fifty-four active Protestant periodicals on the eve of the communist takeover, only one, *Tianfeng* (Heavenly wind), was still publishing after the early 1950s.[7] Founded in 1945 by Wu Yaozong to address social and political issues, *Tianfeng* became, after 1951, the mouthpiece of the TSPM. As the only Christian periodical in the country before the Cultural Revolution, all editorials and important articles in *Tianfeng* were written by core TSPM activists or government officials in charge of religious affairs, though sometimes anonymously or in the name of the journal's "reference room." By the late 1950s, even *Tianfeng* had reduced its publication rate from weekly to monthly, then to bimonthly, because, as one of its editors put it, there was almost nothing to report. Publication of *Tianfeng* ceased in 1965 and did not resume until 1980.

All the church closings and institutional mergers also produced a large "surplus" of ministers, quite a few of whom were senior-level and Western-educated church leaders. One of the TSPM's strategies for making use of them was to establish a Historical Data Unit (*Shiliaozu*) in 1959 for the purpose of exposing Western nations' purported "crimes of imperialism." The unit was composed of twenty-three leaders of various churches, seven of whom held doctoral degrees from British and American universities. The group was charged with collecting and editing historical material regarding the way Western imperialistic powers made use of Christianity against China. One of their chief tasks was to write about their personal relations with Western missionaries and mission societies. The enterprise resulted in the production of a number of booklets and manuscripts, but even this TSPM effort to rewrite the history of Christianity in China was discontinued with the coming of the Cultural Revolution.

All these institutional reshuffles were carried out by the TSPM leaders themselves with strong backing from the government, especially the Religious Affairs Bureau and the United Front Work Department of the Chinese Communist Party's Central Committee, the two official agencies responsible for religious affairs. As a reward, some TSPM leaders were chosen by the government to serve in the National People's Congress and the Chinese People's Political Consultative Conference, a practice that continues to this day.

In the late 1950s, when the whole country was thrown into fanatical campaigns of building a socialist China, this bureaucratic form of indirect control in religious affairs was replaced by much harsher direct controls, and the TSPM's work came to a standstill.[8] It was not until the end of the Cultural Revolution that the importance of religious institutions for the united front work of the party was reemphasized and the TSPM, as a consequence, was rehabilitated, along with the resurrected pre-1949 National China Christian Council, to serve as the established church in China.

Conclusion

Within a few years of its establishment in the 1950s, the Three-Self Patriotic Movement came to monopolize institutionalized Protestantism in China. It did so by attacking all competing Protestant groups and institutions through government-backed political campaigns. Remaining in the wake of all these maneuvers was one church (the TSPM), one theological seminary (the Nanjing Union Theological Seminary), one Christian press (the United Christian Publishing House in China), one Christian periodical (*Tianfeng*), and one history project (the Historical Data Unit). It could be argued that these developments were the only choices for the TSPM, given the prevailing political environment. It is much less convincing and justifiable, however, to describe all these political developments as the TSPM's major contribution to the development of the Protestant church in China.

Perhaps the greatest irony of this period is that the groups and initiatives attacked most viciously by TSPM activists were those that had made the most significant contributions to Chinese Protestantism's realization of the "three-self" principles. Of the Protestant groups that came under attack by the TSPM, the indigenous Protestant movements were treated most severely. The reason is that these groups were truly indigenous and independent and therefore posed the greatest threat to the TSPM's aim of assuming control over all Protestant churches. The political environment during the early 1950s simply did not allow the existence of a church or a church movement independent of the TSPM.

Leading the TSPM in its attacks against other church groups were, for the most part, former YMCA secretaries and St. John's University graduates. Herein lies another great irony. Although the TSPM's leaders found justification for their attacks primarily in the rhetoric of antiforeign nationalism,[9] they themselves, more than any other elements within China's Protestant establishment, were products of Western institutions, particularly in education. Their eagerness to collaborate with China's Communist Party was in large measure a product of the liberal theological training and experience in social activism they received in the YMCA, the Union Theological Seminary, and the Episcopal Church.

Yet the TSPM has paid a price—and continues to pay—for the measures it took to consolidate and reorganize all Protestant churches and institutions in China. By overseeing the systematic dismemberment of the nation's theological schools and the discontinuation of regular theological education, the TSPM robbed itself of the ability to train its own clergy. Although its initiatives were all launched with full government support, the TSPM itself came under attack during various political campaigns. Its own dissolution during the Cultural Revolution created a fertile field for the less supervised local congregations and home gatherings that have proliferated in recent decades.

Moreover, most TSPM leaders had neither strong links with the church body nor pastoral experience. Today they remain separated from the grass roots theologically and socially, as their liberal and urban bent contrasts sharply with the attitudes and beliefs of the largely conservative and rural churchgoers. The tensions between the two were further widened by the TSPM's continuing suppression of opposing views and groups. The TSPM has proved unable to assert its will uniformly upon the Protestant population—its effective urban development being offset by a far weaker presence in rural areas and the interior. As a result, most of the dynamic Christian and sectarian movements in China today are born in the countryside.

Recently, TSPM leaders have attempted to reinvent the movement, describing it as a kind of descendant of China's earlier independent churches. In identifying with these independent churches, the TSPM seeks to play down its political essence by claiming some sort of historical continuity or legitimacy with the earlier, less compromised churches. Indeed, some TSPM leaders have even gone so far as to claim that the TSPM in its current form embodies the three-self principles of all the churches in the whole history of Christianity.

Their efforts have largely failed. When China's Protestants reemerged after the demise of the Cultural Revolution, it was conservative grassroots forces that reaped the harvest. Indeed, the house-church movement laid such a firm foundation for growth during this period that it is quite safe to say that the majority of Protestants in China today are either evangelicals or fundamentalists. The continued devolution of TSPM authority and the declining appeal of theological liberalism among China's Protestants will continue to be the trends in mainland China for the foreseeable future.

Notes

1. This latter argument was initially proposed in Alan Hunter and Kim-kwong Chan, *Protestantism in Contemporary China* (Cambridge University Press, 1993), pp. 105–40.

2. Daniel H. Bays, "The Growth of Independent Christianity," in Daniel H. Bays, ed., *Christianity in China: From the Eighteenth Century to the Present* (Stanford University Press, 1996), p. 308.

3. Zhou Zichen (T. C. Chao or Chao Tzu-ch'en), "Fengchao zhong fenqi di Zhongguo jiaohui" [The Chinese church arising from the storm], *Zhengli yu shengming* [Truth and life], vol. 2 (February 1, 1927), p. 28.

4. Before the end of active denominationalism in China in 1958, the Episcopal Church of China (*Zhonghua Shengong*) consecrated a few more bishops, among them the Reverends Zheng Jianye and Ding Guangxun. In 1988 the Three-Self Patriotic Movement consecrated another two bishops with a view to continuing the Episcopal tradition in China. With the passing away of the two newly consecrated bishops, however, Shen Yifan and Sun Yanli, Bishop Ding Guangxun now is the only Episcopalian bishop on the mainland of China. It does seem that the continuation of the Episcopal tradition in mainland China is questionable.

5. S. R. Anderson and C. Stanley Smith, *The Anderson-Smith Report on Theological Education in Southeast China, Especially As It Relates to the Training of Chinese for the Christian Ministry: The Report of a Survey Commission, 1951–1952* (New York: Board of Founders, Nanking Union Theological Seminary, 1952), p. 93.

6. Union's image as a liberal institution was further enhanced by Song Shangjie's widely publicized experience at Union. Song Shangjie (John Sung), one of the best-known evangelical preachers in China in the twentieth century, earned his doctoral degree in chemistry at Ohio State University before entering Union for his theological studies. While studying at Union from 1926 to 1927, the clash between his conservative beliefs and the liberal theology of his teachers and local pastors brought on a religious and psychological crisis that led him to a period in a sanatorium.

7. The Nanjing Union Theological Seminary started a new journal, *Jinling xiehe shenxuezh*i [Nanjing theological review], in September 1953, but it published only seven issues before the seminary was closed by the Red Guards in 1966.

8. Shen Derong, *Zai Sanzi gongzuo wushi nian* [My fifty years in the TSPM] (Shanghai: National Committee of the TSPM and the China Christian Council), p. 70.

9. For example, see Wu Yaozong's criticism of the church in China being a "duplicate" of American Protestantism in "Jidujiao de shidai beiju" [The present-day tragedy of Christianity], *Tianfeng* [Heavenly wind], no. 116 (April 10, 1948), pp. 1–5, 3.

8

JASON KINDOPP

Fragmented yet Defiant: Protestant Resilience under Chinese Communist Party Rule

The Protestant response to China's newly established communist regime in 1949–50 was fragmented, reflecting the state of the church on the eve of the revolution. As Yihua Xu details in chapter 7 of this volume, a group of theologically liberal Protestants supported the Chinese Communist Party's rise to power and assisted the party-state in creating the Three-Self Patriotic Movement (TSPM). On the other end of the spectrum, outspoken theological conservatives and leaders of indigenous Protestant movements opposed cooperation with the communist regime or its representative organs. On the eve of the communist revolution, for example, Watchman Nee, the founder of the Little Flock, had prayed infamously for the CCP's troops to drown while crossing the Yangtze River, while conservative Protestant leaders such as Wang Mingdao vowed to "not unite in any way" with the TSPM, for which he spent more than twenty years in prison.[1] The majority of China's Protestants remained between these extremes, cautiously hopeful that the CCP would live up to its "united front" rhetoric yet quietly fearful of the policy implications of its resolutely atheistic ideology.

The Communist Party's united front policy created the basis for working with diverse segments of society that were willing to advance its revolutionary agenda. The terms of the CCP's united front with China's Protestants were spelled out in the so-called Christian Manifesto—a document created during a series of talks between a small group of Protestants led by Wu Yaozong and Prime Minister Zhou Enlai.[2] The manifesto set a highly political agenda for the church; its central objectives were to "make people in the churches everywhere recognize clearly the evils that have been wrought in China by imperialism" and to "purge imperialistic influences from within Christianity itself."[3] Party authorities and their Protestant supporters moved quickly to fulfill these pledges. Restrictions on mission activity began almost immediately and tightened dramatically after China's entry into the Korean War in December 1950. By mid-1951, the party-state had nationalized all Protestant institutions engaged in education and welfare services and had decreed that all other foreign mission assets be turned over to the newly formed TSPM.[4] Cut off from their financial lifeline and finding themselves a liability to their Chinese colleagues in the increasingly politicized environment, Western missionaries began a mass exodus from the country. By the end of 1951, almost all foreign missionaries were gone.[5]

Achieving the manifesto's second objective required the establishment of a new mass organization capable of fomenting the party's political campaigns among China's entire Protestant population. The product—the TSPM—was a monolithic, nationally integrated Leninist mass organization. Formally subordinate to the CCP's ruling institutions ("loyalty" to the party was enshrined in its constitution), the TSPM's affairs were determined by a forty-two-member Standing Committee, led by a chairman and several vice chairpersons.[6] Most were liberal Protestant intellectuals with ties to the YMCA or CCP infiltrators appointed to preserve the party's control over the organization.[7] Consequently, the TSPM's initial agenda mirrored the Chinese Communist Party's own policy platform. At the inaugural conference in April 1951, for example, TSPM chairman Wu Yaozong instructed delegates that the church's "central duty" was to support the Resist America and Aid Korea campaign. Other leading priorities were to implement the party's land reform, to conduct political study within the church, and to hold denunciation meetings against the "scoundrels acting as special agents" for the United States and the Nationalist Party within the church.[8]

Coercive Assimilation and Protestant Alienation during the Early People's Republic of China

The party's demands for total control over all social organizations resulted in a coercive assimilation of all Protestant institutions by the TSPM, accomplished through repeated denunciation campaigns. The government issued edicts requiring all Protestant congregations to join the TSPM, but the establishment of local TSPM chapters was contingent on holding "successful" denunciation meetings against "reactionaries" and "counterrevolutionaries" within the church. The result was a massive purging of respected Protestant leaders throughout the country. A 1951 campaign against counterrevolutionaries targeted church leaders who had worked with foreign missionaries.[9] The "three-antis" and "five-antis" campaigns launched later that year catalyzed an attack against autonomous churches and indigenous groups.[10] Dozens of leaders in the Jesus Family, the Little Flock, and the True Jesus Church were arrested, and TSPM activists were dispatched to their headquarters to reorganize the groups and integrate them into the TSPM hierarchy.[11]

The TSPM's final coup in consolidating control over all Protestant institutions came with the Great Leap Forward in 1958. Party leaders eliminated the pastoral role by declaring anyone who was not contributing to material production a parasite upon society and a traitor to the country. The result was a dramatic decline in church life. In the months following the launch of the Great Leap Forward, the number of active Protestant churches in Beijing fell from sixty-five to four, and in Shanghai from more than two hundred to twenty-three.[12] Leaders of the TSPM assumed control over the consolidation process, praising the church closings as a noble effort to "smash the imperialist plot to 'divide and rule'" and issuing notices requiring that the "buildings and property of every church [be] turned over to the TSPM's Standing Committee to administer."[13] Most rural churches ceased to function altogether, as pastors were put to work on communes and church buildings were confiscated and employed for official use. By the early 1960s, fewer than 10 percent of the church's pre-1949 institutions were still employed for church use, with the rest either confiscated by the state or allocated to other work units.[14]

In addition to obtaining control over Protestant organizations, TSPM elites sought to transform Protestantism's very essence. Subordinating the church's mission to that of the ruling Communist Party, TSPM leaders proclaimed that communism held the promise not only to reform society but also to save the church from itself. Bringing the global revolution to fruition was therefore of supreme importance. As Wu Yaozong put it at the time, "The most pressing problem today for China, and indeed for the whole world, is how to destroy imperialism and set up people's governments."[15] Following this reasoning to its logical conclusion, Wu argued astonishingly that the contributions of revolutionary Marxism so outshone

Christianity in its current state that the church had effectively passed its mantle of salvation to the Communist Party. "Christianity," he writes, "must learn that the present period is one of liberation for people, the collapse of the old system, a time when the old, dead Christianity must doff its shroud and come forth arrayed in new garments. It must learn that it is no longer the sole distributor of the panacea for the pains of the world. On the contrary, God has taken the key to the salvation of mankind from its hand and given it to another."[16]

The TSPM's theological adaptations were not merely rhetorical but were employed to transform Protestant beliefs and identities. Church pastors and congregants alike were forced to participate in "small group" study sessions in which they were pressured to voice support for selected themes.[17] Protestants were instructed to refute the principle that "all Christians are children of God [and therefore] must be one big family," on grounds that "the whole of organized Christianity has a class nature."[18] Notions of Christian pacifism and universal love were rejected as "imperialist opiates," while militant revolution and class warfare were extolled as Christian virtues.[19] Wu Yaozong denounced Protestantism's foundational doctrine of righteousness by faith on grounds that the CCP had created a "miracle in the world's history" through its works alone[20] and went so far as to deny the inevitability of sin in the world by reasoning that "if all men are sinners, then every institution of man, including communism, is also sinful"—a notion he dismissed as "anti-communist and anti-Soviet poison."[21]

The TSPM enforced similar adaptations in Protestant services and rituals. Following the 1958 consolidation, TSPM leaders announced a "unified worship program" for all Protestant churches, requiring each church to "surrender its own individual ritual."[22] Certain rituals, such as the Little Flock's women's meetings and the Seventh-Day Adventists' Sabbath observation, were proscribed by name. The TSPM established a committee to compile a single church hymnal and to vet all religious texts used in the church, permitting only those that favored "unity and socialism."[23] By the end of 1958, the TSPM controlled all Protestant institutions and bodies and had imposed a standardized ritual formula upon its diverse traditions.

The denunciation campaigns and forced consolidations purged evergreater numbers of respected leaders from the church. By the early 1960s, most pastors had been attacked, often to be replaced by activists who rose to prominence through their zealous participation in the radical campaigns. Among the new TSPM elites, few had theological training, and many had little direct connection with the church. Quiet resistance grew from within the church body. The vicious denunciations repulsed the faithful, compelling many to abandon the official churches. As church attendance declined, informal house gatherings proliferated. House churches became so widespread that the Religious Affairs Bureau chairman Luo Zhufeng acknowledged the phenomenon in a public speech—a rare admission of policy failure.[24] Meanwhile, attendance in official churches had fallen so sharply that church consolidation was not only forced but necessary.[25]

The Cultural Revolution

Mao-era radicalism climaxed with the Cultural Revolution. In the antireligious fervor that permeated the era, the TSPM was dissolved and even those who had risen within its hierarchy through their zealous implementation of the party's policies were purged. All religious activities were proscribed and all church assets confiscated. Throughout the country, Red Guards defaced church buildings, which were then occupied by government work units or left to fall into disrepair. Countless clergy and ordinary believers came under attack for their faith and were sent to labor reform camps or given other harsh punishment.

In spite of these calamities, many of the faithful continued to worship at home, often late at night in groups of three or four to avoid detection. Pastors and believers who had been sent to the countryside for hard labor evangelized other prisoners and local populations, sowing the seeds for later church growth.[26] By the early 1970s, large-scale clandestine religious activity was already under way in such remote places as rural Henan Province and in the hills surrounding the southern coastal city of Wenzhou—the same areas that gave birth to Protestantism's explosive expansion during the 1980s and 1990s.

Protestantism under Reform

The reform policies initiated during the late 1970s and early 1980s resurrected the Mao-era machinery of religious control, but the new emphasis on social unity and stability created opportunities unknown during Mao's reign. The TSPM was resurrected, and a new Protestant organization, the China Christian Council (CCC), was created to work alongside the

TSPM, owing largely to the legitimacy problems the latter faced as a result of its active role in the radical Mao-era political campaigns. In principle, the TSPM was to continue to function as a "bridge" between China's Protestant population and the party, while the CCC was charged with church management and ecclesiastical affairs. Their division of labor was not clearly articulated, however, and in practice their functions blended into one; thus the two organizations were typically referred to as a single entity—the *lianghui* (two committees).[27] To ensure the lianghui's subordination, the party-state placed the TSPM-CCC under the "administrative control" of the government's Religious Affairs Bureau,[28] effectively reducing church organizations to wards of the state. In addition, political authorities staffed the lianghui with rehabilitated Mao-era elites. By the mid-1980s, the average age of the representatives in the National Chinese Christian Conference—the official church's leading representative body—was over seventy, and the group became known collectively as the Old Three-Selfers.

With the church hierarchy firmly in check, and with strict regulations governing religious activities, political authorities cautiously began to permit a semblance of normalcy in religious life, allowing congregations to reclaim confiscated church properties and hold services. Despite the regime's explicit policy to contain and control the church, however, the new political environment opened enough space for the church to flourish. Church expansion was also attributable, in part, to the nature of Chinese Protestantism. The church's center of gravity has always been with local congregations, which received the least rigorous government supervision. Protestantism's informal ecclesiastical structure also enabled grassroots congregations to ignore co-opted church leaders with impunity. Most significantly, the highly evangelical nature of Chinese Protestantism endowed the church with an élan that the government has been unable to suppress. As a result, local congregations cohered in a way that was impossible during the Mao era. They negotiated with authorities for the return of their properties, and members gave generously to build new church buildings. Although the severe dearth of trained clergy (owing to the neglect of theological education during the Mao era) imposed a heavy burden on the church, it also gave a new salience to the work of church volunteers, which instilled norms of self-sacrifice and participation within the church. As a result of these and other factors, the official church experienced rapid growth, with an average of 1.5 new churches reopened or newly built each day nationwide throughout the 1980s.[29]

Protestants outside the official church took advantage of the relaxed political environment as well. Although TSPM leaders enjoyed considerable success in attracting congregants back into officially registered churches, the majority of China's Protestants continued to worship in informal gatherings, usually in small groups of no more than fifty in a member's home.[30] By the mid-1980s, the number of such "house churches" (*jiating jiaohui*) was expanding rapidly in both urban and rural areas. In the cities, where government control tends to be greater, house churches multiplied as if by perpetual mitosis, splitting into two groups each time one grew large enough to attract the attention of political authorities. Although remaining small was an imperative in the political environment, it also enabled house churches to retain their intimacy and created a perpetual demand for new leaders. In rural areas, many geographically isolated house churches organized into diffuse networks. Regions with rapid church growth—such as rural Henan, Anhui, and the southern coastal provinces—gave birth to networks that have grown to encompass thousands of local congregations and span provincial boundaries.

The indigenous Protestant groups that political authorities and TSPM leaders had worked so hard to suppress during the Mao era also revived, posing additional challenges to the state's strategy of control. Developing strongholds in various regions—the Little Flock in Fujian and Zhejiang, the True Jesus Church in Hunan and northern Guangdong, and the Jesus Family in Shandong—the indigenous groups succeeded in resisting TSPM control by either remaining unauthorized or registering with the government on condition that they would remain free from the TSPM's influence. Other groups returned to the mainland after moving their headquarters abroad during the Mao era. For example, the Local Church was founded after the Little Flock's lieutenant leader, Li Changshou, emigrated to the United States in 1962. Li built up the Local Church primarily in the United States and then, through an aggressive evangelical campaign, exported the movement back to mainland China after 1978. According to official Chinese documents, the Local Church had acquired a following of two hundred thousand adherents by the early 1980s and has continued to grow despite having been banned as a cult in 1984.[31]

Rapid church growth and widespread resistance at the grassroots level also gave rise to elite maneuvering within the TSPM-CCC. Politically astute church leaders adopted a populist stance against the aging leftists who dominated the TSPM. Open rifts emerged between the Old Three-

Selfers—who were concentrated in the TSPM's Shanghai headquarters—and a more moderate faction led by Nanjing-based bishop Ding Guangxun (K. H. Ting), who held the top position in both the TSPM and the CCC until his retirement in 1996. Countering the TSPM leftists' position of total subservience to the regime, Ding championed the church's rights against official abuse, defended the rights of house churches, and cultivated relations with foreign church denominations. In his power struggle against TSPM leftists, Ding also promoted into leadership positions a cadre of dynamic young clergy, who were even more prone to resist government manipulation. The rivalry between Bishop Ding and the Old Three-Selfers intensified throughout the 1980s, culminating in Ding's attempt to dissolve the TSPM entirely—leaving only the CCC—on the eve of the 1989 Tiananmen Square massacre.[32] The coup attempt backfired when the violence of June 4 ushered in a period of conservative retrenchment, strengthening the hand of the leftists within the lianghui hierarchy.

Recent Trends: The Church's Offensive

Sustained rapid church growth throughout the reform era has increasingly put the forces for change in the driver's seat and the bastions of the established order on the defensive. Although the regime's strategy of controlling the church has remained essentially unchanged throughout the reform period, authorities have faced a barrage of new challenges from within the official church, the house-church movement, and, increasingly, from transnational networks that have allied with forces for change within the church. The state has responded to these challenges with a combination of accommodation and repression, but neither has been effective in slowing growth or quelling the church's bid for autonomy.

Pressures within the Official Church

Pressures for change within the official church have emanated primarily from grassroots congregations, reaching up through the lianghui hierarchy. Frictions begin at the level of beliefs, for most Chinese Protestants are conservative in their beliefs, often charismatic, and highly evangelical, in contrast to the liberal orientation of senior lianghui officials. One survey of Protestants in Henan, for example, has found that almost two-thirds of respondents believed that every sentence in the Bible is true.[33] Their theologically conservative and deeply salvational understanding of Christian faith generates strong incentives for believers to learn God's will for mankind more broadly, and for them individually, by attending services regularly, studying the Bible, sharing testimonies, and praying. The belief that conversion is required for salvation also endows the church with an evangelical spirit, as individual believers seek to bring their families, friends, and neighbors into the fold.

Biblically based motivations to learn God's will, to attain spiritual and ethical perfection, and to evangelize the unconverted generate strong norms of active participation within the church. Faced with government-imposed constraints on church operations, local congregations have gradually pushed the boundaries of permitted activities. As one pastor in Shanghai has neatly summarized,

> At first, the government allowed us to hold only one service on Sunday. Then, we began to hold two services, because there were too many people. Then we started holding prayer meeting on Wednesday evenings. Now, we have services each day of the week, for youth, new converts, the elderly, and young married couples. Many churches are even organizing Sunday school classes for children again. This is also the result of a gradual process. First, they told authorities they needed to offer "day care" for children while their parents were in church. Then they began to organize activities for the children. Recently, churches in Wenzhou introduced a formal curriculum for Sunday school classes by age group. Other churches found out about it, and asked for their materials. Now, a number of churches in different parts of the country are using these materials for their own Sunday school classes. All of this happened because the church pushed for it, slowly and gradually. The government did not give this to us.[34]

Today, most official churches are a hub of activity, holding some type of service almost every day of the week and eliciting impressive levels of volunteerism from congregants. Churches hold special services for youth, women, married couples, and the elderly to meet their unique needs. They organize Bible study classes, dividing congregants into groups according to their depth of Biblical knowledge and levels of literacy. A growing number are reaching out into the community by offering welfare and charitable services.

The mutually reinforcing cogent belief system, high levels of individual commitment, and tightly knit communities with strong internal norms, in turn, generate considerable resources—social capital—for defending churches' interests against external manipulation. Congregations have employed a variety of means to defend their organizational integrity against intrusive governance. They have made use of church bylaws for leadership selection to vote compromised church officials from their positions, even those who enjoy strong backing from the Religious Affairs Bureau.[35] Congregations have filed lawsuits against government work units for refusing to return church properties and have sued local Religious Affairs Bureau officials for failing to renew their permit to operate.[36] In a growing number of cases, figures within the church have waged nationwide campaigns to defend its norms against official regulations—such as defending the church's right to hold Sunday school for children.[37] Increasingly robust grassroots congregations have also influenced the selection of lianghui elites. Bottom-up pressures have propelled a number of dynamic young church leaders into the lianghui hierarchy. In some cases, the change has been dramatic, with Mao-era cronies in their seventies and eighties being replaced by popular pastors in their thirties and forties whose deep convictions are matched by an astuteness at maneuvering within the system for the purpose of strengthening the church.

The growing influence of young evangelicals within the church hierarchy has created new cleavages within the church based on theological orientation. Since the TSPM's creation, leading figures within the official church have sought to craft a Christian theology that obfuscates any contradictions between Christian doctrines and communist ideology. The product of their efforts contrasts sharply with the beliefs of most Chinese Protestants and many young church leaders, who remain staunchly conservative and often fundamentalist in their beliefs. Throughout the 1990s, young pastors, theologians, and seminary students penned articles and preached sermons that were increasingly critical of the forced theological position of lianghui elites, on occasion even contradicting the party line on current events. As the lianghui's primary theological expositor in the reform era, Bishop Ding became the principal target of theological dissent within the church despite his more populist policy stance.[38] Much of the criticism came from Ding's own protégés, whom Ding initially promoted in his struggle against the Old Three-Selfers during the 1980s and early 1990s.[39]

As a counterattack, Bishop Ding formed an alliance with his former adversaries, the Old Three-Selfers, and launched a campaign to enforce theological conformity within the church. Convincing political authorities that Protestant fundamentalism posed an imminent threat to social stability and CCP rule, Ding and a small group of aging lianghui elites launched the Theological Construction Campaign in the fall of 1998. Reminiscent of Mao-era political campaigns, the campaign upheld Ding's writings as the official church's new orthodoxy and attempted to bring the entire church leadership in line with his views. Although less extreme than his predecessor, Wu Yaozong, Ding also sought to sanctify CCP rule by advocating justification through good works and depicting party cadres as paragons of Christian virtue while denouncing the core Protestant doctrine of righteousness by faith as immoral.

Throughout the TSPM-CCC hierarchy, church officials were required to participate in small-group study sessions of Ding's *Selected Works*—a throwback to the mass mobilization campaigns of the Mao era. Seminaries were instructed to add classes on Ding's writings. Many within the church who opposed the campaign were dismissed or had their workloads reduced, especially at Nanjing Union Theological Seminary, where Ding remained the school principal. Despite strong government backing and much fanfare within the lianghui hierarchy, however, the campaign faced concerted resistance throughout the church. Local church leaders stymied the campaign by feigning compliance or redefining its objectives or through outright opposition. Church pastors resisted orders to hold discussion sessions on the campaign's themes. Seminary teachers refused to teach Ding's writings. Even six of Ding's own students at Nanjing Seminary left in protest during the 1998–99 school year. Consequently, five years after the campaign was launched, its impact has been scarcely felt beyond the bastions of national lianghui power in Shanghai and Nanjing.

The fate of the Theological Construction Campaign offers a vivid illustration of the shifting balance of power within the official church from the government and co-opted Protestant elites to the church body. During the Mao era, the regime's radical policies dominated the church's agenda. The faithful could resist only by worshipping at home with a few other believers. By contrast, twenty-five years after reforms were launched, lifting the Cultural Revolution's outright ban on religion, grassroots congregations have cohered into robust social units, generating considerable resources for defending their interests against official manipulation. Bottom-up pressures have influenced leadership selection within the lianghui hierarchy, giving rise to a growing number of progressive church leaders. Thus when aging lianghui elites—backed by political authorities—attempted to foment the politicized Theological Construction Campaign, their efforts foundered in the face of concerted resistance throughout the church.

The House-Church Challenge

Continued rapid growth of China's house-church movement poses an even greater challenge to the party-state's system of religious control. House-church resistance to the TSPM is grounded in Protestantism's early development in China and reinforced by enduring demands for control and conformity that compromise the church's integrity. The informal and highly associational organization of house churches can be traced back to the early twentieth century backlash against highly bureaucratized mission organizations and foreign denominations. Identities of dissent were further cultivated during the Mao era, and house-church leaders today view themselves as direct descendants of the "great warriors" of the 1950s, such as Wang Mingdao, Ni Tuosheng, and Lin Xiangao, who chose lengthy prison sentences over capitulation to the TSPM's politicized agenda.[40] Continuing official restrictions and demands for control, including government manipulation of church elites, organizational control, lack of transparency, forced theological adaptations, limits on the number of churches, and constraints on a wide range of activities—from itinerant evangelism to charismatic worship practices to Sunday school for minors—all have reinforced the house churches' principled resistance to the party-state's system of religious control.

In cities, individual house-church congregations meet several times a week. Personal experience is enhanced by highly participatory services and rituals that often include speaking in tongues and faith healings. Although most urban house churches remain relatively autonomous, their leaders have developed active channels of communication with one another. Meetings often begin with an update on house churches in other areas, with detailed reports of recent arrests or other events. Through informal communications and shared experiences, house churches have forged a unified community of memory. Throughout the country, for example, house-church congregations observe specific dates to commemorate recently martyred Chinese Christians and to conduct orchestrated weeklong prayer chains for the soul of the Chinese nation.

The intimacy of house churches, coupled with their strong sense of purpose, gives them a competitive advantage over their large, impersonal, and highly bureaucratized counterparts in the official church. Competition with the dynamic house church is already imposing visible strains on the TSPM, as many of the most active and well-educated congregants are leaving TSPM churches for house churches. As one disillusioned TSPM pastor notes,

Three-Self churches have become a place for old ladies and newcomers. The reason is that they have nothing to say to educated people and active seekers. The message they preach amounts to this: be a good citizen. Lianghui leaders are always saying that the church needs to be able to communicate with intellectuals, but intellectuals who come to church say, "What do I need Christianity for? I can get this by reading the newspaper." That is why intellectuals and believers who are really searching are all leaving the official church. They either find a house church for real spiritual nourishment, or they leave the church altogether.[41]

In the countryside, especially those areas that have seen the most rapid church growth, house churches have harnessed their evangelical zeal to Chinese traditions of religious sectarianism to form large networks that span geographical boundaries. Aggressively evangelical, these Protestant groups have attracted large numbers of adherents and formed multitiered leadership structures resembling the traditional sects that have been a part of rural China's social landscape for centuries.[42] Yet the house-church networks have also been mobilized by a vision of evangelism—originating in the early twentieth century—that is truly global in scope. A house-church network known as the Back to Jerusalem Movement seeks not only to convert China's vast population to Christianity but to continue westward through the Buddhist and Hindu lands of South and Southeast Asia and the Islamic terrain of the Middle East, finishing the global circumference of Christendom with a triumphant "return" to Jerusalem. This feat, they believe, will precipitate the Second Coming.

The strong sense of belonging—reinforced by the subaltern identities house churches cultivate in the face of official repression—and the powerful sense of purpose created by their vision of global evangelism generate high levels of commitment to the house church's mission. Many adherents give all but subsistence-level income to the church; many more leave their homes and families to become itinerant missionaries in remote areas. The church's ranks also include growing numbers of commercial elites, who now underwrite many of its operations. The networks operate an impressive complex of underground seminaries and printing presses to train grassroots leaders and itinerant evangelists and to supply their flocks with Bibles, hymnals, and educational materials.

For young clergy in the official church, the growing organizational sophistication of house churches and their emphasis on evangelism offer an attractive employment alternative to the highly bureaucratized TSPM. A number of students I interviewed in official seminaries, for example, reported that they intend to work in the house church, not the official church. Many more had frequent contacts with house churches and had participated in training seminars or other activities organized by house-church networks.[43]

To be sure, the house-church movement is far from unified. Adherents often define their religious identities narrowly around the group to which they belong. An evangelical-charismatic rift further divides the house-church movement. Evangelicals, who trace their roots to the evangelical doctrines of Western missionaries and to conservative Chinese pastors such as Wang Mingdao, hold literalist views of the Bible and emphasize expository preaching in their worship. China's charismatic Protestants, by contrast, are doctrinally subjective, stressing demonstrations of the Spirit over theological rigor. They are also supernaturalist, relying heavily on faith healings to attract new converts.

Official repression has also created divisions within house-church networks, as periodic arrests of top leaders give way to fractious competition among subordinates seeking to fill the power vacuum. The precarious political status of the house church is matched in many areas by shallow social foundations, making congregations vulnerable to sectarian impulses. In areas of severe official repression, house churches are forced underground, where, in their isolation, they often cultivate lurid, apocalyptic views of the world. The most rapid church growth has occurred in impoverished rural areas among segments of the population with low levels of literacy. In addition, the converts' relatively weak foundation in Christian doctrines is confused by rural society's rich tradition of folk beliefs. Many rural Christians would be hard pressed to offer sound distinctions between Jesus and other deities in the pantheon of local gods. Add to that rural China's history of religious entrepreneurs—a time-honored path to power and wealth—and one begins to understand the sectarian impulses in China's rural church. These centrifugal forces have given rise to a host of offshoot groups. Colorfully named sects—such as the Established King, Eastern Lightning, and the Three-Tiered Servants—have emerged and spread with surprising speed in the Chinese countryside, drawing large numbers of adherents from house churches and official churches alike.

Despite these centrifugal forces, China's house-church networks have struggled to obtain a measure of unity, presenting a united front against the repressive state, on one side, and the threats posed by heretical sects, on the other. One example of their efforts is an open letter issued jointly by leaders of the largest house-church networks to the Chinese government in August 1998. In the letter, the groups claimed that with more than 80 million adherents—compared with the official church's 10 million members—the house-church movement constitutes the "mainstream" of the Chinese church. The statement's authors then demanded that China's leaders "readjust their policies on religion lest they violate God's will to their own detriment." Specifically, they called on authorities to release unconditionally all house-church Christians held in labor camps, to redefine cults to conform to international standards, to end attacks on house churches, and to enter into a dialogue with them.

Three months later, leaders of four other large house-church networks jointly issued two open statements, this time inviting two foreign journalists to be on hand to ensure that the event obtained international exposure. The first was a "Statement of Faith," which drew theological lines between the house church and the official TSPM, on one hand, and the subjective teachings of the more sectarian offshoot groups, on the other. In the second statement, the authors explained why China's house churches refused to register with the government, enumerating the various ways that official regulations violated biblical principles.[44]

House-church leaders have more recently built on these initial acts of collaboration. The six largest networks have formed an alliance, under the rubric the Sinim Fellowship (named after the Biblical reference to the land of Sinim, which some scholars believe to be China), that draws leaders together for monthly meetings to coordinate their operations. Through regular interaction, house-church leaders have formed collaborative ventures in pastoral education, leadership training, and the publication and development of Bibles, study guides, and training materials. Such organizational virtuosity is unprecedented in post-Mao Chinese society, making the house-church networks the only autonomous nationwide civic organizations in China today.

Although the house churches seek to avoid politics, preferring to focus their efforts on evangelism and nurturing the faithful, they have demonstrated a growing willingness to defend their interests against official repression. After years of suffering imprisonment, torture, and other acts of government persecution in silence, leaders of the large house-church networks have been increasingly vocal in drawing international attention to the regime's abuses of their rights. They have also become increasingly sophisticated at working within China's legal and judicial system to defend themselves against official abuse, raising funds to hire high-profile law firms to defend arrested leaders against charges of promoting a "cult" or subverting the state.

Overseas Missions and Transnational Networks

Deepening interaction with overseas mission groups and a multitude of parachurch organizations have further emboldened official and house churches alike. After three decades of Maoist xenophobia and isolationism, China's reform and opening policies were a beckoning call to mission organizations in Europe and North America to resume the task of evangelizing China's massive population. They were joined by counterparts in Hong Kong, Taiwan, South Korea, and Southeast Asia—all of which experienced considerable postwar growth in their Christian populations. Finally, and perhaps most significant, the high rate of conversion to Christianity among Chinese students, scholars, and emigrants to the United States and Europe has given rise to an extensive web of overseas Chinese Christian networks of individuals who conduct mission work in China or revitalize the church upon their return home.

Unlike earlier mission enterprises, whereby Western churches established a wide range of religious, social welfare, and educational institutions within China and exercised authority over them, mission efforts today are geared primarily toward supporting existing activities of the Chinese church. Yet new ventures vary widely in the approach to mission work, the range of activities, and geographical emphasis. Most of the mainline European and American denominational organizations (such as the Lutherans, the Presbyterian Church of the U.S.A., and the Norwegian Mission Alliance) have opted to work through official channels. They support the Amity Printing Press—China's largest publisher of Bibles and other religious materials—and underwrite much of the work of the Amity Foundation, a development and relief nongovernmental organization and English-language teaching service that was founded by the CCC as the monopoly channel for outside resources. Sustained engagement in these authorized activities, however, has led to more direct mission activity. For example, by supporting development and relief work, overseas churches have forged relations with political authorities, who, in turn, have allowed them to fund the construction of new churches, seminaries, and Bible schools.

By contrast, many churches in the United States and Asia tend to be wary of China's official church and focus their efforts on direct evangelism and supporting the house-church movement. Thousands of young English teachers dispatched to China by church groups double as missionaries. Dozens of independent mission agencies have formed to carry out increasingly focused objectives to meet specific needs within the Chinese church. They supply the house churches with Bibles, provide them with materials for leadership and evangelism training, develop Chinese-language Sunday school materials, and help them cultivate a strategic vision for the future. Several large American denominations have even adopted a two-track strategy of working with both China's official church and the house-church movement.

Mission groups from Asian countries tend to concentrate their efforts in geographical regions where they have the greatest influence. Taiwan's churches operate primarily along the southeastern seaboard. Hong Kong's mission outreach is strongest in bordering Guangdong Province. South Korean evangelism is most active among the ethnic Korean population in China's Northeast. By deepening local ties, however, mission groups have been able to expand their geographical scope. Korean missionaries have become particularly active throughout the country and have established many house-church groups and training centers in urban areas. Their range of activities has also expanded beyond traditional mission work. For example, Korean Christian groups organize many of the food aid operations in North Korea and, more recently, have begun orchestrating refugee escapes from North Korea into foreign diplomatic compounds in Beijing, drawing on networks of church contacts within China to execute the daring missions.[45]

High rates of conversion to Christianity among Chinese abroad have given rise to transnational networks of Chinese Christians, which have become a major force in mission work. There are now some fifteen hundred Chinese Protestant churches in North America and several hundred in Europe, many of which support some form of mission activity in China. Overseas congregations form sister churches with mainland churches, supplying funding and materials and offering prayers of support. Pastors trained in the United States or Taiwan make frequent trips to the mainland, baptizing recent converts in house churches that do not have ordained clergy. Many second-generation Chinese American Christians spend a year as student missionaries in China or serve as "tent-making" evangelists (whereby their evangelism is veiled under the cover of commercial ventures).

Leading Chinese intellectuals and high-profile dissidents who converted to Christianity after leaving China have produced a variety of literary and artistic works that offer tremendous psychological support to Christians throughout China. For example, the philosopher and documentarist Yuan Zhiming created a national sensation in 1988 by his participation in the production of the film series *Heshang* (River elegy), a scathing critique of China's inward-looking culture and tradition of authoritarian rule. After being implicated as a "black hand" in the Tiananmen protests the following spring, Yuan escaped to the United States, where he converted to Christianity. In 1999 Yuan produced another film, *Shenzhou* (God's land), which strongly resembles *Heshang* yet critiques China's godless authoritarianism from the perspective of his newfound Christian faith. Despite the official ban on *Shenzhou*, contraband video disks of the film have circulated widely throughout China, in both official and house churches, strengthening believers' sense of Christian unity and their sense of mission to reclaim China for God.

Together, this diverse array of transnational mission groups and networks has formed a bulwark of support and inspiration for the church in China. Overseas funding strengthens the official church's resource base, increasing its leverage in dealing with political authorities. Outside support has more visibly influenced the development of China's large house-church networks, which have been shaped by the materials, training, funding, and even strategic advice of overseas mission organizations. Of course, mission groups' competing theological orientations and financial resources have created competitive pressures among the house-church networks, countering their efforts to promote a united front against the party-state. Cumulatively, however, outside efforts have worked to counter the government's strategy of keeping the church weak and dependent and have helped the church become a viable force in Chinese society.

Official Reaction: Accommodation and Repression

China's leaders have reacted to these mounting new challenges with a mixture of accommodation and repression. Local authorities have accommodated much of the increased activity emanating from the churches, even if only tacitly and in combination with varying degrees of repression. Enforcing the regime's policy platform requires a considerable investment in cadre manpower, and in most locales, political authorities simply lack the capacity or the determination to make that investment. Faced with limited resources (as in most rural areas and smaller cities) or embedded in traditions of more relaxed governance (such as in southern coastal regions), political authorities in many locales turn a blind eye to unauthorized house churches and may even have regular contact with their leaders. Municipal authorities typically instruct the groups to remain relatively small, not to organize with other groups, and to avoid contacts with foreigners. As long as groups meet these criteria, authorities usually do not forcibly disband them. In remote rural areas, local authorities simply lack the resources to prevent the emergence of autonomous religious groups—or may even have religious converts in their own families—and use their authority to protect those groups.

Government officials are also in increasingly frequent contact with leaders in the large house-church networks, and according to some reports, they have become more solicitous recently, inquiring how they might make the house church's situation more "comfortable." In a growing number of cases, local officials have agreed to register house churches directly, allowing them to avoid coming under TSPM control and permitting them to preserve considerable autonomy. China's leaders are reportedly considering this "third wave" of church-state relations as a model for future official policy, which would allow direct church registration with the government and greater church autonomy.

At the same time, the incidence of official repression has risen in recent years. The spate of large-scale arrests of house-church Christians reported in the media in 1999–2000 targeted the leadership structure of signatory groups to the open letters. On August 24, 1999, two days after the first letter was issued, forty leading members of the China Fangcheng Church of Henan were arrested. Almost one year later, on August 13, 2000, the regime conducted another mass arrest of 130 Fangcheng members, presumably to discourage the house churches from making the open letter an annual event. Similar measures were meted out against the other house-church networks. The party-state's campaign to exterminate the Falungong has also spilled over to other forms of unauthorized religion, including house churches. A more recent spike in the arrest of house-church leaders and other repressive measures coincided with the highly sensitive transition of China's top leaders in late 2002 and early 2003. This most recent wave has continued throughout the first half of 2003, perhaps reflecting the party's fears that religious groups may attempt to capitalize on the outbreak of SARS (severe acute respiratory syndrome) to recruit new adherents and perhaps even mobilize them against the government.

Sustained official religious persecution, in turn, has spawned increasingly radical religious sects and cults. Although a wide range of unofficial religious groups now pepper China's social landscape, the most extreme groups initially cohered in the areas of harshest official repression. For instance, a former member of the banned Local Church, Wu Yangming, was jailed several times in Henan and Anhui Provinces during the 1980s for conducting unauthorized religious activities. Each time Wu was released, he resumed evangelizing and attracting adherents but preached an increasingly radical message. He finally broke from the Local Church altogether and established his own sect, the Established King, whereby he claimed to have succeeded Jesus as the "Supreme Savior" and preached the impending apocalypse.[46] Similarly, a disgruntled Protestant Christian named Zhao Weishan broke from his church to establish the Eastern Lightning cult, also in Henan. Claiming that Jesus had already returned (in the form of a peasant woman) and that God had charged him to overthrow the Communist Party in order to establish the Kingdom of God on earth, Zhao quickly attracted tens of thousands of adherents among rural Henan's repressed Protestants, and his message soon spread to neighboring Anhui, Shaanxi, and Jiangsu Provinces. According to Chinese government reports, Eastern Lightning is now active in at least twenty-two provinces and has acquired a following of as many as three hundred thousand adherents, despite a number of large-scale arrests of group leaders.[47]

Political Implications

The state's traditional response of repression and accommodation has alternatively cowed and pacified the church, but neither strategy has been fully successful. Official persecution has produced a theology of martyrdom, particularly among the house churches. China's Christians identify with a savior who suffered unto death, and they often view their own travails as a form of spiritual discipline. House-church networks have even incorporated the spirit of martyrdom into their organizational culture, making individual persecution a valuable form of personal capital, as leadership candidates are ranked by the number of times they have been arrested. This dwindling fear of official repression neutralizes an important asset of the coercive state: the power to intimidate.

The government's efforts to accommodate the church fall short as well. The Chinese Communist Party's suspicion of any autonomous social group compels its cadres to manipulate the church's elites and restrict its activities. Arbitrary constraints on evangelism, the prohibition of services for minors, onerous registration requirements, and a host of other restrictions violate the church's own norms and compromise its values. Until the state gives the church sufficient autonomy to be true to its own principles, relations between them will be marked by tension.

The implications of Protestant challenges to party-state rule remain uncertain. Deepening antagonism may culminate in a Falungong-style crisis. Conversely, the regime may finally forge a mutually acceptable modus vivendi with China's burgeoning Protestant movement. Recent trends suggest that a viable governing arrangement remains elusive. Illicit religious groups continue to expand, and the regime's fitful combination of repression and accommodation alternately hardens religious identities and gives them space to consolidate and expand their operations.

A more certain conclusion is that more than half a century of CCP manipulation has had little lasting impact on China's Protestant population. The party's efforts to refashion Protestant doctrines and identities have failed to take root, and most believers within the official church remain in spite of, or even in direct opposition to, the lianghui's leading figures. More troublesome are the negative implications of the party-state's repression of Protestantism's most popular forms. The fruits of repression—a culture of martyrdom, subaltern religious identities, and the proliferation of increasingly radical sectarian groups—will be the CCP's most enduring legacy for China's Protestant population and will challenge its ability to govern effectively for years to come.

Notes

1. Wang Mingdao, "We, Because of Faith," in Francis P. Jones, ed., *Documents of the Three-Self Movement: Source Materials for the Study of the Protestant Church in Communist China* (New York: National Council of the Churches of Christ in the U.S.A., 1963), pp. 99–114.

2. Francis Price Jones, *The Church in Communist China: A Protestant Appraisal* (New York: Friendship, 1962), p. 52.

3. The manifesto, originally entitled *Zhongguo Jidujiao zai xinzhongguo jianxe zhong nuli di dujing* [Direction of endeavor for Chinese Christianity in the construction of new China], is reprinted in Francis P. Jones, ed., *Documents of the Three-Self Movement: Source Materials for the Study of the Protestant Church in Communist China* (New York: National Council of the Churches of Christ in the U.S.A., 1963), pp. 19–20.

4. Jones, *The Church in Communist China*, p. 58.

5. Ibid., p. 49.

6. Three-Self Patriotic Movement, "Constitution of the Committee of the China Christian Three-Self Patriotic Movement (January 1961)," in Francis P. Jones, ed., *Documents of the Three-Self Movement: Source Materials for the Study of the Protestant Church in Communist China* (New York: National Council of the Churches of Christ in the U.S.A., 1963), pp. 198–99.

7. Alan Hunter and Kim-kwong Chan, *Protestantism in Contemporary China* (Cambridge University Press, 1993), p. 23.

8. Wu Yaozong, "The First Eight Months of the Three-Self Reform Movement," in Francis P. Jones, ed., *Documents of the Three-Self Movement: Source Materials for the Study of the Protestant Church in Communist China* (New York: National Council of the Churches of Christ in the U.S.A., 1963), pp. 34–41, 40.

9. Wu Yaozong, "Report to the July 1954 Conference," in Francis P. Jones, ed., *Documents of the Three-Self Movement: Source Materials for the Study of the Protestant Church in Communist China* (New York: National Council of the Churches of Christ in the U.S.A., 1963), pp. 85–95, 88–89.

10. The three-antis campaign sought to wipe out corruption, waste, and bureaucratism; the five-antis campaign targeted bribery, tax evasion, fraud, stealing of state property, and theft of economic secrets.

11. Bob Whyte, *Unfinished Encounter: China and Christianity* (Harrisburg, Pa.: Morehouse, 1988), pp. 240–43; Deng Zhaoming, "Indigenous Chinese Pentecostal Denominations," *China Study Journal*, vol. 16 (August 2001), pp. 1–12, 17–18.

12. Richard C. Bush Jr., *Religion in Communist China* (New York: Abingdon, 1970), p. 231.

13. "Unification of Worship" (excerpted reports from *Tianfeng*, August, September, and October 1958), in Francis P. Jones, ed., *Documents of the Three-Self Movement: Source Materials for the Study of the Protestant Church in Communist China* (New York: National Council of the Churches of Christ in the U.S.A., 1963), pp. 180–84, 182–83.

14. Jones, *The Church in Communist China*, p. 58.

15. Wu Yaozong, "How the Communist Party Has Educated Me," in Francis P. Jones, ed., *Documents of the Three-Self Movement: Source Materials for the Study of the Protestant Church in Communist China* (New York: National Council of the Churches of Christ in the U.S.A., 1963), pp. 51–54, 52.

16. Wu Yaozong, "The Reformation of Christianity: On the Awakening of Christians," in Francis P. Jones, ed., *Documents of the Three-Self Movement: Source Materials for the Study of the Protestant Church in Communist China* (New York: National Council of the Churches of Christ in the U.S.A., 1963), pp. 12–14, 14.

17. For a thorough analysis of *xiaozu* (small groups) as a form of mass indoctrination, see Martin King Whyte, *Small Groups and Political Rituals in China* (University of California Press, 1974).

18. Wu Yaozong, "How the Communist Party Has Educated Me," p. 53.

19. Dozens of *Tianfeng* articles sought to make a biblical claim for hating one's enemies, citing Jesus' criticism of the Pharisees for support. See Jones, *The Church in Communist China*, p. 89.

20. Wu Yaozong, "Freedom through Truth," in Francis P. Jones, ed., *Documents of the Three-Self Movement: Source Materials for the Study of the Protestant Church in Communist China* (New York: National Council of the Churches of Christ in the U.S.A., 1963), pp. 73–84.

21. Wu Yaozong, "How the Communist Party Has Educated Me," p. 54.

22. Ibid., p. 184.

23. Ibid.

24. Ibid., p. 211.

25. TSPM leader, interview with author, Nanjing, China, April 2, 2001.

26. Tony Lambert, *China's Christian Millions: The Costly Revival* (London: Monarch, 2000).

27. For a discussion of the committees' division of labor, see Hunter and Chan, *Protestantism in Contemporary China,* pp. 58–62.

28. Chinese Communist Party Central Committee, "Document 19: The Basic Viewpoint and Policy on the Religious Question during Our Country's Socialist Period," in Donald E. MacInnis, *Religion in China Today: Policy and Practice* (Maryknoll, N.Y.: Orbis, 1989), pp. 9–26.

29. Bao Jiayuan, "Update on the Church in China," *Chinese Theological Review,* vol. 14 (2000), p. 118.

30. For a detailed examination of China's house-church movement in the reform era, see Jason Kindopp, "The House Church Movement," in "The Politics of Protestantism in Contemporary China: State Control, Civil Society, and Social Movement in a Single Party-State" (Ph.D. diss., George Washington University, 2004).

31. Li Shixiong and Xiqiu (Bob) Fu, eds. and trans., *Religion and National Security in China: Secret Documents from China's Security Sector* (Bartlesville, Okla.: Voice of the Martyrs, 2002), p. 25.

32. See Tony Lambert, *The Resurrection of the Chinese Church* (London: Hodder and Stoughton, 1991), pp. 201–13.

33. An additional 22 percent believed that the majority was true; a mere 3 percent believed that only certain parts of the Bible should be respected. Li Liang, "Researches into the Present Circumstances of Protestant Christianity in China: A Sociological Analysis of Christianity in the Nanyang District of Henan Province," *China Study Journal,* vol. 9, no. 2 (August 1994), pp. 4–10.

34. Interview with author, Shanghai, China, April 12, 2001.

35. Lambert writes that one such case in a large church in northern China resulted in many house-church Christians' returning to the official church because, "as they put it, 'God's temple has been cleansed.'" Lambert, *China's Christian Millions,* p. 170.

36. "Local Christians Take RAB Officials to Court," *Amity News Service,* vol. 5.5 (October 1996) (www.amityfoundation.org/ANS/Past%20Issues.htm [November 13, 2003]); "Christian Lawyer Advises on Church Legal Matters," *Amity News Service,* vol. 7.8 (August 1998) (www.amityfoundation.org/ANS/Articles/ans98.8/98.8_8_1.htm [November 13, 2003]).

37. John Pomfret, "Evangelicals on the Rise in Land of Mao," *Washington Post,* December 24, 2002, p. A1.

38. In his writings, Ding combines process theology with highly idealized accounts of the "cadre." In doing so, he essentially holds up China's Communist Party as a

paragon of Christian virtue. He also criticizes the foundational Protestant doctrine of "righteousness by faith" on grounds that it creates an untenable division between believers and unbelievers. See Janice Wickeri, ed., *Love Never Ends: Papers by K. H. Ting* (Nanjing, China: Nanjing Amity Printing Company, 2000).

39. Mindy Belz, "Caesar's Seminary," *World*, vol. 16 (January 27, 2001), pp. 1–3, 1.

40. House-church leaders jointly publish an underground journal entitled *Dao lu* [The way], with articles glorifying house-church martyrs.

41. Interview with author, Nanjing, China, March 14, 2001.

42. For a recent study, see Hubert Seiwert (in collaboration with Ma Xisha), *Popular Religious Movements and Heterodox Sects in Chinese History* (Leiden, Netherlands: Brill, 2003).

43. The interviews were conducted over an eighteen-month period in 2000–01.

44. English translations of the letters are reprinted in David Aikman, *Jesus in Beijing: How Christianity Is Transforming China and Changing the Global Balance of Power* (Washington, D.C.: Regnery, 2003), pp. 293–307.

45. For one insightful report, see Jasper Becker, "Underground Railway Brings Glimmer of Hope to the Secret Christian Spies of North Korea," *Independent* (London), January 29, 2003, p. 14.

46. Deng Zhaoming, "Recent Millennial Movements on Mainland China: Three Cases," *Inter-Religio*, vol. 34 (Winter 1998), pp. 51–53.

47. "The Bulletin of the Department of Anhui Public Security," in Li Shixiong and Xiqiu (Bob) Fu, eds. and trans., *Religion and National Security in China*, p. 78. See also Paul Hattaway, "When China's Christians Wish They Were in Prison: An Examination of the Eastern Lightning Cult in China" (April 24, 2001) (www.asiaharvest.org/elreport.htm [November 13, 2003]); Tony Lambert, "Lightning from the East: A New Cult," *China Insight* (March–April 1998), pp. 1–4.

PART III

*Religion in
U.S.-China Relations*

9 PENG LIU

Unreconciled Differences: The Staying Power of Religion

Of the several major problem areas that seem to plague U.S.-China relations, differences over religion are among the most persistent. One major reason is that religion is central to the contradictory self-defined public persona or identities of the two countries. The gap between the U.S. and Chinese governments on this issue of religion is huge. With such little common ground, the Chinese government is frequently offended, and the American government is just as frequently frustrated.

If the two parties are going to maintain a healthy relationship, they will have to develop a realistic attitude toward their differences and create a framework for dealing with them, just as they have for other problems. In the wake of September 11, efforts to define areas of possible antiterrorist cooperation have underscored the importance of religion in domestic and world affairs. Both sides are actively seeking ways to cooperate in this arena. If each country takes a constructive attitude, the gap may begin to close.

Friction in U.S.-China Relations

Although preserving stable and healthy bilateral relations is important to both sides, four enduring issues cause tensions in bilateral relations, owing primarily to differences in ideology, history, or geopolitical interests. These are trade, Taiwan, nonproliferation, and human rights. Both governments have made significant efforts to stabilize relations since diplomatic relations were established in 1979, because their leaders realize that even small changes in the relationship will not only directly affect the United States and China individually but will also influence the Asia-Pacific region and even the global structure.

Among these problems, the most visible has been the trade imbalance. This issue has changed for the better, though, with China's entry into the World Trade Organization. As the two economies become more integrated, interdependence forces both parties to work out problems. Moreover, the multilateral mechanisms of the World Trade Organization provide a new means of dealing with them.

Regarding the Taiwan issue, three U.S.-China bilateral communiqués issued in 1972, 1979, and 1982 still function as a minimal framework for setting boundaries for conflict so that disagreement over Taiwan does not destroy the relationship. There is no reason to expect that China will initiate the use of force against Taiwan or that the United States will encourage Taiwan's independence. Although Taiwan may want to initiate fundamental change, there is no realistic path by which it could acquire new international status on its own.

Nonproliferation is an arena in which incentives for cooperation and coordination between China and the United States outweigh differences of approach. As members of the United Nations Security Council, both countries have a sense of heavy obligation—and pressure from other United Nations members—to work together for global stability. For example, China, one of the oldest allies of North Korea, has agreed to make joint efforts with the United States to solve the nuclear crisis. China offered a meeting place for the United States and North Korea to begin to talk about this issue in Beijing in April 2003 and sent a high-level official delegation to Pyongyang to convince North Korea to soften its attitude. In the case of the 2003 Iraq war, China tried to avoid taking action against the United States on any Security Council resolution and is one of only a few countries that allowed no anti-U.S. demonstrations.

In each of these three arenas, despite disagreement and different interests, there is the will to cooperate, a structural framework, and various mechanisms to promote dialogue and cooperation. In the case of human rights, however, contradictions based on deep differences in culture and sociopolitical systems have never been managed well. The agreement to include human rights as an area of potential bilateral cooperation, reached during the 1997–98 summit meetings between President Bill Clinton and President Jiang Zemin quickly fell by the wayside with the 1999 NATO (North Atlantic Treaty Organization) bombing of China's Belgrade embassy and China's ban on the Falungong spiritual movement. The dialogues on human rights and religious freedom were frozen for several years thereafter. In contrast, the structural frameworks and mechanisms created with other Western countries in 1996 and 1997 for human rights and religious freedom dialogues have held and have continued to the present.

Conflicts of Identity

Among various human rights issues that cause bilateral friction, religion may be the most persistent problem. Unlike some other issues, religion does not come and go. Some foreign affairs experts believe that the single most-important cause of cold war tensions between the United States and China was the expulsion of U.S. missionaries from the People's Republic of China in the early 1950s. By the late 1990s, American concern about alleged religious persecution, combined with Chinese suspicion of subversion in the name of religion, was fueling a second Sino-U.S. cold war.

Perhaps the reason is that religion and its secular version, ideology, are central to the conflicting self-defined public personas or identities of both the United States and China. The central tenet of the ideology of the United States—its "civil religion"—is to carry the banner of freedom, including religious freedom, to the rest of the world. China's ideology of socialism is defined largely by opposition to imperialism, including cultural or religious imperialism. China's felt need to redress an alleged history of being "bullied" creates a strong moral identification with other victims of imperialism or hegemonism. The result of these opposing ideologies is a clash of self-perceived moral superiority on both sides.

Religion in the United States

Religion permeates American life. This fact holds true regardless of which political party or which administration is in charge. Changes in trade, arms control, or Taiwanese issues might have a major impact for good or bad upon the quality of the relationship, but religion has been a steady factor throughout. The reasons are deeply rooted and complex. American history cannot be separated from the issue of religious freedom, which was a founding concept in the establishment of the United States. Religious freedom has been deeply rooted in the hearts of the American people since the eighteenth century and is above challenge. It is beyond social conflicts or racial divide or political competition. Religious liberty has been a basic underlying principle in American domestic life and foreign relations from the beginning, though it is made more overt or direct at some times than at others.[1]

Religion also has a broad and deep foundation in American society. More than 90 percent of Americans claim belief in God, and the United States has the highest percentage of church attendance among all Western countries. This situation has remained stable for more than a hundred years. No other country in the world exceeds the United States in the number of religious institutions. Religion and faith-based organizations have played a central role in U.S. society. They influence not only politics, judicial or legal systems, education, and foreign relations but also personal morality and concepts of marriage, family, and community. Religion is an important part of the daily life of many Americans, and the services provided by religious organizations are an essential contribution to many American communities. Much of America's volunteerism and humanitarian work is motivated by religious principles.

Because a majority of Americans are religious believers, and the electoral and political system reflect the opinions and values of the voters, citizens' attitudes toward religion directly influence the results of elections. As representatives of voters, members of Congress cannot pass legislation without considering voters' preferences, including those based on religious concepts. As a representative of all the people, the president has to take account of both congressional and popular opinion when dealing with foreign nations. Government policy toward events in foreign countries that involve religion and arouse a popular reaction must take those popular responses into account. Thus government foreign policy or action does not simply represent political interests but must also reflect values at the grass roots.

Religion in China

Within China, religion is considered quite differently. The ruling Communist Party views religion as a "backward" or even "superstitious" idealist ideology, opposed to and incompatible with Marxist "scientific" materialism. A Marxist government should propagate an atheistic worldview and must not encourage religious belief. At best, the state will tolerate religious teachings that focus on ethics and social service, playing down supernatural elements. China's leaders also view religion as a tool used by foreign powers to exercise undue influence within China. The introduction of the Chinese people to Christianity—Protestant, Roman Catholic, and Orthodox—was closely connected with the unequal treaties of the nineteenth and early twentieth centuries, through which China lost control of its sovereignty owing to its humiliating military defeats by the Western imperialist powers.

China's rulers recognize, however, that religion cannot be ignored or excluded altogether. The history of religion in China is a long one. Many Chinese practice some form of religion, and in some areas of China, religion is an integral part of the people's daily lives and communities. The culture of nearly all of China's ethnic minorities is profoundly influenced by religion. Thus religious issues cannot be separated from ethnic issues. Given these concerns, the party-state cannot easily or quickly eliminate religious belief, regardless of the preferences of China's leaders. Even according to Marxist theory, the predicted gradual death of religion is a protracted process.

Finally, most of the world's population has some kind of religious belief, and China's leaders have been forced to recognize the role religion plays in shaping international affairs. Thus religion and religious freedom and tolerance continually arise as foreign affairs issues that China must address. The state focuses on the practical import of religious diplomacy in the interests of trade and national security.

Given the resilience of religion in China and the pervasiveness of religious concerns in international affairs, the only practical thing for China to do is to shape religious practice and diplomacy into vehicles that serve the political purpose of building a socialist China. Jiang Zemin, as president of the People's Republic of China and general secretary of the Chinese Communist Party, speaking at national religious affairs conferences in 1991 and 2001, stressed that an overriding goal of both religious policy and religious regulations was "to guide religion to adapt to socialism." This statement summarizes the Chinese government's approach to religion; it is a political strategy to unite religious believers at home and overseas behind the Chinese Communist Party.

China's approach to religion drives the structure of its regulation of religion. Government institutions manage religious affairs according to the policies of the party-state, and religious groups have the duty to cooperate and carry out these policies. There are mechanisms for the religious groups to voice their concerns to the party and the government. For example, each religious group has representatives in the national and regional People's Political Consultative Conferences, in which they can talk things over with representatives of the party and the government, and there are periodic informal exchanges between national and local party and government heads and the various religious officials. These avenues only provide a way of exchanging opinions, however, and the concessions given to the religious groups have no legally binding force. The underlying premise of all the interaction and regulation is that the religious groups must accept the leadership of the government to the end of furthering the interests of the party-state.[2] Foreign exchanges with religious groups are encouraged only when they are likely to serve this political purpose.

Thus religion in China is not purely a cultural or private matter; rather, it falls in the category of politics and public affairs. Looking through the filter of its political interests, China logically views any U.S. government statement or action regarding religion as a matter of pure politics.

Mismatched Approaches to Foreign Policy

In the 1950s an ideological approach to foreign policy prevailed on both sides of U.S.-China interaction, pitting "freedom from communism" against "anti-imperialism." During the honeymoon period of the 1980s, after the normalization of relations between the two countries, both governments adopted a more pragmatic approach to the religion issue. They were willing to view religion and ideology in a more instrumentalist fashion, making identity goals secondary to overriding imperatives for geopolitical cooperation. In the post–cold war period of the 1990s, however, this compact foundered. Beijing perceived that the United States was again adopting an ideological cold war attitude targeting China and concluded that religious and other human rights were being used as weapons to undermine the regime. Meanwhile, Washington viewed pragmatic China's domestic or diplomatic initiatives on human rights as purely cynical bargaining tools. This perception was compounded when the Chinese blatantly sought to use offers of Sino-European dialogues as leverage against U.S. promotion of a China resolution in the United Nations Commission on Human Rights.

Promoting Religious Freedom: Other Western Countries

The United States is not alone in its concern about religious freedom issues nor in its communications with the Chinese on the issue. Other Western countries pursue the issue in bilateral meetings and formal dialogues between officials, in multilateral sessions, in informal exchanges and visits, and in various technical cooperative projects. There are differences in approach, though, between the United States and other Western countries and also a disparity in influence, creating a corresponding difference in China's reception and reaction.

A recent example of informal dialogue between Canadian and Chinese officials on religious freedom issues occurred in October 2002 in Mexico at the Asia-Pacific Economic Cooperation summit, at which President Jiang Zemin represented China. Canadian prime minister Jean Chrétien brought to the conference a copy of a resolution that had just been unanimously passed by the House of Commons in the Canadian Parliament. The resolution called on Prime Minister Chrétien to take advantage of his meeting with Jiang Zemin to privately raise the issue of the imprisonment of thirteen Falungong practitioners, specifically named in the resolution, who have close family ties to Canadian citizens.[3] Within four months, five of the thirteen had been released (two of whom were allowed to come to live with family members in Canada), and the treatment of some of the eight still in prison was believed to have improved.[4]

Canada engages in formal bilateral dialogue with Chinese officials through a Joint Committee on Human Rights, which first met in Ottawa in 1997 and has met each year thereafter.[5] The committee provides a formal mechanism for Canadian officials to discuss religious freedom issues with the Chinese, but it addresses a broad spectrum of human rights issues, with religious freedom issues constituting only a small part of the dialogue. The meetings are closed to the public, and no public reports are issued; thus there is no transparency and no accountability as to what was discussed or the results of the discussions—as opposed to the American approach, which would require more openness.

China, Canada, and Norway cohost a Plurilateral Human Rights Symposium, which was initiated in 1998 in Vancouver, British Columbia, and has met since then in China (Qingdao), Thailand (Bangkok), and most recently, in 2002, in Indonesia (Jakarta). The symposium provides a venue in which various human rights issues, including religious freedom, can be discussed before an audience of observers from Bangladesh, Cambodia, Indonesia, Korea, Mongolia, and other Asian countries.

Twice there has been an exchange of what Canada terms the Canada-China Religious Freedom Delegation. The first meeting was in 1999, in China, when representatives from the Canadian Council of Churches, the Canadian government, and the Canadian judiciary met with officials from the China Christian Council and the Three-Self Patriotic Movement. In February 2003 a Chinese delegation headed by Bishop Fu Tieshan, the president of the Chinese Catholic Patriotic Association, and Ye Xiaowen, the director-general of the Religious Affairs Bureau, returned the visit and toured three cities in Canada. The Canadian Council of Churches served as host, and the discussions focused mainly on church-state relations in Canada. The group also met with the Canadian Human Rights Commission and discussed the international human rights and religious freedom covenants.

The activities of the Religious Freedom Delegation share with the Joint Committee meetings the attributes of nontransparency and nonaccountability, in that the delegation's activities were not publicized until after the event and other interested private groups in Canada had no opportunity to participate.[6] Canada financially supports technical cooperative projects in China through the Canadian International Development Agency to further the research into and analysis of human rights in China and the development of the rule of law. So far, religious freedom has not been listed as an issue among the projects.

Norway follows this same general pattern: dialogue between Chinese and Norwegian officials on religious issues takes place during private official meetings and during the Roundtable Conference on the Rule of Law and Human Rights, which first met in 1997 and has met annually thereafter, alternately in China or Norway. Norwegian roundtable participants include government officials and representatives of the Church of Norway, the Parliamentary Ombudsman, the Institute for Human Rights, and the Norwegian Agency for Development Cooperation, and they discuss with the Chinese a broad spectrum of human rights and rule-of-law issues. Religious freedom issues constitute only a part of the agenda. The government-funded Institute for Human Rights has an extensive China program through which Norway supports cooperative projects in China pertaining to rule-of-law and human rights development and also religious freedom.

Norway supports religious freedom in particular through its support of Forum 18, a network of nongovernmental organizations that focuses on freedom of religion and belief, based on article 18 of the United Nations' Universal Declaration of Human Rights. In 2001 the group presented to Norway's Ministry of Foreign Affairs a report on freedom of religion that gave extensive coverage to China's internal practices. Norway also supports the Oslo Coalition, a group of Norwegian religious leaders representing a variety of spiritual backgrounds who have united in their support of religious freedom. The Oslo Coalition visited China in 2000 to share with the Chinese how religious freedom is handled in Norway and to look for ways to discuss religious freedom in China. In 2001 the coalition, in turn, hosted a visit to Norway from a Chinese delegation.

The tone of the Oslo Coalition's visit in China was similar to the visit of the Canadian delegation: officials in China's Religious Affairs Bureau hosted and at all times accompanied the Oslo group. The coalition's official itinerary was restricted to visits with officially registered religious groups arranged by the Religious Affairs Bureau, and they were allowed no contact with unregistered believers.[7]

The Canadian and Norwegian experiences provide a good example of the type of dialogue and interaction that China has with the United Kingdom, the Netherlands, Sweden, the European Union, Australia, and other nations. The Dutch, in their exchanges, continually raise the issue of freedom of religion, fueled perhaps by their national history as a haven for religious dissenters. Since 1996, Chinese officials have met twice each year to discuss human rights issues with officials of the European Union. These meetings include discussion of a broad spectrum of human rights issues, including religious freedom issues, and the European officials have at times made clemency requests for named Falungong practitioners and inquired about the incarceration of leaders of unregistered Protestant groups.[8]

Unlike the United States, other Western governments generally refrain from making strong critical statements about the Chinese in public, and their official meetings with Chinese officials are restrained, thereby minimizing press coverage and the involvement or interference of interested private groups.[9] Over time, most of these countries, in part to protect economic interests in China, have decided against supporting United Nations Commission on Human Rights resolutions critical of the Chinese, though they may voice general comments of concern in various multilateral forums.

Historical and societal differences between the United States and other Western countries also affect the extent to which they promote religious freedom. For example, direct government financial support of initiatives presented by nongovernmental or religious organizations, such as Norway's support of the Oslo Coalition, Forum 18, and the religious projects within the Institute for Human Rights, contrasts with general U.S. practice, whereby traditional interpretations of the principle of the separation of church and state tend to preclude government funding of such projects. Moreover, the Canadian and European peoples are notably more secular and less religious than are the Americans, and religion is not as central to their public personas; this factor moderates the fervor and tenacity of their religious freedom concerns. In addition, because of the tradition of a state church in most European countries, it is natural for them to set up relations with China's registered religious groups, whereas Americans feel a greater affinity with independent, unregistered believers.

The United States is by far the strongest of the Western nations economically, and thus it may feel more confident in expressing its own concerns without fear of economic consequence or repercussions. For China, the United States in fact is more important, politically as well as economically, than other nations, making the religion issue inescapable.

Bridging the Gap with Realism

The gap between the U.S. and Chinese governments on the issue of religion is huge. If each nation considers bilateral religious issues without taking into account the other's perspective, there can be no end to tension and conflict. With no common ground, the Chinese government will always be offended and the American government will continue to be frustrated.

The Chinese government must accept the fact that there is no way to change the faith of Americans or lessen their concern about religious freedom in other countries. There also is no realistic hope that the U.S. government will support or praise China's traditional approach to religion, no matter how much effort is or will be spent on publicity for marginal improvements.

The U.S. government, though it must reflect the values of Americans, should not package religion as an item on the political agenda and should especially avoid using it for political leverage. Using religion as a tool for political bargaining demeans the very nature of religious values. It may be an effective approach in short-term political bargaining between governments or in dealing with politicians, but it will create a negative impression in the long term. It will lead the Chinese people to conclude that the U.S. government is hypocritical and that human rights are purely utilitarian.

The two countries should be able to maintain a healthy relationship if they set six target goals. First, they will need a long-term approach and a realistic attitude toward their differences, with an appreciation of the important positive role of religion for individuals, both in society and in bilateral relations. Religion is a fundamental issue, and the bilateral gap is large, so contradictions cannot be totally resolved in the short term. Yet with a realistic long view, there is room for movement.

Second, they will need a robust policy framework specifically designed for dealing with differences over religious rights. This framework would be coordinated with the broader human rights dialogue and should carefully and consistently integrate the issue of religion into bilateral cooperation to promote rule-of-law and civil society development. As China persists in legal reform to match international law standards in all fields and begins to encourage development of a nonprofit sector, there could be gradual movement from its current attempts to reform religion to suit state goals toward recognition of religion as an autonomous cultural sphere that warrants protection from political interference.

Third, it will be necessary to establish a specific mechanism for religion in China's Foreign Affairs Ministry to promote greater mutual understanding. The existence of such a mechanism would also help the two nations deal with specific incidents involving religion so as to reduce conflict. For example, in the United States, the Office of International Religious Freedom, a special government organ dealing with religious freedom as a foreign policy issue, has been set up within the State Department. However, there is no such relevant organ in the Foreign Affairs Ministry of the People's Republic of China. Religious affairs are supervised by the Religious Affairs Bureau, which is mainly a domestic agency within the Chinese government. Construction of a complementary dialogue framework should be considered the first step in facilitating dialogue. Such a mechanism could keep crises within bounds so that differences over religion cannot undermine the foundations of the relationship.

Fourth, the effort will require two-track diplomacy. Carrying out dialogue on religious problems between the United States and Chinese governments is a necessary—although insufficient—means of ensuring the normal development of Sino-U.S. relations. In addition, the two governments should encourage and assist the nongovernmental forces of the two countries to establish a dialogue mechanism either together with or parallel to the official one. The nongovernmental actors should include not only leaders of religious organizations but also relevant academic experts and institutions, faith-based nongovernmental organizations, and well-known personages. They should be allowed great flexibility to encompass broad representation. If the dialogue between governments breaks off for whatever reasons, the nongovernmental mechanism could still play a certain role in communication. Establishing a nongovernmental mechanism for dialogue on religion would, by itself, promote the development of civil society in China.

Fifth, the United States will need to provide practical aid to improve the Chinese understanding of the Western attitudes toward freedom of religious expression. China has been receiving a lot of assistance from foreign governments, nongovernmental organizations, and international organizations during the process of establishing legal systems and entering the World Trade Organization. The United States and others have helped China make preparations to meet international standards in the economic fields. In the religious field, the situation might be compared with the early dialogue thirty years ago about environmental protection, when great differences in perceptions existed between China and the West. The U.S. government and nongovernmental forces should begin to help Chinese policymakers understand religion's influence and role in society and provide practical assistance in changing the understanding of religion in both government and society in China.

Finally, independent channels of communication will help mitigate traditional handicaps to understanding. Religion is often viewed both in the United States and in China solely as a private matter to be restricted in its activities in the public realm. Although a government may represent nationals with religious faith or religious organizations in foreign affairs, according to a strict interpretation of the principle of separation of church and state, the U.S. government can express the interests of its religious believers only with regard to nonreligious issues. Meanwhile, it is currently impossible for Chinese religious believers to express themselves freely to the outside world.

Relying solely on the Democracy, Human Rights, and Labor Bureau or the International Religious Freedom Office (both under the U.S. State Department), without the Chinese having heard directly from nongovernmental organizations, will make it difficult for the U.S. government to establish a fruitful dialogue. The Chinese government doubts that the U.S. government is raising religious issues solely in response to the genuine concern of its religious population (the majority) and not out of its own ever-changing national interests. The approach of other Western countries, in which religious exchanges take place only within the official religious groups and through the oversight of the government officials, also tends to politicize religion.

Given these traditional handicaps to understanding, the direct expression of religious believers about their own concerns over religious matters would greatly promote dialogue between governments on religious issues. As China increasingly opens up to other nations of the world, more and more Americans come to China for business, tourism, or other kinds of people-to-people exchanges. American nongovernmental and religious organizations can appeal to various levels of government on both sides—based on the firsthand information about China's religious problems they collect in China—so that both governments can hear the voices of the people. If every U.S. enterprise, chamber of commerce, and nongovernmental organization that has invested resources in China would express to both governments the opinions of religious believers in their own organizations, government dialogue would be promoted. In the future, Chinese believers also will have a more direct voice. If the majority of Americans keep raising concerns over religious issues, and these concerns do not vary with changes of administration or party in power, and if the Americans who come to China to work or to stay raise general concerns regarding China's religious problems stemming from their personal faith rather than from the needs of U.S. domestic politics, then the Chinese government will have to consider more seriously how to respond to the U.S. government's request for dialogue on international freedom of religion and how to deal with China's own religious believers and organizations as important factors in Sino-U.S. relations.

Prospects for Positive Change

In the wake of September 11, there are some signs of growing realism, reflected in the resumption in 2002 of U.S.-China dialogues on human and religious rights. Efforts to define areas of possible antiterrorist cooperation have underscored the importance of religion in domestic and world affairs, and the issue of religion has been a priority in meetings between Presidents Jiang Zemin and George W. Bush. Both sides are actively seeking ways to mitigate friction and find avenues of cooperation in this arena.

Policy Trends in China

From the perspective of future development, the Chinese government's change in religious policies is only a matter of time and opportunity. A new generation of Chinese Communist Party leaders has begun to play their role after the Sixteenth Party Congress and the Tenth National People's

Congress. To demonstrate that they are capable of conducting reform, to prove the correctness of the party's choice of leaders, and to gain the acceptance and support of the Chinese people, new leaders will have to take action on political reform, an arena that for a long time has seen little progress. In preparation for its accession to the World Trade Organization, China has already made efforts to accept international standards in the economic field. There is not much pioneering left in economic reform; there is, however, much room for leaders to make some imprint on history by launching new reform initiatives in social policy and the political field. The need to prepare conditions for hosting the international Olympic Games in 2008 and the need to expand and develop the nonprofit sector in order to transfer more social services to nongovernmental organizations are further incentives. Such key issues to some extent require political reform.

For the time being, the essence of political reform in China is to reduce the extent of the party-state's centralization of power and to weaken the traditional official ideology. Compared with other sensitive political demands—such as demands to allow the freedom of political association, to loosen media controls, or to reform the election system—religion is a relatively easy arena in which to make adjustments. If the party can create a more tolerant atmosphere for religion, it will greatly improve not only China's international image, especially with Western countries, but also the party's relations with the religious public (including ethnic minority groups).

Political elites in China are increasingly paying attention to and discussing religion, reversing their traditional tendency to ignore it altogether. In light of the party-state's continued fragmentation and weakening, coupled with the emergence of a more pluralistic society, there will most likely be increasing differences of approach to religion among the competing interest groups in society. The senior leaders of the Chinese Communist Party are mentally preparing for changes in religious policy. The conservative minority within the party, including the officials responsible for administration of religious affairs, along with the leaders of government-led religious organizations are the main forces whose interests pit them against reform of current policies. There are other key actors, however, with different interests to which top leaders must pay attention. These include provincial and municipal authorities needing help with social services, local religious believers with increasing popularity and resources, and the educated urban middle stratum (including academic and policy experts on religion) who are interested in expanding all civil rights. The de facto loosening of the strict controls on believers' contacts with foreign coreligionists that emerges as society continues to open up fuels a growing awareness of religious rights and expectations of government respect and fair treatment. For all these reasons, efforts to maintain current religious policies will give way to the next generation of leaders' political need to win over the broadest internal and external support.

U.S. Policy Review

Under the Bush administration, Congress appears reluctant to criticize the president's handling of religion in domestic and foreign policy. There are also attempts to find more effective ways of dealing with China by both the U.S. Commission on International Religious Freedom and the Congressional-Executive Commission on China.

Policymakers should understand that Sino-U.S. differences in religious matters will exist for a long time. Taking this into consideration, policymakers within the U.S. government should adopt a long-term perspective and persist in dialogue and exchanges with China with a rational, realistic attitude. When judging and responding to Chinese religious policies and practices, the U.S. government should speak as the voice of the American majority's faith instead of serving a few politicians' utilitarian strategy for their own political interests. In the process of dialogue with China, it is important to make careful distinctions between different regions and cases. Any progress in or efforts made on behalf of religious freedom based on the rule of law and legal construction in China should be evaluated and appreciated with positive public recognition. Simply repeating loudly the general concept and goal of international religious freedom can only make a show with little practical achievement for promoting bilateral understanding on both sides.

Ironically, the attempt to exert pressure through bluster about abstract principles of religious freedom can actually aid Chinese conservatives who reject policy reform. Such bravado mainly serves as evidence of what some Chinese view as a "U.S. government plot" to use religion as a lever for political agendas. U.S. politicians may gain votes from this stance, but it will never be a wise solution that brings about change in China. Given the development of China's economy and its political reform, as well as its accelerated attempt to be a full partner in the international community, a realistic and active approach on the part of both governments will promote significant steps toward reconciling the Sino-U.S. divergence in religious matters.

Notes

1. See Leo P. Ribuffo, "Religion in the History of U.S. Foreign Policy," in Elliott Abrams, ed., *The Influence of Faith: Religious Groups and U.S. Foreign Policy* (Lanham, Md.: Rowman and Littlefield, 2001), pp. 1–32.

2. Peng Liu, "Church and State Relations in China: Characteristics and Trends," *Journal of Contemporary China,* vol. 5 (March 1996), pp. 69–80.

3. Canada, House of Commons, *Debates,* October 24, 2002, vol. 138, no. 014, 10:35.

4. Canada, House of Commons, Statement of the Honorable Scott Reid, citing the release of Bo Qiu, Yang Yueli, Peng Tianxiong, Sun Changzheng, and Huang Guangshou, *Debates,* February 28, 2003, vol. 138, no. 070, 13:30–40.

5. Canada announced in 1997 that it would no longer cosponsor the China resolution before the United Nations Commission on Human Rights. See International Centre for Human Rights and Democratic Development, "The Bilateral Human Rights Dialogue with China: Undermining the International Human Rights Regime," sec. 2 (serveur.ichrdd.ca/english/commdoc/publications/globalization/chinaBilatDialogue.html [November 10, 2003]).

6. Joint Committee on Human Rights, "Religious Freedom Delegation Visited Canada, February 2003," press release issued to the religious press in Canada, March 24, 2003.

7. Lena Larsen, ed., "Report from the Oslo Coalition: Visit to China (21.03—01.04.00)" (www.oslocoalition.org/html/project_china/report_china_visit_2000.html [November 10, 2003]).

8. European Council of Ministers, "Joint Answer to Written Questions P-0444/01 and P-0481/01," *Official Journal* C 340 E, December 4, 2001, p. 30; European Commission, "Answer Given by Mr. Patten on Behalf of the Commission," *Official Journal* C 309 E, December 12, 2002, p. 46.

9. The European Parliament is a notable exception, and its members are often vocally critical of the Chinese. The Parliament is the least powerful of the European institutions in regards to foreign affairs, however, and its direct impact is limited. The members of the European Commission and the Council of Ministers are required to publicly respond to questions posed to them by members of the European Parliament. See note 8 to this chapter, referencing specific responses to questions of European Union parliamentarians.

10

CAROL LEE HAMRIN

Advancing Religious Freedom in a Global China: Conclusions

Most observers of U.S.-China relations view religion, and especially religious freedom, as a recent and contentious bilateral issue. However, tensions between China and the West over religious matters have existed since long before the start of the cold war, and China has had longstanding internal tensions between religion and politics, especially when external actors have been involved. The expulsion of American missionaries after 1949 may have been the single most-important factor in turning U.S. public opinion against China, and the People's Republic of China's continuing attacks on missionary history are an obstacle to change.

Religion has also played a positive role, however, in uniting the two societies at the grassroots level. In the post-Mao era, the toleration of religious practice in China was a significant supporting factor in the renormalization of relations with the West. When China and the United States first negotiated the resumption of formal diplomatic ties in 1979, President Jimmy Carter asked Vice Premier Deng Xiaoping to grant greater freedom to Chinese Christians. Shortly thereafter, at Easter time in 1979, churches began to reopen across China. The warm welcome given families of former missionaries upon return visits to their Chinese hometowns and the rebuilding of religious exchanges have helped renew the unofficial ties that buffer U.S.-China relations from periodic government clashes.

For most of the 1980s, from the Carter through the Reagan administrations, China was not a major target of concern regarding religious and other human rights abuses, despite evidence of them in the State Department's annual worldwide review. The geopolitical cooperation between the

United States and China against the Soviet Union put these and other contentious issues on the back burner. This policy was sustainable only because the American public and its religious leaders perceived that Deng Xiaoping's reform program was heading in the right direction and yielding greater protection for civil rights. Deng and his protégé, party leader Hu Yaobang, formulated a new religious policy in 1982 to serve as a model for other social reforms. Class struggle against religious groups and other "enemies" of communist goals was to give way to "peaceful coexistence" between the party-state and all social groups in the name of patriotic cooperation in pursuit of economic development and other nationalistic goals.

Throughout the 1980s there was a growing appreciation in Chinese society of American values and institutions. Nongovernmental ties between U.S. and Chinese religious groups were becoming an increasingly important factor in the overall bilateral relationship. Foreign religious organizations and faith-based international nongovernmental organizations brought much benefit to China's post-Mao renewal efforts by rebuilding houses of worship, teaching seminarians, supporting social welfare projects, and helping Chinese scholars in the United States.[1] The positive contributions of religious groups to bilateral understanding and cooperation continued to grow in all sectors through the 1990s. Privately, Chinese officials have welcomed and applauded these efforts. Yet rarely have such contributions been noted by the U.S. government or given public acknowledgement by the Chinese government.

It seems logical to ask why there is not a more positive appreciation of the role of religious believers in China and in bilateral relations, either in the United States or in China. Why has religion become a "problem" and religious organizations "troublemakers" in Sino-U.S. relations? Are there policy options that could enhance the potential for faith-based contributions to both religious freedom in China and bilateral cooperation?

The Impact of American Culture Wars on China Policy

In the period immediately following the end of the cold war, the United States developed a secular ideology of globalization that led to major efforts to promote global free trade and political democracy, and in the Clinton era, China was deemed the last major holdout against American-style market economics and democratic politics. Both the U.S. government's human rights policymakers and the human rights nongovernmental organizations tended to give priority to political and labor dissidents—an understandable tendency in the China context in the aftermath of the Tiananmen tragedy of 1989. These secular groups, unconsciously echoing the views of China's leaders, viewed religious rights in the narrow context of ethnic minority issues, such as the preservation of Tibetan culture and the defense of Muslim Uighurs, rather than in the broader context of freedom of religious belief and practice for all Chinese. Religious rights were at best a secondary issue in policy considerations, owing partly to a lack of understanding of the positive causal linkages between religious and sociopolitical development and partly to a thinly veiled disdain for religious belief.

In part as a backlash to this attitude toward religion, the United States in the 1990s experienced an acceleration of interest in politics by Christian cultural conservatives, which influenced not just domestic politics but also related foreign policy issues. James Dobson, the founder of Focus on the Family, was perhaps America's most prominent spokesman for these "family values," along with former Richard Nixon associate Chuck Colson, the chair of the Prison Fellowship Ministries.

Growing concern in the United States over domestic social trends such as legalized abortion and the exclusion of religion from public life began to be projected into foreign policy, at first as single-issue policies but later focused on China policy. For example, Representative Christopher Smith, strongly committed to the antiabortion stance of his Roman Catholic faith, worked hard and successfully to prohibit U.S. funding for China's coercive population policy through the United Nations Population Fund. Representative Frank Wolf joined with Smith in publicizing the Chinese persecution of underground Catholics and house-church Protestants, with whom Wolf, as an evangelical, claimed affinity.[2] These members of Congress were at the center of an expanding bipartisan congressional coalition that came to include Representative Nancy Pelosi, champion of political dissidents, and others who focused on labor rights or Tibetan autonomy.

A key focus of debate and coalition building regarding China was the annual review of most favored nation status (later renamed normal trade relations) for China, required for granting such status to any communist country. The "religious right," so named by their critics for their radical and uncompromising political stances, lobbied the federal government to use tactics of economic pressure and verbal shaming against the Chinese government. Thus, ironically, religious groups that champion limited government at home turned to the U.S. government as the primary defender of religious rights in China. Seemingly unaware of the rapid change under way in China and the presence of many faith-based business, academic, and cultural groups in China, they ignored these groups' potential for direct influence. Reasons for this myopia include the reality that leading think tank activists such as Michael Horowitz, of the Hudson Institute, and Nina Shea, of Freedom House, had more experience in domestic lobbying than in international affairs and that the general public and media remained ignorant of the complex religious situation in China and the extent of faith-based work in China, in part owing to the necessity to maintain a low public profile for such work.

Internal Feuding

There was continual tension in the United States between this relatively radical wing of religious conservatives and a more moderate wing of "new evangelicals" who were actively involved in moral or humanitarian engagement overseas, including leaders of the chief mission agencies and coalitions. The two wings worked together to launch the movement on behalf of the persecuted church, beginning as early as 1992 but hitting the headlines with the release of the National Association of Evangelicals' manifesto on January 23, 1996. Their consensus on the goal did not extend, however, to strategy and tactics, including in regard to China.[3]

During the debates of 1997 and 1998 around most favored nation status for China, for example, there were countervailing lobbying efforts in Congress. On a given day in April or May, one might observe leading spokespersons for cultural conservatives like Dobson and his close associate Gary Bauer, of the Family Research Council, entering a congressional meeting room with political dissidents like Harry Wu, the founder of the Laogai Research Foundation, to argue against granting most favored nation status to China. Coming out the door would be Representative Joe Pitts, who supported most favored nation status for China, with letters from mission leaders in hand and accompanied by like-minded spokespersons for mainland Chinese Christians.

There was further tactical disagreement over the celebration in the United States of the International Day of Prayer for the Persecuted Church. This initiative by the World Evangelical Fellowship, headquartered at the time in Singapore, was intended to raise consciousness on the issues and bring people around the world to prayer and action of various kinds. However, domestic lobbyists, such as Michael Horowitz and others, saw this as a way to generate mainly political action and used the day of prayer as a means of mobilizing backing for international religious freedom (IRF) legislation.[4] Domestic political tactics, including lobbying, appeals to the electorate, and alarmist media portrayal of the problem, which dominated over the method of prayer, proved ineffective and even counterproductive as part of a China policy by fueling Chinese resentment of U.S. moralistic "preaching."

The U.S. government human rights policymakers and the human rights nongovernmental organizations viewed with suspicion, if not hostility, the sudden emergence of the issue of the persecution of Christians, rightly stressing that such concern should extend to all religious believers. Meanwhile, reaction by Protestants and Catholics was also split between groups such as the National Council of Churches and the U.S. Catholic China Bureau, which were willing to work with the Chinese government and the officially authorized religious organizations, and others such as Voice of the Martyrs and the Cardinal Kung Foundation, which sought to be the "voice for the voiceless"—Protestant house churches or underground Catholics. Because of this polarization regarding religion in China, the United States was never able to adopt and sustain the European approach (documented in chapter 9 of this volume). Lack of consensus also meant that conflicting messages were received by the government of the People's Republic of China.

Direct Engagement

Ironically, it was the U.S. government that got religious groups directly involved in advocacy for international religious freedom. The Clinton administration's first response to advocates was to deflect their attacks with measures that gave them a voice but not genuine power. This included the creation in 1996 of an Advisory Committee on Religious Freedom Abroad and a special representative on international religious freedom, with a tiny budget and staff buried in the midlevels of the Department of State, where they remain under the Bush administration.

After the Washington summit in October 1997, President Bill Clinton also extended the personal invitation of President Jiang Zemin to three prominent religious leaders to visit China in early 1998. The White House helped organize and raise funds for the visit. The chosen leaders were representatives from prominent groups in the Jewish, Roman Catholic, and Protestant traditions that were raising the issue of persecution.[5] The religious leaders' six-city visit included a stop in Tibet and raised high-level and midlevel Chinese attention to religious rights abuses. For example, Shanghai officials responsible for foreign affairs privately admitted to surprise and shock when they were exposed to facts about the backwardness of their "model" city in this area.

Unfortunately, neither the political nor the religious sector conducted much coordinated and structured follow-up to take advantage of this rare entry at the top, although the religious leaders individually made some sporadic efforts to build on their new contacts in China. Sustained cooperative engagement might well have helped limit recent abuses in China and would have better represented the internationalist preference of thousands of American Christian organizations involved in ministry and social services in China.[6]

Instead, throughout the year 1998, personal scandal leading to the effort to impeach the president further inflamed and polarized debate about China policy, especially its religious freedom and human rights components. The positive atmosphere created for Clinton's state visit to China that June moderated the attacks only for a brief period. As the presidential election year of 2000 loomed closer, "China bashing" became more and more "Clinton bashing" by another name. Michael Horowitz, who had served in the government under President Ronald Reagan, was a key figure in linking the several wings of evangelicals with Jewish leaders and media figures, such as Abe Rosenthal of the *New York Times*, as well as with other former "Reaganauts" who have come to be known collectively as neoconservatives, such as Elliott Abrams, John Bolton, and Jeane Kirkpatrick, then the U.S. ambassador to the United Nations.

In the highly politicized atmosphere of the late 1990s, the contradictions within the movement for international religious freedom became acrimonious and plagued the creation of IRF legislation and the setting up of the U.S. Commission on International Religious Freedom in 1998. These same contradictions continue to hinder IRF policy in the Bush administration.[7] Horowitz was the primary author of the Freedom from Religious Persecution bill, less formally known as the Wolf-Specter bill, which was introduced in Congress in May 1997 but became bogged down in committee until the next May, when it was passed by the House of Representatives. When it became apparent that the Senate and the White House would never move the bill further, a group of congressional staffers, led by John Hanford, from Senator Richard Lugar's office, who had long worked on the persecution issue quietly and behind the scenes, took the initiative to draft an alternative, more moderate bill. In March 1998 their

International Religious Freedom Act, also known as the Nickles-Lieberman bill, was introduced in the Senate and, after months of negotiation with the administration, was passed in October. By that time the bill had earned broad support from religious groups along the whole spectrum of politics, with the exception of liberal Protestants.[8]

The two bills were quite different in tone: Wolf-Specter reflected a tendency toward isolating the perpetrators of extreme cases of persecution, whereas the International Religious Freedom Act reflected a desire to spread religious freedom more broadly. Specifically, the International Religious Freedom Act included a focus on changing governmental behavior both in the United States and overseas rather than solely punishing persecution. The focus was on strengthening rather than undermining or bypassing international organizations, avoiding any hierarchy of religious rights over other rights, and addressing concerns about special pleading for Christianity over other religions.[9]

The International Religious Freedom Act upgraded the special representative on international religious freedom to an ambassador-at-large, with an office in the State Department and an annual reporting requirement. The act also established an independent U.S. Commission on International Religious Freedom to monitor the issue and advise the government. The first ambassador, appointed in May 1999, was Robert Seiple, who, as the former president of World Vision International—the world's largest faith-based relief and development agency—represented the more internationalist wing of evangelicals.[10]

Following these successful efforts to institutionalize the concern about international religious freedom as an integral part of the U.S. foreign policy agenda in late 1998 and the failure to impeach the president in February 1999, the steam seemed to go out of the IRF movement as religious conservatives began to rethink the efficacy of legislating morality. In May 2000 the focal point of the annual debate on most favored nation status disappeared with the granting of permanent normal trade relations status to China. The political compromise included yet another mechanism for monitoring human rights—the Congressional-Executive Commission on China.

The strong desire among American religious conservatives for change abroad made them potential supporters of the faith-based U.S. and international organizations on the ground in China that were actively promoting and supporting social and cultural change there. The attempt to use the U.S. government as a bullhorn, however, turned the U.S.-China dialogue into a dissonant exchange—with little effect on China other than to feed the mind-set growing among the Chinese people that the Americans were against them.

A Resurgence of Chinese Nationalism Targeting the United States

Social sentiment in China that viewed U.S. frontal attacks on rights abuses as self-interested hostility toward the Chinese nation and people, not just the government, was spurred by the disastrous results of "shock therapy" in Russia and bolstered the regime's continued repression of liberal democratic thought. In the 1990s China experienced a confluence of state promotion of authoritarian nationalism and disillusionment among the intellectual elite with the democratic idealism of the 1980s. There is a widespread awareness in China that economic collapse and national disintegration have followed the collapse of communism and other authoritarian regimes, and that outcome is something all Chinese want to avoid. The U.S. moral crusade appeared oblivious, at best, to this concern and intentionally subversive, at worst. This alienated urban Chinese, especially the younger generations, and put progressive reformers on the defensive. Mutual ill will helped produce broad elite support for a pragmatic but illiberal "neoauthoritarian" program in China.

A search was under way among the social elite for a new path to modernization, one better suited to Chinese tradition than either Soviet-style communism or American democratic capitalism. Cultural nationalism surfaced, as reflected in the New Confucianism and talk of "Asian values."[11] The state sought to manage the globalization process for its own ends, and the influx of Western culture inspired intellectuals to search for the roots of Chinese culture and traditions to forge an alternate Chinese identity. One policy researcher even proposed the resurrection of Confucianism as a state religion—an idea that fell on deaf ears, given the rapid pluralization of culture and religion already well under way in China.[12]

Politically, while the state preferred Asian authoritarian models like Singapore's, more liberal intellectuals looked to European social democratic models, such as the New Labor Party's "Third Way" in the United Kingdom. It was no longer politically or socially acceptable to propose the U.S. model in planning for reforms. As a result of this anti-American trend among the elite, China's leaders paid no domestic political penalty when it froze the U.S.-China religious and human rights dialogues through 1999 until late 2001 in protest over several bilateral political-military crises and the U.S. promotion of resolutions on China's rights abuses in each annual session of the United Nations Commission on Human Rights.

Windfall Gains for the Chinese Communist Party

In this context, the U.S. government's effort to confront the central government in China over a number of issues, including religious and human rights abuses, ironically helped strengthen the regime and prolong its life as the "defender" of Chinese national interests against American "bullying." The theme of vigilance against alleged U.S. efforts to Westernize, divide, and weaken China was pervasive in internal government communications, especially in the security sector. During the increasingly harsh "strike hard" anticrime campaigns, the government was not only fighting crime and cults but was also secretly watching for "hostile elements." This included the search for unregistered but orthodox Catholics and Protestants with "illegal" foreign ties and for "hostile infiltrators" in the business and academic worlds, including American foundations working in China.[13]

China's heavy-handed approach to religion in the late 1990s reflected a legitimacy crisis after the collapse of European communism and a growing insecurity about rapidly changing state-society relations. With the development of the economy and wider access to information, the old means of social control—party patronage through a monopoly on resources and enforcement of ideological conformity—gradually eroded. The government put new mechanisms into place to regulate all nongovernmental, nonprofit organizations—mechanisms, enforced by fines, bans, and arrests, that are marked by corruption and abuse of power and have resulted in an unequal playing field for social actors. Although the Chinese government favors indigenous religions and is relatively lenient toward charitable work and even consumer or environmental advocacy, it tightly controls religious, labor, political, and youth organizing.

Blowback to Globalization

China's suspicion of religion stems in part from a legitimate concern about the dark side of globalization. A warning bell sounded for policymakers in late 1997 when the Asian financial crisis contributed to a flagging economic growth rate and produced a rise in unemployment, a surge in the income gap, and an explosion of social disturbances. The collapse of the

Russian economy in 1998, and later of Indonesia's sociopolitical order, gave Chinese leaders cold feet, and movement on social and political reform ceased. In addition, the rapid expansion of the Falungong spiritual movement presented the governing structure with a problem it was ill equipped to handle—the worldwide spread of new religions or spiritual movements that combine aspects of traditional folk religion with postmodern means of networking and communication, attracting mass followings. Thus in 1999 China's final steps toward joining the World Trade Organization coincided with an upsurge in social tensions, including a burst of activity by millennial movements preaching catastrophe.

These developments, combined with preparation for the selection of new party successors and policies for the next five years, highlighted the short-term risks involved in reforms related to China's membership in the World Trade Organization, despite the promise of long-term gain. Fixated on fears of social and political instability, the government took a step backward in social policy reminiscent of China's long tradition of intolerance in the face of foreign intrusion. Instead of initiating legislation to protect civil rights—the logical next step in creating the rule of law—there has been an attempt to resurrect party as well as police controls over social groups. Formal reinterpretations of the criminal law and harsh anticrime campaigns have made outlaws of groups that refuse to go along. There has been political interference in religious doctrine—the promotion of "prosocialist" theological reform—and the condemnation of religious dissenters as promoters of heretical cults, separatists, or even terrorists. Banning groups justifies their total eradication. Critics of these policies are labeled unpatriotic and therefore antigovernment or even threats to national security.

The anti-infiltration campaign is clearly intended to keep the Chinese social structure in quarantine even as the economy opens up. Even reformers in the government are looking to Europe for guidance, especially to France, for ways to shore up state-backed monopoly religious organizations and outlaw new religions as cults. This approach reflects both China's historic statist tradition and the modern pre-1949 Chinese legal and judicial structure, which is more continental than Anglo-American in origin.

Fears of foreign intrusion combine with insecurity over internal state-society relations to fuel the state's ambition to monitor and constrain all unsanctioned organizational activity and to counter a resurgence in China of both local and international identities. This conservative approach, however, sets China on a collision course with global trends toward social and cultural pluralism and the rapid growth of religion, especially new religious movements. These trends are too powerful for China to stifle or ignore.

Prospects for Change:
Religion Moves up on the International Agenda

The September 11, 2001, terrorist attacks on the Pentagon and New York's World Trade Center towers sobered the leaders and citizens of China as well as the United States. The salience of religion in national security, not just in diplomacy, became immediately obvious to all. Just a few months later, at a previously planned work conference on religious affairs held in Beijing, President Jiang Zemin stressed that religion is here to stay as an important issue affecting all societies and international relations.[14] One positive result of the media coverage of the conference was the demise of a long-standing taboo against public discussion of religion in today's China. Previously, scholars and the media had been allowed to discuss religion only as it pertained to other countries or to other time periods in China. The implication from most media coverage since the conference, however, has been that religion is still a problem, an even bigger one than was thought, outweighing any positive elements. In the United States, too, there is much more attention to religious conflict and its dangers than before.

This shock at first tended to bring the two countries together, as both sides tried to address the new imperative of cooperation against global terrorism. Immediately after the September attack President Bush seized the chance to improve relations with Russia and China, and in his 2002 State of the Union address he spoke of "a common danger easing old rivalries . . . to achieve peace and prosperity"—themes that the Chinese could welcome. Yet President Bush posited other themes less favorable to the People's Republic of China, including new programs to fight tyranny and to counter a "frame of mind that fosters hate, including hating Christianity."[15]

The war on terrorism, followed by the Iraq war, greatly complicated the IRF equation in U.S.-China relations. On one hand, the United States was reluctant to give carte blanche to the Chinese regarding the crackdown on Muslim extremists in China's Far West, even though at least one small group of separatists was deemed to fall into the category of international terrorists. On the other hand, Chinese suspicion of the long-term strategic intentions of the U.S. military presence in Afghanistan and Central Asia was greatly heightened by the advent of the Bush doctrine of preemptive war and regime change, which appeared to put North Korea a close second behind Iraq on the list of enemy states.

U.S. policy toward China is under pressure from two extreme approaches to the religion issues, either of which would be mistaken. Some experts on foreign affairs and on China have proposed a resurrection of the early 1980s U.S.-China protoalliance against a common enemy to dissolve the animosity of recent years. If there were such a single-minded focus on combating "religious extremism," however, domestic security and national security officials in both countries would dominate policymaking with their worst-case scenarios. Yet an alternative of promoting education and antipoverty efforts to prevent extremism—based on purely secular values and slighting the importance of religion—would also be a mistake. It could even be counterproductive if it fueled fundamentalism against such "modernity."

New Thinking about Religion in International Circles

Worry about the negative potential for radical religious movements must be balanced by recognition of the positive and essential role religion can play in modern (and postmodern) societies. Decisionmakers in the United States need to absorb the foreign policy implications of recent research concerning the positive role that religion plays in creating a civil society able to sustain economic development and promote democratic political development. One scholar outlines the largely unrecognized but resounding success of past Wilsonian (idealist) foreign policies in the United States in support of faith-based (missionary) and secular (philanthropic) activities overseas, which he credits with the creation of today's expanding global civil society. Others highlight the important role of religion in conflict resolution and peacemaking.[16]

Scholarly insights from all the social sciences posit a major role for the interplay of sociology and economics. Nonprofit organizations, especially religious associations, proliferated in the 1990s and have become partners with the state in providing social services. Greater regulatory attention to nonprofits in the wake of financial scandals and their misuse of funds to bankroll terrorists is both necessary and proper, but this underscores rather than denigrates their importance. There is now a budding awareness, including among the Chinese elite, that a successful capitalist democracy is far more than a country with markets and elections, that a vibrant civil society is the necessary "third leg" of the overall structure.[17]

In concert with this broader rethinking of religion, human rights experts are realizing that the freedom of religion and belief is essential, not peripheral, in human rights advocacy and diplomacy, given its function as the conceptual and historical source of many other individual and associational rights.[18] Social scientists are finding that social virtues, usually based in religion, function as social capital and are the essential cultural glue of successful societies.[19] Protestant charismatic and evangelical movements, in promoting individual choice and voluntary association, have been indirect but important catalysts for transition from traditional authoritarianism to democratic modernity worldwide. The Roman Catholic Church has also contributed to the latest historic wave of peaceful democratic transitions in Latin America and Eastern Europe.[20]

Practical Incentives for a More Positive Chinese View

Economic globalization brings with it many powerful motivations for Chinese leaders to explore new mechanisms for state-society and political-religious relations.[21] There are practical rewards for a state that promotes new ways of accommodating religious pluralism and tolerance rather than repressing proselytizing to prevent growth of religion through conversion. There can be payoffs in sustaining development, protecting national security, and promoting peaceful political change as well as eliciting international approval. These need to be explored within the bilateral dialogue on international religious freedom to encourage their incorporation into Chinese religious policy.

Some Chinese leaders are now beginning to realize that to be truly competitive in the global economy, China will have to pursue a number of goals. First, attracting the highly educated and creative professionals and managers who are in great demand in the global market will be essential. This will require reform of China's educational system as well as provision of an environment protective of civil liberties that can reverse China's brain drain and attract other professionals overseas. Religious freedom is especially important given the great numbers of overseas Chinese and returning citizens of the People's Republic who have a faith commitment. Second, China will need to spur the growth of its third sector, the nonprofit sector, including domestic and international faith-based organizations, to gain more resources for development.

Third, public morality will need to be rebuilt by engaging rapidly growing religious groups in ways that promote moderation and cooperation, not extremism and religious warfare. Debates on corruption in China have focused on the need for honesty, altruism, and trust, which can only be built on the basis of respect for minority interests and rights, including religious practices. Both social capital and personal significance must come from the grass roots, through learning how to work together in voluntary organization, and not from the top down, through state-sponsored ethics campaigns. Finally, China must seek constructive and peaceful ways of conciliation with democratizing Taiwan and Hong Kong and better protection of religious and human rights as part of that process.

Alternative Policy Prescriptions

The further opening up of Chinese society and politics in the next decade offers an array of new U.S. policy options to move beyond current reactive and sporadic efforts on behalf of international religious freedom. Creating a sustainable religious rights policy that promotes steady progress toward the rule of law in church-state relations in China will require a sophisticated coordination of short-term and long-term approaches. Critical publicity and advocacy must continue to address immediate egregious abuses; at the same time, there should be long-term engagement to promote cultural tolerance and institutional change. This engagement must come from networking with groups that have a stake in human rights protection, both inside and outside of China and at all levels and in all sectors of society. Actors in the United States should consciously plan to incorporate religious freedom goals into persistent engagement activities with rising forces in China—new generations, new social and economic elites, and grassroots social groups, all of which will increasingly be interacting directly with outsiders.

This multifaceted approach will be far more effective than political and economic pressures aimed solely at the top of the system. Blanket condemnation of the Chinese central government for religious rights abuses has had limited utility since as early as 1994, when trade and human rights issues were effectively separated. Continued wrangling over foreign policy priorities within the ranks of political conservatives is a distraction from the job at hand.[22] China has become too complex and the central government too limited in its reach for real change to come from the top down. There is a window of opportunity before the 2008 Beijing Olympics for a more nuanced U.S. policy to align with the growing domestic consciousness of

Chinese rights and expectations for democratization under new leaders. Following are some suggested guidelines for a more effective policy.

First, domestic consensus in the United States can be built by revising assumptions and expectations. Until there is evidence of a strong IRF policy consensus in the United States, backed by the American public, China will have little incentive to meet U.S. demands or expectations. To build consensus, Americans need to better understand the facts of the situation on the ground in China. There is rapid change beneath China's surface appearance of rigid authoritarianism; younger officials and policy advisers are interested in new approaches to modern, accountable, and nonideological governance. They want practical solutions to the problems they face. Meanwhile, expectations for overnight improvements in human rights should give way to understanding the long-term nature of cultural change. There are highly negative as well as positive social trends under way: corruption and authoritarianism infect both official religious circles and unauthorized religious groups. Neither should be viewed through rose-tinted glasses.

The goal and outcome of change in China will most likely not be an American-style society. The strong Chinese tradition of state control of religion, as illustrated in chapter 2 of this volume, as well as its pre-1949 legal structure and heritage, suggest that China will follow other statist models, whether European or Asian, in the initial stages of building democracy.

Second, the United States should focus on provincial and sectoral decisionmakers. One key element of any policy revision should be to create local incentive structures that reward positive behavior as well as sanction abuses. Beijing city officials, for example, are already improving religious facilities and researching Olympics' requirements and precedents in providing for the religious needs of athletes and spectators. Technical assistance could help create new policy precedents.

The single most-effective initiative would be to organize monitoring and reporting of both abuses and improvements in rights practices at the level of provinces and their capitals. Given the serious need and desire for foreign resources of all types in China, this would engender the dynamics of competition and transparency that are so evident in other sectors.

The whole array of U.S. government programs could be used to reward certifiable progress. At the same time, giving businesses, tourists, or nonprofits the information they need to invest—or disinvest—in certain geographic areas would add a rights component to their risk analysis. The same logic would pertain to the further development of bilateral "sister-state" and "sister-city" ties. To protect their own interests, outsiders would prefer to work with progressive officials who abide by international standards. Thus the natural consequences from failing to meet international standards—unofficial and informal local "boycotts"—would be much more effective than threatening, but never using, the blunt instrument of a U.S.-China trade war.

Bilateral governmental interaction will need to be restructured. An effective policy must begin with widespread public recognition of the properly limited role of the federal government in IRF work and the strong potential role of nonstate actors. Given the historical memory of "gunboat diplomacy" and "cultural imperialism" (partly myth and partly fact) in the Chinese public mind, unilateral political pressure will continue to be counterproductive. Several structural changes would serve to make government efforts more effective. Dialogue on international religious freedom requires counterpart organizations in the U.S. State Department and the Chinese Foreign Ministry that can communicate regularly about concerns and questions both large and small and expand into track-two exchanges that include more voices from social groups affected (see chapter 9 in this volume).

Religion needs to be thoroughly integrated into existing U.S.-China programming in democracy, human rights, and the rule of law, including public diplomacy and foreign assistance. These programs should be depoliticized, or they will merely fortify barriers to progress. Religious freedom issues should also be incorporated carefully into cooperation on countering terrorism. To make fundamental gains against global terrorism, China and the United States need to work together on the causes as well as the symptoms of a backlash against globalization. One defense analyst has pointed out the need to fight terrorist networks with antiterrorist networks rather than with traditional warfare, proposing that such networking against terrorism should center on "fostering a global civil society that promotes democracy and protects human rights."[23] Religious freedom is the best antidote to religious extremism, for such freedom contributes to the construction of social justice and national security—two sides of the same coin. Those countries that actively promote freedom of religion make the best allies against terrorism.[24]

It would be worthwhile to explore a new initiative to conduct dialogue on domestic issues arising from globalization. Allen Choate, of the Asia Foundation, has offered creative suggestions for a U.S.-China dialogue on common domestic policy concerns that would go beyond the language of individual rights to include community responsibility and the exercise of citizenship.[25] Any such programs that address social reforms should include the promotion of sustainable religious freedom and societywide religious tolerance.

Third, independent business and nonprofit initiatives should be encouraged. Businesses and nonprofit organizations, including faith-based organizations, need to assume more responsibility for the health of the bilateral relationship. Nongovernmental diplomacy, such as business initiatives, might well be more effective than state efforts in addressing concerns about international religious freedom. Ironically, IRF activists who accuse the U.S. government of favoring profit over principle have done little thus far to influence business, educational, or media leaders or even mission agencies and faith-based nonprofits to use their considerable presence and influence in China to improve the rights and conditions of believers there.

Such nongovernmental efforts should be made aware of, and where possible work in tandem with, transnational Chinese business, educational, philanthropic, and religious networks. Chinese churches and temples are filled with highly educated clergy and lay professionals with family members scattered globally who regularly interact with counterparts in China. Chinese religious networks help open up the market for values and ideas, along with goods and services. A new modern Chinese cultural identity is being constructed among the diaspora. In American West Coast cities, for example, up to one-third of the Chinese population belongs to independent nondenominational Protestant churches.[26]

Finally, cooperation with regional and international religious rights agencies and initiatives should be strengthened, and international, not American, norms emphasized. Positive Chinese response to any outside effort would be easier to mobilize and justify if it were not primarily an American initiative. Chinese citizens have high expectations for China to become accepted as a "normal," responsible member of the global society of nations. As China becomes integrated into the global community, the World Trade Organization sets a precedent for allowing limits on sovereignty in order to conform to international norms in noneconomic arenas, from nonproliferation to human rights. The United States should coordinate consistently with other countries' efforts and take the lead in reshaping multilateral efforts. Specifically, the United States might explore the application to Asia of the model of the Organization for Security and Cooperation in Europe, which links regional security and human rights, and find ways to restructure United Nations human rights mechanisms to become more effective in advancing religious freedom worldwide.

Conclusion

The escalation of China bashing in the United States in the 1990s was met with equally strong America bashing in China. In both countries, the end of the cold war with the collapse of European communism fostered an identity crisis and focused internal politics on issues of cultural identity. The search for new core values led each to stereotype the other as a potential adversary; one might even say there was a "clash of identities" between the American celebration of the systemic victory over communism and the Chinese hubris in expectation of regaining a "rightful" historic status as a major world civilization and power. This dynamic has fueled a dangerous negative cycle, and it needs to be addressed by creative leadership on both sides to reshape public opinion.

Fortunately, there are trends regarding the issue of religious freedom that could be used to help break out of the negative cycle in relations. The global downsizing of government and the rapid growth of the nonprofit sector in the 1990s led to a new understanding in the United States that faith-based institutions are central, not peripheral, actors in society. Meanwhile, China is experiencing a wave of interest in the role of the third sector and in how to develop a healthy society, which has led to a revived interest in the American model and openness to contributions from faith-based nonprofits. New awareness of the benefits of partnership among business, government, and nonprofit sectors has begun to replace more simplistic assumptions, both in the United States and China, about oppositional relations between state and society. These new dynamics, if used to explore areas of common interest and build public and international opinion behind win-win solutions, could foster the growth of religious freedom in China.

Notes

1. Carol Lee Hamrin, "Faith-Based Organizations: Invisible Partners in Developing Chinese Society," paper presented at the Issues Roundtable conference, To Serve the People: NGOs and the Development of Civil Society in China, Congressional-Executive Commission on China, March 24, 2003 (www.cecc.gov/pages/roundtables/032403/Hamrin.php [November 7, 2003]).

2. Smith and Wolf made their first visit to China in 1991 (Smith returned in January 1994), during which they had polite but tense exchanges with a number of Chinese officials, linking continuation of most favored nation status for China with the

issues of coerced abortions and sterilizations, prisoners of conscience and religion, prison labor exports, and the rights of the unregistered church. For further information on the 1991 visit, see Wolf's report of his trip to the People's Republic of China, *Congressional Record*, vol. 137, no. 62, daily ed. (April 25, 1991), p. H2557, and Smith's report of his trip, *Congressional Record*, vol. 137, no. 62, daily ed. (April 25, 1991), p. H2560–63. For information on the 1991 and 1994 visits by another member of the delegation, see Steve Snyder, president of International Christian Concern, "Statement Concerning Revocation of Most Favored Nation to China," paper presented in the United States Capitol, June 5, 1997 (www.persecution.org/whitepapers/mfnchina.html [November 7, 2003]). By the mid-1990s, Smith and Wolf had become persona non grata in China and were unable to get visas; Wolf made a secret trip to Tibet in 1997, using a tourist passport. See U.S. Rep. Frank R. Wolf, "Tibet: A First-Hand Look, August 9–13, 1997" (www.house.gov/wolf/issues/hr/trips/Tibet08-1997.pdf [November 7, 2003]).

3. Telephone conversation with Richard Cizik, director of the National Association of Evangelicals' Washington office, Washington, D.C., February 15, 2002. Cizik's former associate Brian O'Connell launched the Religious Liberty Commission for the World Evangelical Fellowship in 1992; at a later conference on the topic, held in the United Kingdom, delegates from the third world asked that something be done on behalf of the persecuted. An ensuing day of prayer for Iran sparked the idea for the International Day of Prayer for the Persecuted Church in the minds of O'Connell and World Evangelical Fellowship director Dwight Gibson, who proposed it to the National Association of Evangelicals, along with John Corts of the Billy Graham Evangelistic Association.

4. Telephone conversations with Dwight Gibson, Washington, D.C., February 3, 2002, and June 7, 2003, recalling strategy meetings on the day of prayer involving Horowitz, Shea, Bauer, Colson, Bill Bright of Campus Crusade, and Richard Land of the Southern Baptists. Gibson made the point that different groups tend to favor different types of action, all of them valid: prayer, politics aimed at elites, social reforms aimed at building middle-class civil society, and grassroots humanitarian assistance.

5. Appeal of Conscience Foundation, "Initiatives in China" (see www.appealofconscience.org/initiatives/china.htm [November 7, 2003]). The leaders were Rabbi Arthur Schneier, the president of the Appeal of Conscience Foundation; Theodore McCarrick, the Roman Catholic archbishop of Newark, representing the Conference of Catholic Bishops; and the Reverend Don Argue, the president of the National Association of Evangelicals and an Assemblies of God minister, who presented a Bible to Jiang Zemin during their visit. They were accompanied by the Reverend Richard Cizik, of the National Association of Evangelicals' Office for Governmental Affairs, who had served in missions in Taiwan, and Brent Fulton, the managing director of the Institute of Chinese Studies at Wheaton College, which served as a clearinghouse of information and networking for evangelical ministries involved in China. The National Council of Churches bitterly contested the National Association of Evangelicals' participation in the trip, because for decades it has viewed itself as the traditional "representative" of Protestantism in global affairs. However, the council's reputation for being uncritically friendly to China's religious establishment worked against it in the political context of the day.

6. See Nicholas D. Kristof, "International Aid, for Heaven's Sake," *International Herald Tribune,* May 22, 2002, for rare objective secular press coverage of the growing international involvement of the evangelical movement.

7. T. Jeremy Gunn, "The United States and the Promotion of Freedom of Religion and Belief," in Tore Lindholm, W. Cole Durham Jr., and Bahia G. Tahzib-Lie, eds., *Facilitating Freedom of Religion or Belief: A Deskbook* (Netherlands: Kluwer Law International, 2001), pp. 161–88. For continuing polemics on the issue of international religious freedom during the Bush administration, see the exchange between Ambassador Robert Seiple, Michael Horowitz, and T. Jeremy Gunn (who worked for Seiple at the State Department), in Robert A. Seiple, "The USCIRF Is Only Cursing the Darkness" (www.christianitytoday.com/ct/2002/140/31.0.html [November 7, 2003]); Michael Horowitz, "Cry Freedom," *Christianity Today,* vol. 47 (March 2003), pp. 48–51; and T. Jeremy Gunn, "Full of Sound and Fury," *Christianity Today,* vol. 47 (March 2003), pp. 51–54.

8. Allen D. Hertzke, "The Political Sociology of the Crusade against Religious Persecution," in Elliott Abrams, ed., *The Influence of Faith: Religious Groups and U.S. Foreign Policy* (Lanham, Md.: Rowman and Littlefield, 2001), pp. 69–94.

9. John Hanford, Steve Moffitt, Laura Bryant, and William Inboden, "The International Religious Freedom Act (IRFA): A View from Congress," in Rosalind I. J. Hackett, Mark Silk, and Dennis Hoover, eds., *Religious Persecution as a U.S. Policy Issue: Proceedings of a Consultation* (Hartford, Conn.: Trinity College, Center for the Study of Religion in Public Life, 2000), pp. 7–17.

10. Activists from 1998 have been prominent in these new mechanisms. Rabbi David Saperstein and Elliott Abrams became, respectively, the commission's first and the second chairman; Nina Shea and Archbishop McCarrick were members. John Hanford became the second ambassador-at-large for international religious freedom.

11. Liu Qingfeng, "The Topography of Intellectual Culture in 1990s Mainland China: A Survey," in Gloria Davies, ed., *Voicing Concerns: Contemporary Chinese Critical Inquiry* (Lanham, Md.: Rowman and Littlefield, 2001), pp. 47–70.

12. Kang Xiaoguang, "Wenhua minzu zhuyi lungang" [On cultural nationalism], *Zhanlue yu guanli* [Strategy and management], vol. 2 (March 1, 2003), pp. 9–27.

13. See China, Department of Public Security of Anhui Province, "The Bulletin of the Department of Anhui Public Security" (March 6, 2001), in Li Shixiong and Xiqui (Bob) Fu, eds. and trans., *Religion and National Security in China: Secret Documents from China's Security Sector* (Bartlesville, Okla.: Voice of the Martyrs, 2002), p. 40–70.

14. See chapter 4, this volume.

15. "The State of the Union Address by the President of the United States," *Congressional Record,* vol. 148, no. 1, daily ed. (January 29, 2002), pp. H98–H101.

16. See, generally, Walter Russell Mead, *Special Providence: American Foreign Policy and How It Changed the World* (Knopf, 2002); Douglas Johnston and Cynthia Sampson, eds., *Religion: The Missing Dimension of Statecraft* (Oxford University Press, 1994).

17. Lester M. Salamon, in his introduction to *America's Nonprofit Sector: A Primer* (New York: Foundation Center, 1999) and in his other writings, has inspired social theorists and nongovernmental activists in China, where he is a popular speaker.

18. On the importance of religious rights in protecting other rights, see John Witte Jr. and Johan D. van der Vyver, eds., *Religious Human Rights in Global Perspective: Religious Perspectives* (Boston: Martinus Nijhoff, 1996), pp. xvii–xxxv, 1–46, 455–84.

19. For the linkage between religious values and socioeconomic development, see Lawrence E. Harrison and Samuel P. Huntington, eds., *Culture Matters: How Values Shape Human Progress* (Basic, 2000); and Francis Fukuyama, *Trust: The Social Virtues and the Creation of Prosperity* (Free Press Paperbacks, 1995).

20. Peter Berger terms evangelicalism one of the most dynamic global cultures, but along with Huntington he also credits the "new" Roman Catholicism for its contributions. See Peter L. Berger and Samuel P. Huntington, eds., introduction to *Many Globalizations: Cultural Diversity in the Contemporary World* (Oxford University Press, 2002), pp. 1–16.

21. In 2000 a researcher in the Chinese Communist Party's United Front Work Department called for a rethinking of the "delicate relations between religion and politics," given that "everything in the world is moving in the direction of pluralism," as reported in a commentary by Peter J. Barry, *Asia Focus* (newsweekly from the Union of Catholic Asian News-UCAN, Hong Kong), vol. 18 (January 11, 2002), p. 3.

22. For complaints by activists for international religious freedom about the Bush administration's handling of the issue in the wake of September 11, see Rachel Zoll, "Protecting Persecution?" Associated Press, January 30, 2002; for criticism of the record of the Commission on International Religious Freedom, see Patricia Zapor, "Religious Rights Commission Needs Sharper Role, Critics Say," Catholic News Service, May 16, 2002.

23. John Arquilla, "Terrorism: It Takes a Network," *Los Angeles Times*, August 25, 2002.

24. Telephone conversation with Tom Farr, director of the International Religious Freedom Office, Department of State, Washington, D.C., February 5, 2002.

25. Allen C. Choate, "Building Trust in the United States–China Relationship," Working Paper 4 (San Francisco: Asia Foundation, October 1997).

26. See Yang Fenggang, conclusion to *Chinese Christians in America: Conversion, Assimilation, and Adhesive Identities* (Pennsylvania State University Press, 1999), pp. 186–200.

Suggested Reading

Religion Policy in the People's Republic of China

Anagnost, Ann S. "Politics and Magic in Contemporary China." *Modern China*, vol. 13 (January 1987), pp. 40–61.

Chan, Kim-kwong. "A Chinese Perspective on the Interpretation of the Chinese Government's Religious Policy." In Alan Hunter and Don Rimmington, eds., *All under Heaven: Chinese Tradition and Christian Life in the People's Republic of China*, pp. 38–44. Kampen, Netherlands: J. H. Kok, 1992.

Kindopp, Jason. "China's War on 'Cults.'" *Current History*, vol. 101 (September 2002), pp. 259–66.

MacInnis, Donald E. *Religion in China Today: Policy and Practice*. Maryknoll, N.Y.: Orbis, 1989.

Madsen, Richard, and James Tong, eds. "Local Religious Policy in China, 1980–1997." Special issue, *Chinese Law and Government*, vol. 33 (May–June 2000).

Spiegel, Mickey, and James Tong, eds. "Documents on Religion in China: Central Government Policy." Special issue, *Chinese Law and Government*, vol. 33 (March–April 2000).

The Church in China before 1949

Bays, Daniel H., ed. *Christianity in China: From the Eighteenth Century to the Present.* Stanford University Press, 1996.

Cary-Elwes, Iris Columba. *China and the Cross: A Survey of Missionary History.* New York: P. J. Kenedy and Sons, 1957.

Cohen, Paul A. *China and Christianity: The Missionary Movement and the Growth of Chinese Antiforeignism, 1860–1870.* Harvard University Press, 1963.

Fairbank, John K., ed. *The Missionary Enterprise in China and America, 1880–1950.* Grand Rapids, Mich.: Eerdmans, 1976.

Gernet, Jacques. *China and the Christian Impact: A Conflict of Cultures.* Translated by Janet Lloyd. Cambridge University Press, 1985.

Wiest, Jean-Paul. *Maryknoll in China: A History, 1918–1955.* Armonk, N.Y.: M. E. Sharpe, 1988.

The Church in China since 1949

Bush, Richard C., Jr. *Religion in Communist China.* New York: Abingdon, 1970.

Chan, Kim-kwong. *Struggling for Survival: The Catholic Church in China.* Hong Kong: Christian Study Centre on Religion and Culture, 1992.

———. *Towards a Contextual Ecclesiology: The Catholic Church in the People's Republic of China (1979–1983)—Its Life and Theological Implications.* Hong Kong: Photech Systems, 1987.

Charbonnier, Jean. *Guide to the Catholic Church in China.* Singapore: China Catholic Communication, 2000.

Hanson, Eric O. *Catholic Politics in China and Korea.* Maryknoll, N.Y.: Orbis, 1980.

Hunter, Alan, and Kim-kwong Chan. *Protestantism in Contemporary China.* Cambridge University Press, 1993.

Lambert, Tony. *China's Christian Millions: The Costly Revival.* London: Monarch, 2000.

———. *The Resurrection of the Chinese Church.* London: Hodder and Stoughton, 1991.

Leung, Beatrice. *Sino-Vatican Relations: Problems in Conflicting Authority, 1976–1986.* Cambridge University Press, 1992.

Lozada, Eriberto P., Jr. *God above Ground: Catholic Church, Postsocialist State, and Transnational Processes in a Chinese Village.* Stanford University Press, 2001.

Madsen, Richard. *China's Catholics: Tragedy and Hope in an Emerging Civil Society.* University of California Press, 1998.

Tang, Edmond, and John-Paul Wiest, eds. *The Catholic Church in Modern China.* Maryknoll, N.Y.: Orbis, 1993.

Uhalley, Stephen, Jr., and Xiaoxin Wu, eds. *China and Christianity: Burdened Past, Hopeful Future.* Armonk, N.Y.: M. E. Sharpe, 2001.

Whyte, Bob. *Unfinished Encounter: China and Christianity.* Harrisburg, Pa.: Morehouse, 1988.

Religion in Civil Society and in Foreign Policy

Abrams, Elliott, ed. *The Influence of Faith: Religious Groups and U.S. Foreign Policy.* Lanham, Md.: Rowman and Littlefield, 2001.

Berger, Peter L., and Samuel P. Huntington, eds. *Many Globalizations: Cultural Diversity in the Contemporary World.* Oxford University Press, 2002.

Fukuyama, Francis. *Trust: The Social Virtues and the Creation of Prosperity.* Free Press, 1995.

Harrison, Lawrence E., and Samuel P. Huntington, eds. *Culture Matters: How Values Shape Human Progress.* Basic, 2000.

Johnston, Douglas, and Cynthia Sampson, eds. *Religion: The Missing Dimension of Statecraft.* Oxford University Press, 1994.

Lindholm, Tore, W. Cole Durham Jr., and Bahia G. Tahzib-Lie, eds., *Facilitating Freedom of Religion or Belief: A Deskbook*. Netherlands: Kluwer Law International, 2001.

Mead, Walter Russell. *Special Providence: American Foreign Policy and How It Changed the World*. Knopf, 2002.

Witte, John, Jr. and Johan D. van der Vyver, eds. *Religious Human Rights in Global Perspective: Religious Perspectives*. Boston: Martinus Nijhoff, 1996.

Contributors

DANIEL H. BAYS is a professor of history and the chair of Asian Studies at Calvin College and professor emeritus at the University of Kansas. Bays has written numerous books, articles, and reviews on the influence of Christianity in China and the impact of missionary movements in both China and the United States. He is the editor (with Grant Walker) of *The Foreign Missionary Enterprise at Home: Explorations in North American Cultural History*. He holds a doctorate in history from the University of Michigan.

KIM-KWONG CHAN is the executive secretary of the Hong Kong Christian Council and honorary research fellow at the Universities Service Center for China Studies, Chinese University of Hong Kong. He is the author or coauthor of ten books and numerous academic articles, including *Protestantism in Contemporary China* (with Alan Hunter) and his most recent work, *Holistic Entrepreneurs in China* (with Tetsunao Yamamori). He holds two doctorates and three master's degrees from the University of Ottawa and St. Paul University in the areas of theology, economics, and China studies and history and has studied agricultural economics at the University of London.

CAROL LEE HAMRIN is a Chinese affairs consultant, currently advising on social, cultural, and political change; U.S.-China relations; and human rights and religious policy development. She served for twenty-five years at the U.S. Department of State, becoming its senior Chinese affairs specialist. A sought-after speaker and writer, her major publications include *China and the Challenge of the Future* and *Decision-Making in Deng's China*. Hamrin has taught at the Nitze School of Advanced International Studies at Johns Hopkins University and currently serves as a research professor at George Mason University, working with the Center for Asia Pacific Economic Cooperation and the Institute for Conflict Analysis and Resolution. She holds a doctorate in comparative world history from the University of Wisconsin–Madison.

JASON KINDOPP is resident scholar at the National Committee on United States–China Relations and was previously a civitas research fellow at the Brookings Institution. Kindopp recently finished his doctoral dissertation, "The Politics of Protestantism in Contemporary China: State Control, Civil Society, and Social Movement in a Single Party-State," and has written a number of articles and commentaries on religion and politics in China, including "China's War on 'Cults'" (*Current History*) and "Religious Repression in China: New Revelations on an Old Policy" (*Ethics and Religion Newsweekly*). He holds a master's in international affairs and a doctorate in political science, both from George Washington University.

PENG LIU is a professor at the Institute of American Studies at the Chinese Academy of Social Sciences and a senior fellow in the Religion and Law Program at Emory University. He has traveled extensively throughout China and Europe, examining the impact of religion on society and comparative patterns of politics and religion. Liu's most recent publication is *Religion in the United States Today* (in Chinese). He holds a master's from the Department of World Religions at the Graduate School of the Chinese Academy of the Social Sciences, Beijing.

RICHARD P. MADSEN is a professor of sociology at the University of California, San Diego, and codirector of the Ford Foundation project, Social Development in China. Recent publications include *Popular China: Unofficial Culture in a Globalizing Society* (coedited with Perry Link and Paul Pickowicz) and *China's Catholics: Tragedy and Hope in an Emerging Civil Society*. He holds a doctorate in sociology from Harvard University and a master's in theology from Maryknoll Seminary.

MICKEY SPIEGEL is a senior researcher in the Asia Division of Human Rights Watch, with responsibilities for work on China and Tibet. Among the many reports she has written or cowritten for Human Rights Watch are a series on religious freedom in the People's Republic of China, including "China: Persecution of a Protestant Sect," "China: Religious Persecution Persists," "China: State Control of Religion," "Tibet since 1950: Silence, Prison, or Exile," and, most recently, the 117-page monograph *Dangerous Meditation: China's Campaign against Falungong*. She received her master's in Anthropology from Columbia University.

JEAN-PAUL WIEST is a visiting scholar at the University of Hong Kong's Center of Asian Studies and a visiting professor at Tsinghua University's Center for the Study of Morality and Religion, and has served as director of the Center for Mission Research and Study at Maryknoll. He is currently codirector of a research project on the Catholic Church in Zhejiang Province. Major publications include *The Catholic Church in Modern China: Perspectives* and *Popular Catholicism in a World Church: Seven Case Studies in Inculturation*. He holds a master's in theology from the Pontifical Gregorian University in Rome and a doctorate in Chinese history from the University of Washington in Seattle.

YIHUA XU is a professor in the Center for American Studies at Fudan University in Shanghai, China, and editor in chief of *Christian Scholarship*. His most recent publications include *Religion in America*, volume 1 (in Chinese), *Christian Colleges and Theological Education in China* (in Chinese), *International Relations at the Turn of the Century* (editor; in Chinese), and *Education and Religion: St. John's University as Evangelizing Agency* (in Chinese). He received his master's in history from Wuhan University and his doctorate in religion from Princeton University.

Index

Abortion conflicts and foreign policy, 167
Agricultural sector, 60, 64–65
Aluoben, 78
Amity Printing Press, 137
Amity Foundation, 137
Ancestral rituals, 85–87, 90
Anhui Province, 6, 128, 141
Arrests/detentions. *See* Persecution tactics *entries*
Arrow War, 88
Asia-Pacific Economic Cooperation, 12, 58, 155

Back to Jerusalem Movement, 134
Banking sector, 60
"Basic Viewpoint and Policy on the Religious Question . . ." (Document *19*), 40–41, 44, 49, 51, 52, 96–97
Bays, Daniel, 13–14
Beijing: Franciscan missionaries, 81; municipal religious regulations, 45; Protestant groups, 62, 115–16, 124; *2001* conference, 65–69, 175
Bibles, restrictions, 51–52
Bishops (Catholic): control strategies, 47–48, 49–50; first indigenous, 90; papal authority and, 41, 94, 102; underground churches, 98–99. *See also* Persecution tactics *entries*

Board of Rites, 26–27
Boone University, 113
Boxer Uprising, 89
Buddhism: imperial era, 26, 78, 79, 80; reform era, 1, 5, 42
Bush, George W., 11–12, 58, 175

Canada, 155–56, 157
Canada-China Religious Freedom Dialogue, 155–56
Canton (Guangzhou), 28
Cardinal Kung Foundation, 104–05
Carter, Jimmy, 165
Catholicism: overview, 1–2, 16, 96–97; clergy control strategies, 47–48, 49–50; Mao's regime, 93–96; open churches, 47–48, 97–98, 100–01; before Opium War, 28–29; papal authority, 41, 94, 102; reform era recognition, 42; rites controversy, 85–87; statistics, 1–2, 83, 86, 91, 93, 95; underground churches, 5–6, 47–48, 95–96, 98–99, 98–103, 126, 128, 135. *See also* Missionaries; Vatican
Catholic Patriotic Association (CPA), 43, 94–95, 97–98, 101–03
CCC. *See* China Christian Council
Chan, Kim-kwong, 14–15
Chaote, Allen, 180–81

195

Chapdelaine, Auguste, 88
Cheng Jingyi, 114
Chiang Kai-shek, 33, 89
China Christian Council (CCC), 69, 126–29, 137, 156
Chinese Independent Church, 108
Chrétien, Jean, 155
Christian Manifesto, 115, 122–23
Church of Christ, 110, 115
Church of the East. *See* Nestorians
"Church Order for Chinese Protestant Christian Churches," 46
"Circular on Some Problems Concerning the Further Improvement . . ." (Document 6), 44–45, 52
Clergy, regulations, 49–50. *See also* Persecution tactics *entries*
Clinton, Bill, and administration, 169–70
Colson, Chuck, 167
Confucianism, 83, 84–87, 89, 90, 172
Congress, U.S., 167–69, 170–71
Constitutional guarantee of religious freedom, 41
Corruption, 6–7, 103
Costantini, Celso, 89
CPA. *See* Catholic Patriotic Association
Cult policy, 48, 53, 67, 69–70
Cultural Revolution, 14, 35, 40, 95, 119, 126

Daily Knowledge Society, 113
Daoguang emperor, 87–88
Demographics: Catholics, 83, 86, 91, 93, 95; Protestants, 91, 110; religions compared, 1–2; work force characteristics, 59–60
Deng Xiaoping, 35, 96, 165, 166
Detentions/arrests. *See* Persecution tactics *entries*
Ding Guangxun, 112, 113, 114, 129, 131–32
"Direction of Endeavor for Chinese Christianity . . ." (Christian Manifesto), 115, 122–23
Dobson, James, 167

Document 6. *See* Circular on Some Problems Concerning Further Improvement . . ."
Document 19. *See* "Basic Viewpoint and Policy on the Religious Question . . ."
Dong Jianwu, 113

Eastern Lightning cult, 141
East Germany, 9
Economic issues: globalization, 166–67, 173–74; U.S. trade relations, 149–50, 167, 168, 171. *See also* World Trade Organization,
Edict of Toleration *(1692),* 84
Elliot, Harrison S., 114
Episcopal Church, 112–13, 114
Established King sect, 141
European Union, 157

Falungong, 5, 7, 48, 102, 155, 174
Fangcheng Church, 53, 140
Fa Xian, 80
Folk religions, 42, 64, 109, 135, 153
Foreign Affairs, Department of (imperial era), 78
Foreign Affairs Ministry (reform era), 159
Forum *18,* 156, 157
Fosdick, Harry Emerson, 114
France, 88–89
Franciscan missionaries, 77, 80–81
Freedom from Religious Persecution bill, 170–71
Fujian Province, 53, 64, 83, 128
Fu Tieshan, 156

Globalization, 166–67, 173–74. *See also* World Trade Organization
God-Worshippers Society, 29–30
Gong Pinmei, 94, 104
Great Britain, 28–29, 88
Guangdong Province, 128, 138
Guangzhou, 28, 45, 49
Guizhou Province, 6, 83

Hamrin, Carol Lee, 18–19
Hanford, John, 12, 170

INDEX

Han Wenzao, 112
Heavenly Soldiers Fraternal Army, 7–8
Hebei Province, 1, 52–53, 96
Heilongjiang Province, 6
Henan Province, 6, 53, 126, 128, 129–30, 140, 141
Heshang (film), 139
Historical Data Unit (TSPM), 117
Hong Kong, 138
Hong Xiuquan, 9, 29–30
Horowitz, Michael, 168, 170
House churches (*jiating jiaohui*), 5–6, 126, 128, 133–39, 140. *See also* Underground churches
Human rights. *See* Religious tensions
Hunan Province, 128
Hundred Flowers movement, 94
Hu Yaobang, 166

Imperial China: Buddhism, 26, 78, 79, 80; missionary movement, 28, 32, 78–89; regulation tradition, 13–14, 25–31
Imperialism (Western), and Christianity, 28–31, 33
Independent churches, 107–10
Industrial sector, 60–61
Innocent IV, 80
Institute for Human Rights, 156, 157
International Day of Prayer for the Persecuted Church, 168–69
International investment, 59, 61
International Religious Freedom, U.S. Office of, 11–12, 159
International Religious Freedom Act, 11, 170–71
Iraq war *(2003)*, 150
Islam, 1, 5, 42, 80, 81

Japan, 90, 111
Jesuits, 77, 82–87
Jesus Family, 32, 109, 124, 128
Jiangsu Province, 45, 83
Jiang Zemin, 65–66, 68, 153, 155, 169, 175
Jingxian County, 52–53
John Paul II, 87, 103

John XXIII, 95

Kangxi emperor, 84, 85–86
Kang Youwei, 31
Korean missionaries, 138
Kuhn, Philip, 25, 26

Langrené, Théodore de, 87–88
Lebbe, Vincent, 90
Lianghui hierarchy, 127, 128–29, 131–32
Li Changshou, 128
Lin Xiangao, 133
Little Flock, 32, 33, 109–10, 122, 124, 128
Liu, Peng, 18
Liu Tingfang, 114
Li Zhizao, 83
Local Church (Shouters), 42, 128, 141
Luminous Religion, 78–80
Luo Zhufeng, 126
Lu Xiaozhou, 50

Macao, 28, 81
Madsen, Richard, 16
Mao Zedong, 14
Mark (Nestorian monk), 79
Mazu cult, 64
Mergers/consolidations as control, 50, 125
Ming dynasty, 81–84
Missionaries: bans and expulsions, 34, 86, 90–91, 123, 151; Franciscans, 80–81; historical summary, 15, 28; house church, 134–35; imperial era, 28, 32, 78–89; Jesuit, 77, 82–87; Nestorian, 78–80; reform era, 52–53, 137–39; Republican era, 32–33, 89–91; rites controversy, 85–87; and Taiping Rebellion, 29–31; three-self movement, 108–11; unequal treaty period, 87–89. *See also* Religious organizations; Three-Self Patriotic Movement
Mongol Empire, 79–81
Montecorvino, Giovanni da, 81

Nanjing Union Theological Seminary, 116, 132

National Association of Evangelicals, 168
National Catholic Administrative Committee, 97
National Chinese Christian Council, 69, 127
National Christian Conference, 32
National Christian Council of China, 32, 110, 115
National Committee of the Three-Self Patriotic Movement, 115–16
National Conference of Chinese Independent Churches, 108–09
Nationalism: and foreign Protestantism, 33, 34, 89; and U.S. human rights pressures, 172–75; and WTO accession, 68–69
Nationalist Party, 31, 33, 89
National Union Theological Seminary, 116
Nestorians (Syro-Persian Church), 77, 78–80
Netherlands, 157
Nickles-Lieberman bill. *See* International Religious Freedom Act
Ni Tuosheng (Watchman Nee), 32, 122, 133
Nonproliferation, 149, 150
North Korea, 150
Norway, 155, 156–57

Official churches, defined, 101
Olympic Games *(2008)*, 58, 178, 179
Open churches: described, 47–48; growth of, 97–98; Vatican acceptance, 100–01
Opium War, 28–29
Oslo Coalition, 156–57

Patriotic religious organizations. *See* Catholic Patriotic Association; Three-Self Patriotic Movement
Pelosi, Nancy, 167
People's Political Consultative Conferences, 153–54
Persecution tactics: imperial era, 25–28, 29–30, 80, 81, 87, 88–89; Mao's regime, 94, 95–96, 124–26, 133

Persecution tactics, reform era: overview, 5–8; and constitutional guarantees, 42; cult definitions, 48, 53; detentions and arrests, 49–50, 99, 140–41; and house churches, 135–37; as nationalism defense, 173; and rule of law approach, 44; Theological Campaign, 132
Pius XII, 90, 93, 94
Plurilateral Human Rights Symposium, 155
Poland, 9
Portugal, 82–83
Preparatory Committee of the Chinese Protestant Resist America . . . (TSPM), 115
Protestantism: autonomy trend, 129–32; church growth, 1–2, 5–6, 127–28; communist suspicions, 33, 34, 122–23; development summarized, 31–34; house churches, 5–6, 47, 48, 126, 128, 133–39, 140; missionary movement, 28, 29–31, 32, 77, 90; reform era recognition, 42; statistics, 1–2, 91, 110; three-self movement, 107–11. *See also* Regulatory practices, reform era; Three-Self Patriotic Movement
Publications, religious, 51–52, 53, 116–17, 137
Public Security, Ministry of, 7, 43, 48, 70
Pu Huaren, 113

Qianlong emperor, 25, 26
Qing dynasty, 9, 28–30, 84, 85–89
Qinghai Province, 47

Record of facts to ward off heterodoxy, 88
Registration requirements: imperial era, 26–27; Mao regime, 35, 45; reform era, 46–48, 51; Republic period, 31
Regulatory practices: overview, 2–11, 13–14, 35–36; imperial era, 25–31; Mao regime, 34–35, 115–20; Republic period, 31, 32–33
Regulatory practices, reform era: overview, 14, 40–42, 53–54, 96–97, 126–27, 153–54; activity restrictions, 50–51;

INDEX

arrests and detentions, 140–41; bureaucratic structure, 43; clergy controls, 48–50; limitations 127–28, 129–32, 139–40, 141; as nationalism defense, 173; publication approval, 51–52; registration requirements, 46–48; rule of law approach, 43–46; and WTO accession, 65–72
Religion, Office of, 78
Religious Affairs Bureau, 35, 43, 46–47, 52, 66, 97, 117–18, 127
Religious organizations, international: as Document 6 justification, 44; reform era regulations, 52–53; and underground churches, 104–05; and WTO accession, 62–63, 68–69. *See also* Missionaries
Religious publications, 51–52, 53, 116–17, 137
Religious tensions, U.S.-China: overview, 11–12, 17–19, 104–05, 149–51, 165–66, 182; and Chinese nationalism, 172–75; international comparisons, 154–58; proposals for improvement, 158–63, 176–81; religious identities compared, 151–54; and U.S. political pressures, 166–72, 175–76
Republic period, 31, 32–33, 89–91, 108–09
Riberi, Antonio, 93
Ricci, Matteo, 82–83
Rites controversy, 85–87, 90
Roots, Logan H., 113
Roundtable Conference on the Rule of Law and Human Rights, 156
Ruggieri, Michele, 83
Rule of law approach, 43–46

Sacraments, 97–98
Seiple, Robert, 11, 171
September *11* attacks, 175
Shaanxi Province, 64, 83
Shandong Province, 6, 109, 128
Shanghai, 45, 49, 111–13, 124
Shanxi Province, 83, 95, 99
Shea, Nina, 168

Shengyang, 61
Shen Yifan, 112
Shenzhou (film), 139
Shouters. *See* Local Church
Sichuan Province, 83, 86
Sinim Fellowship, 136
Sino-Japanese War, 111
Smith, Christopher, 167
Society of Jesus. *See* Jesuits
Sorcery scare, 25, 26
Soulstealers (Kuhn), 25, 26
South Korea, 138
Spain, 82
Spence, Jonathan, 29
Spiegel, Mickey, 14
St. John's University, 112–13
State, U.S. Department of, 11–12, 171
Syro-Persian Church. *See* Nestorians

Taft, William H., 111
Tain/Shangdi controversy, 85–87
Taiping Rebellion, 9, 29–30
Taiwan, 138, 149, 150
Taizong emperor, 78
Tamerlane, 80
Tang dynasty, 78–79
Taoism, 26, 42
Theological Construction Campaign, 132
Three-self movement, 17, 107–09. *See also* Three-Self Patriotic Movement
Three-Self Patriotic Movement (TSPM): overview, 16–17, 43, 107, 118–20, 122–23; background, 107–15; Canada dialogue, 156; institutionalization, 115–18, 123–26; reform era, 45–46, 126–29, 131–32, 133–37
"Three Sentences," 66
Tianfeng (periodical), 117
Tian Gengxin, Thomas, 90
Tianjin massacre, 89
Tibet, 1, 7, 65
Trade relations, U.S.-China, 149–50, 167, 168, 171. *See also* World Trade Organization
Transnational interaction, 62–63. *See also* Religious organizations

Treaties, 28–29, 33, 82, 87, 88–89. *See also* Unequal treaty system
Treat of Tordesillas, 82
Treaty of Nanking, 87
True Jesus Church, 32, 33, 109–10, 124, 128
TSPM. *See* Three-Self Patriotic Movement

Underground churches, 5–6, 47–48, 95–96, 98–103, 126, 128, 135. *See also* House churches
Unequal treaty system, 28–29, 33, 87–89, 152–53
Union Theological Seminary, 113–15
United Christian Publishing House, 117
United Front Work Department, 35, 43, 97, 117–18
United Nations, 150, 157, 167
United States: support for China's Christians, 104–05, 137–39, 166. *See also* Religious tensions
Unofficial churches, defined, 101. *See also* House churches; Underground churches

Valignano, Alessandro, 82–83
Van Dusen, Henry Pitney, 114
Vatican: acceptance of open churches, 100–01; anticommunist stance, 93, 94; canonization conflict, 102–03; negotiations with Ding regime, 102–03; rites controversy, 85–87; underground churches, 98–99. *See also* Catholicism

Wang Mingdao, 122, 133
Wang Zuo'an, 66
Ward, Harry F., 114
Watchman Nee (Ni Tuosheng), 32, 122, 133
Wenzhou, 6, 61–62, 65, 126
Wiest, Jean-Paul, 15
Wolf, Frank, 167

Wolf-Spector bill. *See* Freedom from Religious Persecution bill
Work force characteristics, 59–61; mobility of, 60, 63, 64–65
World Evangelical Fellowship, 168
World Trade Organization, China's entry: overview, 14–15, 58; economic effects, 59–61; government policy challenges, 65–70, 161–63, 174–75; religious implications, 61–65, 70–72; and U.S. trade relations, 150
Wuchang, 113
Wu Yangming, 141
Wu Yaozong, 114, 115, 116, 117, 122, 123, 124–25

Xinjiang, 1, 7
Xu, Yihua, 16–17
Xuan Zang, 80
Xu Guangqi, 83

Yang, C. K., 8–9
Yang Tingyun, 83
Yenching Union Theological Seminary, 116
Yenching University School of Religion, 114, 116
Ye Xiaowen, 46, 69, 156
YMCA, 111–12, 114, 116
Yongli emperor, 83, 84
Yongzheng emperor, 86
Yuan dynasty, 79–81
Yuan Zhiming, 139
Yu Bin, 93
Yu Guozhen, 108
Yunnan Province, 6

Zhao Wieshan, 141
Zhao Zichen, 116
Zhejiang Province, 83, 128
Zhou Enlai, 113, 122